the cat's whispers

CAT HARVEY

the cat's whispers

The Real Breakfast Diaries Uncut

Black & White Publishing

First published 2006
by Black & White Publishing Ltd
99 Giles Street, Edinburgh, EH6 6BZ

ISBN 13: 978 1 84502 105 4
ISBN 10: 1 84502 105 3

A CIP catalogue record for this book is available from
The British Library.

Printed and bound by Creative Print and Design Group Ltd

acknowledgements

I'd like to thank the girls for their continued support and friendship, my family for absolutely everything and Scott for putting up with me.

Special thanks to my co-presenter Robin Galloway at Real Radio who is the kindest and funniest workmate anyone could wish for.

The Real Radio team of Billy Anderson, Jay Crawford and Baz have all helped me tremendously, while my mate Tam Cowan and the *Offside* team also deserve a grateful mention.

Thanks to everyone at Black & White Publishing. They've made this latest adventure a relatively fun and painless one.

But most of all a big thanks goes out to the Breakfast Show listeners – the 'Real' stars of the show . . .

For Mum and Dad. Thank you . . .

'The man o' independent mind,
He looks an' laughs at a' that.'
                    Robert Burns

foreword

by Robin Galloway

It's been pointed out to me by many people that I spend more time with Cat than I do with my wife, a wonderfully warm and witty human being. And my wife's 'not too shabby' either.

We have worked together for three years and it has been an absolute pleasure. She makes me laugh just being Cat.

Like the times she comes to the studio wearing a swimsuit under her jeans when she runs out of clean pants or breaks the flap off her fridge freezer's ice compartment because the door won't close due to lack of defrosting. And of course I love the many wonderful tales that come from meeting her beloved 'troops' when they rip up the West End of a Saturday night.

Delivered to Real Radio through the Cat Flap in the autumn of 2004, The Catster was an instant hit with the listeners. Her girl-next-door qualities make her appealing to everybody.

Cat possesses the rare quality of being exactly the same person off air as she is on. She does exactly what it says on the tin. Working and sometimes socialising, for all the time we've spent together, there's never been as much as a raised voice.

We are great friends who are lucky enough to work together. For me, it is the ultimate on-air partnership.

It was quite by chance that I found out about this book. Cat has always been a doodler and constantly sits with pen and paper scribbling away during the show. I noticed back in January that the doodling had progressed to 'jottings'.

This, of course, was the beginning of what you are about to receive. I have a feeling you'll be truly thankful.

Disclaimer

The views in this book are mine alone and nothing to do with the management of Real Radio or GMG Radio. They are clever, sensible, responsible adults who never sleep in and eat food that is not from a microwave.

why the cat is
sharing her whispers

Wednesday,
21 December 2005

It was whilst sipping champagne wearing reindeer horns, having just asked Scotland's First Minister Jack McConnell if he secretly enjoyed wearing Speedos, that it began to dawn on me how unusual my life had become.

Presenting a breakfast show is never going to be routine, but at that instant, in the luxurious surroundings of Bute House, Edinburgh, the official residence of the most powerful man in the country, at his private invite-only Christmas bash with the collective glowers of the assembled broadsheet hacks and chosen political allies, the bells on my bobbled antlers tinkled as I enjoyed a silent chuckle at the amazing events of the past year.

With my partner in crime Robin Galloway, we are the *Real Radio Breakfast Show* – officially the biggest breakfast show outside London in the UK. And unofficially a pair of similar-minded chancers, joyously broadcasting each day until we are found out and forced to get proper grown-up jobs.

Our invite to this salubrious affair came after an entertaining set of circumstances. Robin, who is famed for his wind-ups, called up the Scottish Parliament with a delivery of cannabis when the legalisation debate was on-going. Jack, being driven to work to run the country, thought it was hilarious and called to congratulate him off air. Naturally, we think we are being wound up and are exceptionally cheeky to . . . 'THE FIRST MINISTER? AYE RIGHT.'

The exact conversation makes me blush now and I'm afraid I can't possibly reveal the extent of our naughtiness or we would surely be beheaded or sent to live in England or something.

Anyway, the day before Jack had to meet George Bush off his plane and play host to the world's mighty powers at the G8 summit in Gleneagles, his people asked if he could come on our show. Naturally, we didn't delve into the inner workings of international politics and global salvation, but set about having a laugh and finding out what kind of a bloke he is away from that big daud of concrete known to architects as the Scottish Parliament.

Intellectual gems like the great roasted or toasted cheese debate and his murky past as a 'Wishy' (nickname for his home town of Wishaw to our foreign readers not au fait with fluent Lanarkshire . . .) councillor unfolded. I read out a text saying: 'Good luck our Jack, you're doing really well.'

Despite showing obvious signs of nerves, he was visibly encouraged by this message of goodwill, until I revealed it was actually sent in by his sister, who clearly thought a morning with Robin and Cat a more difficult challenge than a day with George 'W'. Nice wee touch, though, and he took a cracking beamer.

I had just returned from a holiday in Bulgaria and we always bring everyone on the show a silly wee gift. Before I left, Robin shocked the nation by confessing his preference for Speedos, those horrible tight Lycra trunks that make even the fittest of blokes look squashed and somehow pervy.

Poor Mr W., our producer, was done out of his quality present as Robin asked for his while Jack was still there and on air. Despite frantic eye gestures to signify that this might not be an entirely appropriate moment for this exchange, Robin again asked for his gift and I was forced to do the honourable thing and make our First Minister open HIS new present – a spanking new pair of extra-skimpy Speedos with a Bulgarian flag transfer. Disturbingly, he loved them. 'These are sensational,' he beamed. I suggested he could wear them the following day at Gleneagles, to which he promptly replied: 'No chance. I need to get myself a pair with the St Andrew's flag on it.'

Anyway, the Christmas card was next, handwritten: 'To Cat, hope Santa brings YOU some nice new swimwear! Best wishes, Jack.' Say what you like about his politics, he's a good bloke with a cheeky sense of humour.

And so it came to pass, as is often the case in books much better written than this one, the invite arrived two days later and we somehow ended up schmoozing with Scotland's sagacious and significant people. As I mentioned, it was at this moment I began to reflect on some recent highlights in a magnificently absurd few months. They included:

Growing Old Disgracefully

Every now and then the age difference between Robin and me (twelve years) leads to entertaining exchanges when we reminisce about our respective upbringings. We some- how stumbled upon the great 'I know I am getting old when . . . ' chat and were flooded with brilliant answers. These included:

I know I'm getting old when . . .
    'I make a noise involuntarily bending down.'
    'I take cod liver oil by choice.'
    'I prefer pubs with no music.'
    'Friday nights IN are appealing.'
    'I look at scantily clad girls in the pub and think they should be covered up!'

The call that had us on the floor, though, and perhaps showed us once again the benefits of pre-recording calls during songs, was an elderly gent called Andy from Whitburn. In his gruff voice he told us: 'I knew I was getting old when I started having DRY dreams and wet farts.' Ah, culture, you cannae beat it . . .

Beetroot

Surveys provide endless fun for us. They are printed on a daily basis in the papers and range from the sublime to the totally ridiculous. My favourite was the great piece one. Apparently only twenty-three per cent of people take sandwiches to their work nowadays.

E-mail of the day came from a lady in Hamilton; her brother-in-law has taken cheese and beetroot pieces on white bread every day for fifteen years. Last year, his workmates asked how the bread remains white and doesn't go soggy. Perplexed with this dilemma he finally asked his wife how, for fifteen years, five days a week, she created his favoured snack. 'I just sook oot the juice before I slice them . . .'

Not the answer he was looking for but it's had me in stitches ever since . . .

The Day We Nearly Got Sacked (Part One)

The skip sitting outside the studio window was empty. In a moment of spontaneous comedy genius Robin offered its services to any listeners with stuff to dump. Now, knowing a clear out of the office was about to commence, this was clearly a very bad idea indeed. But like most very bad ideas it proved to be hilariously funny.

Within five minutes a man arrives with a broken Dyson and makes a splendidly dramatic gesture of throwing it into the empty skip. I begin to give live commentary as the madness unfolds. A taxi stops and the driver drops off his McDonald's wrappers, a small van appears with a mangled racer bike and the driver begins chatting to fellow dumpers. This continues at an unbelievable rate until the Glasgow City Council cleansing van appears with an entire defunct central heating system complete with twelve feet of silver ventilation tubing. It takes four guys eight minutes to empty their van by which point our once-empty skip is stuffed with junk – and not our junk. Oops.

Our MD's lovely secretary Maggi called in on the internal – you know you are in trouble – line. She was almost teary. 'Tell me you are kidding. That cost a fortune and we need to use it TODAY. Please tell me you are kidding!'

With Real Radio staff now unable to park in the car park for listeners dumping garden waste and bin bags of rubbish now getting placed around the base of the overflowing skip, we knew we were in trouble. We officially 'CLOSED' the Real Radio skip as Mr W., our producer, began to look exceptionally worried. The High Heid Yins were not at all pleased and wanted to see us later.

Thankfully, with eight minutes of the show remaining, the skip company phoned up and offered to replace the skip and remove all the junk. They were doubled up laughing at our antics and were delighted that skips, for possibly the first time ever, were the most talked about subject of the day.

It's the last time we intentionally talked rubbish for a while.

The Great Farting Enquiry

I knew by the scowl on Real Radio programme director Jay Crawford's face when he summoned me into his office that something was wrong.

'We've had an official complaint about you. The man is absolutely furious and he's planning to go to Offcom.'

I sat replaying the show in my head on super fast-forward and couldn't think of one single contentious comment. A few wee cheeky one-liners maybe, but that's what I do.

'Mr Paterson has phoned reception four times and he is furious.'

What had I done?

'He says you farted on air and then had the audacity to laugh afterwards.'

At this point Jay and I dissolve into fits. Unfortunately Mr Paterson is not so easily amused. I'm not sure if a car backfired near his house at some point during our show, but I know for a fact I NEVER and have never (yet) let one slip on air. Poor Nadia our receptionist can't keep her face straight as she answers his fifth call. He is getting more and more irate after Jay's backing: 'Cat did not fart on air. We have a recording of the show and we can go through every link and check.'

'She did, and she laughed,' he screams, apoplectic.

Now the best bit . . .

'And what is worse is that it's not the first time she has done it. I know we all do it but there is a time and a place and she is a bad influence on younger listeners. It is disgusting.'

By now, word has filtered round the building that the great pump enquiry is under way. Mr Paterson hangs up enraged, claiming to have a tape of the show which he is going to listen to before contacting the broadcast industries' governing body. Despite a love of vegetables, curry and sultana cake, I'm pleased to report I still await my phantom farting summons. Aye, it's an ill wind that blows no one any good . . .

Big in Falkirk

As a Partick Thistle fan who ran a supporters' bus at the age of seventeen (Milngavie and Summerston . . . leaves the station 12.15, non-members welcome, nae carry outs mind . . .), standing on stage wearing a Falkirk top and leading 35,000 in a chorus of 'Amarillo' at 'Big in Falkirk 2005', the open air festival, evokes mixed emotions of euphoria and guilt. The fact that crooner of the moment Tony Christie felt my not insubstantial arse backstage is perhaps another reason this day stands out, and not in a good way!

Other memorable facts from that weekend: Heather Small from M People seemed like a grumpy cow and pop strumpet Javine is a lovely looking lass in dire need of a fish supper. To me, though, Big in Falkirk the previous year was funnier. McFly had a cracking backstage water-fight, we all drank far too much, Bossman Jay nearly fell off the stage while introducing Deacon Blue and we found out the following Monday the closing firework display was apparently spectacular!

The Injury

It is almost predictable that if I were to be injured in the line of duty, it quite simply had to be undertaking something daft.

The Royal Highland Show is a grand annual agricultural affair at Ingliston Showground and my job for the day was to meet the Royal Marines (oh yes please!) and the kids taking part in the Army's assault course. I have perhaps been a tad vague with the specifics here; they were taking part in the standard assault course, and I was to participate in the Army's *inflatable* assault course.

Two days after my narrow defeat to 'Big Mad Mental Rambo' from Leith, it was off to the National Medical Centre at Hampden, where I received splendid treatment for my left knee's torn ligament and severely damaged cartilage. Filling in my records in the waiting room packed with SPL footballers, the receptionist boomed: 'INFLATABLE ASSAULT COURSE? WHAT, LIKE A JUMPY CASTLE?'

Not since my car was fixed at the garage for 'monkey damage' after a trip to the Safari Park, have I taken such a reddie.

The Sausage Scandal

Our marketing strategy for the *Breakfast Show* involved a picture of Robin and me, with large cartoon upturned sausages superimposed on our smiles. The fact that Robin is a strict vegetarian appealed to me lots. At one stage forty per cent of the buses in Glasgow, Edinburgh and Fife had this delightful image. Oh yes, thank you media gurus. I was finally the back end of the bus I'd had the potential to be for years.

Daily shouts of: 'Awright, Cat, don't recognise you without a sausage/bit of meat in your mouth . . .' etc. followed. Just as well I'm naïve and don't understand the implication. I'm not sure if it has had a significant psychological impact on me, but I have now not eaten a link sausage in over a year. Thank God it wasn't a tattie scone on that fork . . .

The Veritable Mixed Bag

Other notable moments include the nation learning that my first cuddly toy was a scruffy cat unfortunately named 'Pink Pussy', dial-a-song-on-the-accordion day when I murdered Sidney Devine's classic 'Tiny Bubbles' (I know there's a cheap gag here but I think he's a legend so I shall resist), bug-eating *I'm a Celebrity Get Me Out of Here* style (fear not, Robin – I told you I would never tell that the African water-bug crunch was really a packet of cheesy Quavers), a trip to Tunnock's factory (two weeks' all-inclusive not an option unfortunately) and a bizarre walk-/dance-on part at the Edinburgh Playhouse in the musical *Oh What a Night* with Noel from Hear'Say and Faye from Steps. I wish I could expand and explain that one, but I'm afraid I still don't have a clue what it was all about. They seemed nice, in a disillusioned pop star kind of way. And of course simulating Hogmanay with the toured-out boys from Franz Ferdinand in a Portakabin in Waverley Gardens next to the train track on a rainy August afternoon (they were abroad for the real bells, and needs must, people). I was delighted to find out that the hottest band on the planet met fighting over a bottle of vodka at a party, and they love Irn Bru and Shareen Nanjiani, but not necessarily at the same time.

The Telly Stuff

The great thing about coming off air at nine is that I can still keep up my telly work. After five years at Scottish TV working as a reporter on *Scotsport*, *Extra Time* and *Scotland Today* and presenting *Champions League Extra*, I finally admitted to myself that I wasn't terribly good at doing sensible sport.

When the Comedy Unit asked if I'd like to work on BBC Scotland's *Offside* programme with Tam Cowan I jumped at the chance. I could keep up my interest in football, but only shoot features about interesting people and the lighter side of our beautiful game instead of constantly keeping track of injured groins up and down the country (not guilty for any of them!).

Two shoots stand out for various reasons. Scotland legend Gordon Strachan was top of my hit list. I should point out at that in February 2005, he had just lost out on the Scotland manager's job to Walter Smith and Martin O'Neill was still happily bounding about the touchline at Parkhead.

It took roughly thirty phone calls and three e-mails to get him to agree. I spoke to him on his home phone, his mobile, when he was loading the car at the supermarket and even hoovering.

'What are you going to ask me? What is the piece about? E-mail me your questions, I need to clear it with the wife, we are only meeting in a hotel . . .' etc., etc.

He is confident, cheeky and not going to be taken for anybody's fool. I liked him. This was going to be a game of wits and I was looking forward to it. After flying to Southampton on an Airfix plane (I detest flying and that's what it felt like) I was met by the cameraman from BBC Southampton who warned me, 'He's a grumpy little shit.'

With the camera and lights set up in the drawing room of a plush hotel, we got started. He told me he had no plans to return to Scottish football (aye, cheers), Walter Smith was the right man for the Scotland job, and that he was a passionate member of the Tartan Army. So much so that he spent his honeymoon dancing on the pitch at Wembley in the infamous goal-post-breaking game v. England in 1977. When I asked if his wife was with him he quickly replied: 'It was my honeymoon, I'd have been a bit of a bloody weirdo if she hadn't been.'

His other cracking yarn involved a flight back from the World Cup in 1986, when Scotland had to share a flight with Ireland. Both teams were 'choking for a drink' and were queuing in the aisle to get booze off the trolley. Alan Rough took it upon himself to clear the chaos. Clearly under the influence of a shandy or two, he took control of the tannoy system and announced: 'Would anybody who has NOT been in THREE World Cups please return to their seats.' Scotland might not be very good, but we are certainly gallus.

Lorenzo Amoruso's Guide to Love

The other memorable shoot was at former Rangers captain Lorenzo Amoruso's house in Blackburn. He was clearly annoyed at being left on the bench and when I phoned on the off chance that he might do something for the show he said yes straight away.

I was most surprised to see he shares his designer living room with a life-size cardboard Lorenzo Amoruso in a Rangers strip. The pictures in his living room walls are of Rangers winning the SPL, Rangers winning the Cup, and all the players celebrating at Ibrox. Say what you like about him, he is one of the foreign players who genuinely fell in love with a club.

Now Lorenzo anticipated an interview about life away from Rangers and his current situation; however, in my head I was hoping to shoot a fun feature to be broadcast on Valentine's Day. The fact that he was a hot Italian renowned for having the biggest boaby this side of a German porn flick added to the occasion.

I've interviewed him before and despite the flash lifestyle he has always been a really nice guy. This trip proved no different. He laughed at my film ideas and played along spectacularly. He even revealed his top three tips for hot loving:

1. Food – seduce her with some home cooking, possibly with a recipe from the Lorenzo Amoruso cook book! (I then served him a pie, some Irn Bru and a Mars bar on a plate.)

2. Romantic music – for which he stuck on a CD labelled *Pulling Tunes* with the Proclaimers blasting out.

3. A present – he suggested a girl will be blown away if she gets an unexpected gift and concluded his guide to love with sincerity: 'It is the thought that counts, size really doesn't matter.'

I left with the finest line of my TV career in the can, and the poor soul didn't even know.

From Six Foot Cock to Eight Foot Squirrel

Let me first point out, this has NOTHING to do with the last story!

I was the only person in the *Offside* office when the phone rang. 'Where is Jock the Cock? We are all waiting for him.' Jock, the show's mascot, a six-foot multi-coloured cockerel, had apparently been booked for a football mascot charity pancake race for Cancer Research and was late. Jock, now I shall break it to you gently, is not actually real. It is a costume with a wee man inside. No, really. The wee man, an architect called Andy, had obviously not been informed.

'But we have Hoopy the Huddlehound and Broxy Bear and we need Jock, there's a crowd of kids waiting at Royal Exchange Square,' pleaded the man. I reluctantly agreed to help and jumped in a taxi to the BBC, picked up the large cock costume and arrived at the big race.

'Quick, get changed, you still have time,' the man barked as I stumbled out the taxi with a chicken head tumbling on to the pavement. Now this was not part of the deal: I was simply delivering the costume; I am the reporter on the show, not the cock, I explained.

'Well we have nobody else and you look the right size,' he shouted, and so it came to pass that instead of booking premier league players for the next programme, I dressed up as a large chicken, picked up a rusty pan and tossed pancakes through the centre of Glasgow against six fellow mascots.

'Jock, you're shit,' commented a lovely young lad of about six in a Rangers top as I hobbled in last. It was only then I realised I'd been duped. I was one of just two mascots to wear the correct animal footwear. I had size fourteen chicken claws to run in, while Hoopy, the victor, was wearing very smart white Nike trainers in his size!

Taking my cock head off to reveal a very sweaty face and a mop of blonde, sticky hair, quote of the day went to the builder hanging off scaffolding in the square who shouted: 'No way – Jock the Cock's a burd!'

As I recounted this tale on the *Breakfast Show* I had no idea what was about to unfold. Alyson Gray, one of my best friends, who works for The Sports Business, sent this text to the show: 'We shall pay £1000 to Cancer Research if Cat agrees to be Nutz the Squirrel at the CIS Cup Final.' Thanks pal! Robin naturally announced this on air through peals of laughter, catching a glimpse of my stony face, and I had no choice but to agree.

So on a lovely sunny day in March, I found myself squeezed into an eight-foot squirrel costume with tiny peep-holes with the instruction: 'Out you go and entertain the crowd.' Eh? What do big squirrels do? How do I get myself in such ridiculous situations? I only answered the bloody phone!

Well I got over the initial shame by dancing, waving and shimmying like a maniac (it is actually quite liberating when people can't see your face). I fell off the pitch on to the track (not planned) and rolled about a bit (try getting up when you are as round as a barrel and have Tufty feet for digits). I then went back to lead Rangers and Ayr United out the tunnel and bop about in the background as the toss was made on live television in front of one million viewers and 54,000 supporters in the stadium.

Reflecting back on this whole escapade, I struggle to believe it actually happened. It's like a trippy sixties' dream, hey man, I answered the phone man, and next thing I knew I was a six foot cock in the centre of Glasgow and then an eight-foot squirrel on the telly at the football. Still, at least when I'm seventy I can look back and say I've played Hampden . . . Wow, do I go off on tangents or what?

Returning back to the warmth of Xmas 2005 at Jack's Bash and wearing the reindeer horns our lovely listeners asked us to wear, I had a quick look around to see what was available as a wee souvenir (they also asked us to pinch something, naughty lot!).

The personal Christmas card from Tony and Cherie Blair sitting on a cabinet looked tempting, and I must've been looking shifty, for Jack's aide, aware of our challenge, approached with the line: 'So, anything caught your eye yet?' Sense prevailed, and we left the bash having certainly left an impression of sorts. Jumping on the train at Haymarket, we never even got to our seats when a well-dressed lady with her family smiled: 'So Cat, what did you nick then?' I went to Girls' Brigade you know . . .

Increasingly we exist in a blame culture and for that reason I am now pointing the finger vehemently at booze and the government. Champagne goes to my head (via my 'I think I can sing and play piano' gene) and crazy ideas develop. If

I hadn't had that Cat-out-of-water feeling at Jack's glitzy do, your poor relative/friend/secret lover would still have their cash instead of this catalogue of nonsense.

For what it's worth, deep down I know Mr McConnell loves his new super-clingy swimwear but the fact that his wife Bridget never came over to chat suggests she probably prefers shorts.

Could 2006 be any more surreal? Here are the Cat's whispers . . .

January

Monday the 9th

First day back in 2006 and I get off to a splendid start. I forget my key fob and have to stand in the freezing cold for nine minutes as Robin and Willie Docherty, our overnight legend, chat merrily in the warmth of the studio wondering why the old guy who delivers the *Metro* newspaper at this unearthly time keeps ringing the bell. My brain has also turned to mush as my log-in fails. I need my bed like a footballer's wife needs fake tan.

After a quick look at the papers it becomes obvious that Roy Keane is having a much worse time of it then me. The Man United legend shocked the international football world by quitting Old Trafford to join Celtic. His debut, a third round cup tie against lowly first division Clyde, was expected to be a stroll in the park. A shock 2–1 victory for the underdogs makes tabloid heaven. 'DestROYed,' screams the *Mirror*, while the *Scottish Sun* pictures the jubilant Clyde squad under the headline 'Roy WHO?' I knew he should have gone to Partick Thistle.

We somehow stumble on to the subject of driving tests, a topic my poor mum still gets stressed thinking about after overtaking a funeral party back in 1965. In her defence, the rearmost car was going at fifteen miles an hour and she couldn't have known when she pulled out that there were seventeen vehicles in front of it.

Curly from Edinburgh calls to inform us his pal recently sat his test and was asked what hazard lights were used for. His reply: 'They're for when you stop the car and nip in for a newspaper.' It comes as no surprise to learn he failed.

Talking of failing, today I have signed up for the double torture of gym induction and fat class – or Scottish Slimmers as they prefer to call it. To avoid this becoming a Bridget Jonesesque tome, only incidents of extreme interest or severe pain will be recorded.

I wonder if Roy Keane fancies becoming my personal trainer. One swatch of that fuming coupon at the final whistle and I'd be sprinting like an athlete in no time . . .

Tuesday the 10th

It's a fairly quiet Scottish news day which pleases me greatly. Quite often the most entertaining debates and enthusiastic responses come from discussing day-to-day trivialities.Today's major talking point was kicked off by an e-mail from Harry Davidson in Edinburgh whose little girl Gemma wanted to know why there's no such thing as banana jam. Right up there with what happens to turkey eggs and why do I find myself physically unable to watch Gary Lineker on the telly. With raspberries, strawberries, gooseberries, rhubarb, oranges, lemons, pineapples and even exotic fruits like guava now becoming jam, it had me stumped. The general consensus was that bananas go off colour too quickly.

However, Robin caused a stooshie by doubting the existence of pineapple preserve and for the next fifteen minutes poor Mr W., our six-foot-four baldy English producer, had to field calls cataloguing the location (including which aisle), price, make and availability of every solitary jar of pineapple jam in Scotland. He now believes.

As a seasoned pro, Robin very rarely makes mistakes. As an on-air liability (or 'character' as the bosses write in complaint sheets to Offcom) I particularly enjoy pulling him up when something IS amiss.

This text arrived at 8:17 a.m.: 'Robin it is the 10th of January, not 10th January. This is Scotland NOT America.' As a very vocal hater of DJs who've adopted the transatlantic drawl, he was mortified. To rectify the situation he announced in his finest RP voice,

'Good morning and a very warm welcome to Monday the 10th of January.' Oh how I chuckled, as the texts poured in reminding him it was TUESDAY. As I've mentioned, a VERY quiet Scottish news day.

After the reprimand for his lamentable Americanism, it was slightly ironic that we then went into a trail for our holiday giveaway VACATION station. Yeehah!

Wednesday the 11th

I am in shock. As part of the *Breakfast Show* sponsorship deal, every now and then the lovely people at Arnold Clark drop off new models of cars for us to test drive. Sir Uncle Arnold, as we like to call him, is clearly in humorous spirits. A top of the range Lexus awaits Robin, a wee Nissan Micra C+C is waiting for me and unfortunately it is PINK. Not pink as in pastel pink, but pink as in luminous, visible from space, stop and gawp in the street jaw-dropping pink.

We have a laugh on air about my new wheels, with the Pink Panther tune and Barbie Girl playing in the background. As a result, my trip home along the M8 could not have been more embarrassing if I was in a soft top tartan combine harvester. With toots from lorry drivers, waves from chuckling couples and kids bouncing about mental in the back of cars, I had to smile graciously despite being absolutely mortified. The van full of joiners who all put on their sunglasses to pass did make me laugh out loud.

Parking on Byres Road at night time, two sniggering, chip-munching Neds eyed up the motor with glee and asked the question on most people's lips: 'Haw missus, do you no' feel like a pure fanny driving that?' I suspect you know the answer . . .

Thursday the 12th

Angelina is having Brad's baby. It is official, and our female listeners are not pleased. She is a marriage wrecker, a harridan and a psycho according to our irate lassies. 'Ah but she is A-MAAY-ZING,' says Robin in a 'she is DIRTY but in such a good way' voice. Every male on the planet apparently feels the same way.

'It's those lips,' say the texts. Dead or Alive singer Pete Burns is grabbing headlines in *Celebrity Big Brother* this week. I wonder if they feel the same way about him.

Turns out Robin's kids have been telling all their neighbours and school pals that MP George Galloway, who is also in the *Big Brother* house, is their uncle. I try to think of any famous relatives I could invent and give up after a six-foot imaginary rabbit is as good as it gets.

As part of a promotion with the Hong Kong tourist board, we are broadcasting the show from there over the Chinese New Year. We've known about this since November, but it's only weeks away now and today we have our first official meeting. The trip sounds amazing, and with the time difference, we shall be on air in the afternoon from 1.00 p.m. until 6.00 p.m. which is FANTASTIC.

Without doubt the worst thing about doing breakfast radio is the sleep deprivation. I get up at 3.45 a.m., with a view to being in at 4.30 a.m. for a 5.00 a.m. to 9.00 a.m. show. As I live in the centre of Glasgow, people are usually walking home half-cut, eating kebabs and snogging randoms (ah, the good old days) while I am driving to work. Jings, I could even have a Canton Express (Glasgow's late-night metropolis of fine dining) for breakfast.

Bedtime is between 8.00 p.m. and 9.00 p.m., although most folk who work this shift suffer from sleeping problems at some stage. Not only have I aged fifty years in the two years I have worked breakfasts, I have put on almost three stone. Extreme tiredness and needing something to eat at about 6.00 a.m. and then lunch at about eleven leads to snacking. But that, of course, was the old me; now I have joined Scottish Slimmers, I shall be fine.

That reminds me, I have not been back to the gym since the induction and tonight we have our belated Christmas dinner with the Arnold Clark team. The show was so successful last year that champagne is apparently on the cards. I shall be ordering PINK, of course, that'll teach them. This fitness lark may be tougher than I thought . . .

Friday the 13th

Ah, the power of radio. A box packed full of pineapple jam and banoffee spread is waiting for us. The good people from Dobbies Garden Centres PR department are obviously listeners. Robin concedes he was wrong and spreads it thickly on some of his lo-carb, fat-free, vegan wholegrain baked-by-orphans health bread.

We are both a bit sleepy after last night's Arnold Clark night out. In a moment of madness, or perhaps to prove a point, I turned up at the Thai Fountain in pink pyjamas, pink diamanté sandals and sporting a waist-length, pink and purple highlighted wig. My new look went down a storm, they appreciated my point (PINK bloody car – I ask you!) and I've decided PJs are the most comfortable clothes to wear in restaurants ever and may start a campaign to advocate such behaviour. Fancy another course? Simply loosen the drawstring. Lovely.

The wig began to get a bit scratchy and hot after an hour, but it remained on, and when a two-foot-long curly purple lock was found floating on a sweet-and-sour prawn dish, we could not blame it on the kitchen.

Today is Friday the 13th and we debate superstitions. I have to tap the outside of a plane three times at the top of the gangway before going on board while Robin HAS to have his trousers on BEFORE his socks. As ever, the listeners provided a fascinating insight. Texts included:

'I put my boots on at home but NEVER tie them until I get on site, done it for years and don't know why.'

'I always put my right shoe on first. I put my left on first once and crashed the car, so never again.' John, Motherwell.

'Spare me a thought. I am very superstitious with a phobia for dentists and I have an appointment at 8.45 a.m. Help.' Debbie Mac.

'When I buy shoes I always put them on the wrong feet for two days. I have done this for ten years.' Scott Reid.

'My mum and dad got married on Friday the 13th and they celebrate twenty-five years together today so it can't be all bad.'

Alan Rough popped into the studio to join in the discussion, and as he's a former international goalkeeper, we knew there would be some belters. Turns out Roughie had a bag full of lucky trinkets in his goalmouth – including a garter; he also had to bounce the ball seven times off the wall in the tunnel before running out and had to eat seven bits of chewing gum during the game. It was always three bits in the first half, and four in the second (no doubt 7–0 to the opposition by then).

He laughed as he recalled tales of his former Partick Thistle boss Bertie Auld who was exceptionally superstitious. Now Bertie enjoyed a drink, and could look a bit rough some mornings according to Roughie. On this occasion, he was bouncing about the dressing room and staggering all over the place looking stressed during the team talk. Turns out he hates standing on white tiles and with the newly decorated changing rooms floored in black and white ones like a chess board, he was simply trying to avoid bad luck. As manager of my beloved team he certainly had his work cut out in that department.

I still haven't returned to the gym, had pizza for lunch and was peeped at about forty times in THAT car – it HAS to go. Squashed a black cat and smashed a mirror on the way home. I shall now probably have it for life . . .

Monday the 16th

Forget Christmas, Hogmanay and St Andrew's Day – today, January the sixteenth, is the new BIG one for your diaries. Oh yes, for it is on this fine day, so the press release sitting in front of me informs, we must celebrate National Soup Day. A cunning marketing ploy from Ena Baxter and her soup empire, or a genuine bid to give our favourite winter warmer the respect it firmly deserves? Who cares, we love soup and so does the whole of Scotland.

Every conceivable soupçon of soup is discussed from the best homemade soup in cafés across Scotland to the best bread to dunk in it. In the interest of brevity, I shall sum up the findings; we love lentil best, it has to be made by an elderly relative and despite celebrity chefs and their current penchant for blending everything, we still like our chunky bits.

Talking of which, I was up at the Comedy Unit today discussing my wardrobe for *Offside*. Turns out, now that I am to be in the studio with Tam, there's a woman whose job it is to buy my clothes to fit in with the lighting and the set.

To some women this must be heaven – a personal shopper providing the latest fashions: to me this is absolute torture. As a self-confessed label 'chopper-offer' the thought of someone knowing what size I'd really like to wear is horrific. But I know that giving the wrong size could be disastrous. Visions of me sitting in a Girls Aloud-sized crop top with it all hanging out calls for drastic action.

I physically bundle Cath (the poor unfortunate) into an empty room with my list of demands. No bare arms, nothing tight, no cleavage, no patterns, black, black and nothing but black. I can tell she is more than a little bit scared and I can't help it. Clothes do this to me. Thankfully, Cath is used to dealing with flaky actors with body hang-ups and assures me she will pick wisely.

With that sorted I head to fat class (a pound and a half off) and vow to eat nothing but bloody soup until it is all over . . .

Tuesday the 17th

Now then, now then, guys and gals. Mr W.'s mate Sir Jimmy Savile has entered the *Celebrity Big Brother* house and is granting wishes left, right and centre.

From the catchy theme tune, 'Your letter was only the start of it . . .' to the lush red shiny ribbon on those to-die-for medals, I loved *Jim'll Fix It* almost as much as *Wonder Woman*. The fact that he never let me play for Partick Thistle or meet Dexy's Midnight Runners back in the early 1980s is irrelevant.

We open the phones to find out what our listeners would ask Jim for if they could. Robin wants lunch with Sir Paul McCartney (not with that new icy wifey of his thankfully); I'd like a night out with smouldering Chelsea boss José Mourinho. Actually, make that a night in. Oh my.

It turns out the great Scottish public have some very odd ambitions. Helen in Springburn phoned full of enthusiasm: 'I've always wanted to drive a car through a showroom window really fast like they do in movies.' Hmm. I know just the car she can practise on. Texts include:

'I'd like an amphibian boat to get me to work from Leven to Leith'. Allie.

'I'd like a life-size David Beckham hot water bottle, as long as it doesn't speak.' Karen in Stirling.

'When I was ten I wrote to Jimmy Savile to dance with Five Star. He never got back in touch and I am scarred for life.' Vikki in Falkirk.

For reasons of decency this final one will remain anonymous.

'I'd like Jim to fix it for me to have an affair with my mother-in-law. She is hot.'

Oh dear.

Robin asks how my fitness campaign is progressing and I have to admit I've not been since the induction eight days ago. The thing is, the girl is planning to assess my fitness next week to add to the programme, so I'm now well behind schedule.

Andy from Edinburgh, who's been suffering from cancer for fifteen years, phones during a song. He says he's proud of me for trying and is going to sponsor me fifty quid if I run the Race for Life in June. Talk about pressure. I feel humble and embarrassed with myself again. The trainers will definitely be coming out today.

I wonder if Jim could fix it for me to be Paula Radcliffe. I'm always bursting so I'm half way there . . .

Wednesday the 18th

I've been thinking about an e-mail sent to the show yesterday. Wendy McGaw from Rosyth in Fife sent a heartbreaking note about her little boy Ivan. To understand the effect it had on us I shall reprint it in full:

Dear Robin & Cat,

You may have read our story in last week's newspapers. We live in Rosyth with our two children Ivan and

Sean. Ivan, who's 6, has a severe developmental delay as well as a partial diagnosis meaning the link between the two halves of his brain is missing. These conditions mean that as well as functioning like an 18 month old child, he's unable to speak and has very bad eyesight caused by cataracts. He gets so frustrated at not being able to communicate and it's heartbreaking for us all.

Ivan attends a special school in Dunfermline and is trying so hard to find some means of communication. In fact any progress he makes, no matter how small, brings a tear to our eyes as he tries so hard. He's had so many operations since he was born and we're constantly trying additional therapy in the hope it improves his life. Recently while on holiday in Majorca, we visited a marine park and he was able to touch the dolphins – prompting a level of excitement we've never seen in him before. It was almost like they knew how special Ivan was.

On our return from Majorca, we've looked into therapies available related to dolphins and found one such project in Key Largo, Florida. They offer speech-therapy, motor-neurone therapy and physiotherapy to mention just a few but it's a very expensive treatment. We're determined to do everything we can to send Ivan on the course in the hope of any improvement to making his life a little easier. Ultimately, it would mean so much to all of us just to hear our little boy speak a few words and escape the silent and frustrating world he's lived in all of his life.

Yours truly,

Wendy & Alan (Ivan's loving parents)

I read this out as part of our newspaper review segment and immediately the phones go into meltdown. Wendy needs £7,000 to take her wee boy for a week of treatment and we think we can maybe help raise this.

We speak to her on air at half past seven and I can already feel myself getting teary and emotional. Ivan can't communicate at all, so his mum never knows if he is happy, in pain or hungry. She admits, 'Our dream is that one day he will say a few words.'

Scottish people are somehow tarnished with the reputation of being miserly and this has always perplexed me. We are a generous nation and today our listeners are the best people in the world. Within an hour we have five grand, ranging from businesses donating £1,000 to wee Rebecca who phoned in to donate her £2 pocket money.

The unofficial appeal gathers momentum at a rate of knots. Wendy gives us account details of an appeal fund she's started and we continue to be bombarded with pledges. By nine o'clock we get her back on the line with the news we have raised over ten grand. Her wee boy WILL go to Florida for treatment, Direct Holidays have donated free flights, and three people have offered their personal villas for nothing.

Naturally, Wendy is stunned, as are we. She is very emotional on air thanking everybody for their donations and best wishes. Her final line before she broke down in tears was: 'Hopefully one day he will be able to say mummy or even thank you.'

Texts flood in about people greeting on the bus, in their cars and on the train. I come off air emotionally drained and walk into the main office in a daze. Bossman Jay gives me a hug and I burst into tears. I managed to contain myself until now but I'm completely emotionally spent. Hopefully we have made a difference to this wee boy's life. For all the fun, frivolity and nonsense we get up to, it's days like this that show me how powerful radio can be and how bloody fantastic the Scottish public are.

A producer from the news desk at Scottish TV's *Scotland Today* programme phones at 9.01 a.m.: Ivan's story will be shown tonight. A real-life story as touching as this puts everything into perspective and I need to be by myself. I've decided to go and gather my thoughts in Greens' swimming pool.

For the record, I can't bend down courtesy of my two-hour gym visit yesterday. Andy in Edinburgh – I hold YOU responsible!

Thursday the 19th

It's all celebrity baby chat this morning. Angelina's had a wee scare, Holly Hunter has dropped twins at forty-seven, and Katie Holmes continues to be plagued by weird behaviour from loopy father-to-be Tom Cruise. For her birthday, lucky thing, he gave her the entire back catalogue of his films, including three starring his ex-wife Nicole Kidman and one with his ex-girlfriend Penelope Cruz, and he signed them! What an arse.

Inappropriate gifts become our subject of the day. My mum, who can't see very well, got me aloe vera cream from Lanzarote when I was about seventeen. She didn't read the small print, it was an anti-cellulite formula. I could use it now right enough.

Willie McNiven calls: he was given a colour TV by his mum and dad who beamed with pride telling him they had paid in full for the first month's rental! It was returned after thirty-one days. Texts included Brian from Wishaw who got hair gel from his mum for Christmas despite having shaved his head for ten years. Anne from Musselburgh was given a diary by an aunt, FIVE years out of date. My favourite gaffe gift was given to Davie from Barrhead on his wedding day – a cow bell. I'm sure his wife is lovely though.

After the show I can't find my mobile so pop out to the pink car to see if I've left it there. When I open the door two teenage girls scream at me like Beatlemania and snap with camera phones. Well not quite, as it turns out I've just fired past Lee Ryan, former Blue hunk and singing sensation, in reception. Slightly embarrassing when I get back in and he instantly smiles: 'Hiya, I've met you before haven't I?' The only previous time we could possible have caught eyes was at the Blue concert in the SECC in 2003 where my mad mate Kaza and I were in row C and the only people over fourteen and five foot tall.

Having had a bit of a Duncan and Simon fetish, I've also described him on air as the 'ugly one from Blue'. Thankfully, he is unaware of this and I can only assume the old Shelly-from-*Corrie* lookalike thing has thrown him (I can't see it myself but everyone else does). We chat about drink and singing karaoke and bond when we discover we both sing Guns N' Roses as our song of choice. I murder 'Sweet Child of Mine', he no doubt smoulders through 'November Rain'. He's definitely much, MUCH better in the flesh and a nice lad as well.

I do what most media-savvy nonchalant radio presenters do after meeting a pop star – I text my pal Alyson in a 'na na na na na' stylee and e-mail her a picture. I'm sure I shall grow up soon.

Friday the 20th

There is a bit of paper fluttering on my windscreen when I go to my pink car parked on the road outside my flat at 4.20 a.m. I have the parking ticket dread, but no, it is a birthday request – Ian McPherson from Glasgow is forty today. The car HAS to go!

Kenny Miller is the talk of the steamie. The twenty-six-year-old Scotland striker has signed a pre-contract agreement to join Celtic in the summer from Wolves and as an ex-Rangers player this causes a right commotion. Photos of Miller playing for the Gers are removed from the walls of the Loudon Tavern, and Alfie Conn, the first post-war player to do the same (years ahead of Mo Johnston) predicts he is in for thirty years of misery.

I've interviewed Kenny loads of times and reckon he is a bright enough lad to know what he has let himself in for. My dad took me to an Old Firm game on the day of my sixteenth birthday to show me WHY I was a Partick Thistle fan. It was my most memorable present ever. I love Glasgow to bits and I love football, but there is a sectarian minority following each side that spoils it for everybody.

Right, enough of this serious stuff. In other news Angelina is now thought to be having twins, and Keira Knightly is in a huff for not being nominated for a BAFTA. *Brokeback Mountain*, better known in Scotland as *The Gay Cowboy Movie* or *Bareback Boaby*, is tipped to win best picture. Robin was dragged kicking and screaming to see it by Mrs G, and loved it.

This is quite a timely revelation because tonight I'm going to the King's Theatre to see *Footloose*. Now there is a story here. When I go on a girlie holiday I always make up a CD with each adventurer choosing three tracks. My friend Janis always picks 'Footloose' and it is the one song in the world that absolutely does my head in. I exert editorial control and NEVER put it on. However, at Christmas I felt a bit guilty for being so mean and bought tickets for all of us to go. This opened the floodgates about events we dread that turn out OK.

Golden Baz, our very weegie and masculine stand-in producer, is mortified when I reveal that he enjoyed a Michael Bolton concert with an ex so much he now has an M.B. key ring!

The number of anonymous texts today makes me chuckle. I suspect most are from men taking their mums/other halves to Daniel O'Donnell, Tom Jones and Sidney Devine and subsequently loving it. Gerry in Lanark was taken to the Royal Concert Hall three years ago with fellow trainee architects. To get in to see the building they had to pay to see the only concert on – a three-hour show with Russian folk dancers. He's not sure about the building but reckons Cossack dancing is the future. Other stoatirs include:

'I was dreading the mother-in-law at Christmas, but she turned out to be OK.' Anon.

'I was dragged to *Sing-A-Long-A Sound of Music* at the Theatre Royal, but it was fantastic. I sat next to a steaming nun with a hip flask and the guys in front of us had made lederhosen from curtains like my mum's.' Loreen. My favourite was:

'My girlfriend dragged me to a big day out that I was desperate to avoid. However, when I got there everyone bought me drinks and I got steam-boats for free. It was our wedding.'

It must be fate. Cath the *Offside* wardrobe lady calls to meet up. She's bought me 'interesting outfits' for the show and suddenly going to *Footloose* seems like fun . . .

Monday the 23rd

I'm feeling quite perky this morning on the back of a successful weekend. The pink car has gone and I can drive anonymously again, which means that any annoying wee dangly bogeys I find at the traffic lights are now not such a major personal dilemma. I swapped it at Arnold Clark Nissan, Linwood, where all the staff ran out to greet its arrival.

'We knew it was pink but not THAT pink!' said Steven the manager. They'd put on 'I'm a Barbie Girl' in the showroom especially for me. The car caused such an instant commotion they decided to mount it on a plinth in their forecourt for all to see and kids have been getting their picture with it all weekend. It's been an adventure but I'm delighted normal service has been resumed.

Today the papers are full of the Euro lottery. There's been another rollover and the prize is now £100 million. This would earn £3.5 million a year in interest by simply banking it. We open the phones and our listeners suggest ways to spend the riches:

'I would make a hostile takeover of my work.' Peter in Falkirk.

'I'd start my own dream team of footballers – and drool over them every Saturday.' Karen from Stirling.

'I'd buy a South Sea island filled with dozens of dusky maidens – after I've divorced the wife of course.' Steve Baxter.

'I would buy a massive house and take the rest of the cash in pound coins. I'd then happily spend my days shovelling them from room to room naked.' Hawk.

Offside starts on the telly this evening and I am now bricking it. I've never been in studio in front of an audience before and Robin tries to ease my nerves by setting me a challenge. He reckons I should squeeze in a secret word and asks for suggestions. Well, every swear word you could think of is texted in along with: balloon, onomatopoeia, heehaw, stramash, neuroscience, heebie jeebies, Munchkin and jobby. The latter is a naturally funny word that makes people chuckle but I'm not sure I could squeeze it out on air . . .

Munchkin seems VERY popular and within minutes the challenge is set. In a football show on BBC1 primetime I have to say Munchkin. Great. I love Robin dearly, but sometimes I could punch him in the face.

I give a special wee mention on air to Alan Porter, a builder from Glasgow, who I met with his girlfriend at *Footloose* (I loved it and danced in the aisle, so predictable . . .). Alan meets his mates every Friday in the pub and told them he was ill. He is adamant that I CAN'T say they were there, west-of-Scotland masculinity issues obviously. His girlfriend whispers his name to me and winks as they return to their seats. Her sweet revenge for lonely Friday nights, I suspect. I am more than happy to oblige in a moment of Girl Power solidarity. I can be a pesky wee Munchkin too sometimes . . .

Tuesday the 24th

Four hours' sleep and up and at 'em again. Despite my nerves, *Offside* was fine last night and I completed my task. Following an interview with former Rangers and Barcelona star Giovanni Van Bronckhorst, Tam asked me if I thought Partick Thistle had any youngsters with any chance of playing in the Nou Camp.

'No, we are a team full of Munchkins . . .' I replied to his blank look and muffled sniggers throughout the audience.

It was weird not having an autocue, but I think I'll get used to it in the forthcoming weeks. The show is recorded an hour before transmission, and unfortunately we ran way over. This means the producer is forced to edit bits out in a frantic bid to make the allocated time slot. I was stunned to watch the final programme being broadcast and realise that my momentous Munchkin moment was chopped for time reasons. I know this morning I am in for pelters.

A new survey out today has listed the top ten feel-good films of all time. They are:

1. *Some Like It Hot*
2. *Billy Elliot*
3. *The Odd Couple*
4. *Bringing Up Baby*
5. *Grease*
6. *My Fair Lady*
7. *Singin' in the Rain*
8. *It's a Wonderful Life*
9. *Strictly Ballroom*
10. *The Gold Rush*

We think the new survey is rubbish. I've not heard of several of these and where is *Dirty Dancing, Shrek, Mary Poppins, Toy Story, Bridget Jones, The Blues Brothers, Debbie Does Dennistoun,* etc.?

Billy from Glasgow phones in with a cracking yarn:

'When *Top Gun* was out my pal and I chatted up two Dutch girls in the Excelsior Hotel and pretended we were fighter pilots. We knew terminology from the film and anything we couldn't answer, we told them we couldn't divulge any further information for security reasons. Turns out they were trolley dollies and knew more about planes than us. However, we sang the song from *Top Gun* like Tom Cruise did in the pub to Kelly McGillis, and they were taken in. We pulled, so *Top Gun* turned out to be a feel-good movie for me quite literally.'

Robin teases me endlessly about my failure to deliver my line on telly. Texts of disappointment flood in, and my 'It was edited out, honestly' chat is met with disbelief. Thankfully Davie from Glasgow was in the *Offside* audience and texts to my defence. Hopefully this wee game doesn't continue for the whole ten-week run.

I come off air and shamefully cancel my catch-up session at the gym. I make up a terrible excuse and everyone in the newsroom laughs at my outrageous fibbing. Give me a break; I have the stress of finding a new fat class today because *Offside* clashes with my regular one. I wonder how many other mentally fragile dieters have to swap slimming classes for TV commitments. I must call Vanessa Feltz . . .

Wednesday the 25th

I'm really sleepy again this morning. Stayed up to watch *Celebrity Big Brother* for the first time in ages and sat in disbelief as the house imploded. Scraps left, right and centre and without doubt the finest night of reality TV ever. Pure car-crash telly with Michael Barrymore, Dennis Rodman, Preston, George Galloway and Chantelle, the non-celeb, all dissolving in front of our eyes.

I wouldn't go on one of these shows for all the money in the world, but we have had our own similar experience. Last year we did a Real Radio House at the Ideal Homes exhibition in Glasgow. There were ten presenters, ten days, a lot of pool, a lot of laughs and a lot of booze. Unfortunately we all got on. Robin was the winner which pleased me loads. No fitness DVD or *Heat* magazine column for him, though. Shame really. He's quite athletic for an old bloke.

Today we are celebrating Burns Night, and have a wee mini-Burns supper in the studio. Two people from Hall's Haggis turn up, or should that be turnip, and prepare an early morning feast. We have bagpipes, the address and then get stuck in. Fantastic, even the veggie one tastes great. Our listeners share their Burns Day plans:

> 'St Vincent School for the Deaf are having Burns Day, with dancing, poems and haggis. The kids are really excited about it all.' Mandy, their teacher.
>
> 'Would you please tell my wife Evelyn that haggis, tatties and butternut squash is getting there, but not quite right.'
>
> 'We had haggis on Monday, it would've been out of date today so it's liver and onions instead.' Scott, Edinburgh.
>
> Bert Jenkins e-mails from Sweden: 'I am so homesick listening to your Burns supper chat that I am now pining for Scotland.' Minutes later we receive another e-mail:
>
> 'Hi, I sit next to Bert in Sweden, I wish he would stop with this greeting about haggis and just f*** off back to Scotland and give us all peace!' Ah technology.

When the trendy young Hall's Haggis man asks Robin for a photo, he smiles and puffs out his chest thinking he's a hit with the hip and happening crew. 'It's for my mum,' he adds, as I snigger into my sleeve.

Thursday the 26th

Quelle surprise, George Galloway has been booted out of the *Big Brother* house. His political career is in the balance with constituents complaining that their elected representative should not be pretending to be a cat, or wearing red Lycra in theatrical role-playing situations with a gender-confused ex-pop star. They have a point. He's been sensational to watch, a right nippy wee stirrer, as my gran would have commented. That said, I would not trust him as far as I could throw him. He still manages to sneak into a poll released today by *Reader's Digest*, listing celebrities we trust. Granted he is number 96 out of 100, narrowly ahead of kiss and tell guru Max Clifford and the perpetually slippery Peter Mandelson. The top ten are:

1. Sir David Attenborough (comforting velvety voice, knows lots about bugs and stuff);
2. Sir Trevor McDonald (ice cool newsreader, trustworthy but not very endearing);
3. Rolf Harris (Rolf rocks. I met him in a lift once at the Press Ball with my pals. We invited him to join our table for a laugh and he did. Fabulous company, he got up and sang 'Two Little Boys' and 'Tie Me Kangaroo Down' with the bemused band and spent the rest of the evening happily sketching drunk journalists on napkins and little Rolfaroos. A legend.);
4. Bill Oddie (former Goodie, a keen ornithologist and a little bit weird);
5. Sir Cliff Richard (my mum loves him. I don't.);
6. Michael Palin (happy with this choice, he's great and his travels are fascinating);
7. Dame Judi Dench (good actress, surprised at her listing though);
8. Gary Lineker (ARRGH. I can't stand him. Smarm smarm smarm. Trustworthy? If he told a result on telly I would check it on Ceefax. Crisp-selling slimeball.);

9. Alan Titchmarsh (gardening guru with dirty-book-writing hobby. No wonder he looks so happy in his thigh-length rubber wellies. A bit annoying.);

10. Esther Rantzen (her ChildLine campaigning makes her a worthy inclusion).

My list would include STV anchor Shareen Nanjiani, football legend Arthur Montford, Lorraine Kelly, Philip and Fearne and the lovely old bloke from the *Antiques Road Show*. Robin reckons *Reporting Scotland* front-woman Jackie Bird is the most trustworthy in Scotland followed by Carol Smillie. I am noticing a pattern. He is mentioning Jackie and Carol quite a lot these days.

Our listeners add to the collection. Ant and Dec, David Jason, Ewan McGregor, STV newsreader John McKay, Cat Deeley, Nelson Mandela and woolly-bunnet-wearing hill-walking pensioner Tom Weir (awww) all get the big thumbs up. Anne Robinson, Richard Madeley and our own *Football Phone In* host Ewen Cameron fail to make the honesty grade. Ewen will love this.

Great news: Ivan's mum Wendy has been in touch. The *Real Breakfast Show* listeners have raised over £12,000 for his dolphin appeal and he will be going for THREE weeks' worth of intensive therapy in March. We initially tried to raise enough for one week so this is absolutely brilliant.

Tonight we are speaking at the NCH Burns Supper in Edinburgh. Robin will toast the lassies and I shall reply.

There's just not enough time in this week and I feel a tight ball of tension in my tummy with the amount of things I've still to do. I've still to visit the Comedy Unit, shop and pack for Hong Kong, write a speech and spray Febreze on the armpits of my only evening gown that zips. Still, things could be worse, at least I'm not George Galloway . . .

Friday the 27th

Oh dear. Sleep deprivation again, finally got back to Glasgow at 1.00 a.m. from the big NCH Burns Supper and had to be up at half three as usual. Yuk. I really am beginning to resemble Chi-Chi the Panda, a look that should go down well in Hong Kong I suppose.

Robin and I were on our best behaviour last night given the very posh Edinburgh audience. I had hoped Bossman Billy, our esteemed MD, would let his hair down and show his true larky colours, but alas real haloes all round.

The room was full of lawyers, bankers and property people who thankfully all listen to the show. It's usually the mental truckers who phone in but it's nice to see we have a broad appeal. The people were lovely, although I admit I did tone down my speech a little bit.

Comedy moment of the evening was the immaculately dressed woman who spoke like Camilla Parker-Bowles telling Robin: 'Oh Robin, I absolutely adore Boaby!' I bet she does. For those of you not familiar with the show, Robin has a camp character for his wind-ups called Cecil who has a pet mouse called Boaby who just happens to get into some very sticky situations.

We are pretty hyper on air today ahead of our Far East adventure, although my pre-flight nerves are beginning to kick in.

Great story in the *Record* today: Kelvingrove Art Gallery in Glasgow is reopening after three years with an exhibition of Kylie's pants. Glasgow councillors are 'spinning around', and Robin 'can't get them out of his head'. Suggestions for further exhibits flood in:

'We should have an exhibition celebrating everything that Scottish people have invented.' Margaret, Balmore.

'Cat's holiday snaps from age sixteen to present day.' Shirley, Edinburgh.

Several lads ask if the Kylie's Pants exhibit can be scratch and sniff. Then we answer a call with a cracking tale to top them all:

'I WAS the last exhibit in the Art Gallery before it closed for refurbishment. I've been a life model for seven years. One of the local artists painted me and it was the last picture remaining in the gallery before they closed it. Anyone that's been to Art School in Glasgow will know me. I'm BIG Eric.'

Suddenly painting seems like fun!

After a frantic packing session, Robin, Mr W. and I meet at Glasgow Airport. Robin's case is so large all three of us could fit in it. Thankfully, the BA girls checking us in at Glasgow are fans of the show and we somehow manage to sneak an upgrade. We love you! Sitting in club class made the flight bearable (two Niteol tablets and sixteen drops of herbal nerve calmers help too). However, my scabby travel hoodie (black and extra baggy for in-flight comfort) and zebra-faced Totes Toasties draw curious glances from the stewardesses who are still trying to work out how we made it into the posh bit.

I fall asleep after dinner and wake up with the captain's dulcet tones informing me there are only fifteen minutes until landing. Superb, I must go to Burns suppers the night before every flight from now on.

Robin somehow makes it through customs despite the Pablo Escobar prison-like photo. And our adventures begin . . .

Saturday the 28th

I don't usually fill in weekend diary entries, to keep my friends and their crazy antics anonymous. Obviously, I am an angel always. However, I've never been to Hong Kong before and I don't want to forget any of our adventures.

We arrive in Hong Kong at four in the afternoon and check into the Marco Polo Hotel, Kowloon. This is a fabulously positioned five-star joint overlooking the skyline of the island. I open my bedroom door, thank the footman, wait a respectable thirty seconds before running and taking a flier at the luxurious bed big enough for twenty. My room is in fact larger than my flat in Glasgow. There is no time to relax, though, because we have an appointment with Raymond Lo, a highly revered feng shui master.

By checking charts based on the time and date of my birth, Raymond informs me I am an exceptionally loyal friend, highly intelligent, can communicate well (I'm loving this guy) and I'm attractive to the opposite sex. José Mourinho, he regrettably informs me, will unfortunately NOT be mine. He also tells me I am exceptionally destructive – but only to myself. I think this last bit is particularly spot on. I have major problems concentrating on mundane tasks and burn/maim/cut myself numerous times in the kitchen. I also have a host of broken bones from sheer stupidity whilst 'breengeing about' to use a wonderful Scottish phrase.

He also works out, from our respective elements, that Robin and I have the perfect Yin–Yang relationship. 'You are like a perfect married couple.' He smiled, as we chuckled along. 'Except, Robin, YOU are the wife.' Ha. Plenty of opportunity for on-air banter with that one.

Robin's over-excessive male grooming routine and bizarre love of shopping has finally been explained. Not too sure I'm happy wearing the trousers, but for the time being I shall enjoy my more dominant role.

Next up is a visit to Sam the Tailor in a pokey wee back shop in a run-down shopping centre where they make made to measure suits for buttons (sorry!). Sam is actually about the third generation Sam, and is Indian not Chinese. Still, he is world famous and his shop is like a gallery from *Hello* magazine. Robin asks for a cashmere suit, I order a shirt because I feel I have to. Thankfully, he is professional enough not to shout the measurements out to his helper.

Our first meal is in a swanky restaurant called Signature. Little dishes are plentiful with a variety of interesting specials, steamed fish, seasoned scallops, and iced pak choi. Despite being knackered, we soldier on because it is Saturday. We go to Dragon-I nightclub, where the beautiful people pose and sup extortionate drinks to trendy sounds. We last about five minutes.

Over the road is a much cheesier establishment called Insomnia and the atmosphere is much better. We walk into the pub to the sound of Simple Minds' 'Don't You Forget About Me' being covered by the Chinese house band. Bloody good it was too, or maybe that was the vodka. Anyway, splendid night had by all and we make it home for about half three. Not a bad effort given that we have been up for about six weeks . . .

Sunday the 29th

I really want to stay in my bed. My alarm goes off at eight o'clock and I have no idea where I am or why indeed I have to get up.

To give us plenty to talk about on tomorrow's show, we are cramming in a day of sightseeing like you wouldn't believe. We are off to Lantau Island, a forty-five minute drive away. Denny, the local tour guide employed by the tourism board, is proving to be a real character. We climb almost 300 stairs to see the biggest outdoor seated Buddha in world. It is covered in fog and we can't see a thing. Still, it looks very impressive in the postcards.

It is traditional for the Chinese to have a vegetarian meal on the first day of the New Year to cleanse the system. We ate another multi-coloured buffet of weird and wonderful vegetarian food, and let me tell you it certainly worked for us!

Watching the monks chanting in the monastery was an amazing experience, although the ethereal atmosphere was slightly broken by three guys in Celtic tops, one shouting, 'Ma camera's totally f***** by the way.' I lit an incense stick and prayed for his filthy mouth and memory card.

We then walked along the Wisdom Path, a short figure-of-eight shaped trail with free-standing wooden pillars carved with words of wisdom. The top pillar is blank, working on the premise that by the time you reach it you will have pondered long and hard about life enough to have come up with your own conclusion on what wisdom is. Again, the fog gave the place a slightly other-worldly feel and I'm still waiting for my new-found acumen to kick in.

Tonight we visited the official Chinese night parade, where different acts from all over the world showcase their country against a backdrop of fireworks and pyrotechnics. I loved the Beijing lantern balancers and the little Hong Kong children dressed as bees on flashing roller blades. Robin liked the cheerleaders, each one more plastic and pneumatic than her predecessor.

Robin was actually one of the stars of the night despite 3,000 people from all over the globe cramming into the stadium. He wore his kilt with the world's biggest sporran and managed to smile and say 'Happy New Year from all your friends in Scotland' to every TV crew and video camera within a five mile radius. A true professional and charm personified, the fact that he finally got asked to pose for a picture beside the stunning Cathay Pacific air hostesses I'm sure had nothing to do with his motivation.

Monday the 30th

We are woken early to experience a traditional Chinese morning ritual. Thai Chi on the quayside with William and Pandora. I can't believe that at half seven in the morning I am outside wearing a tracksuit being shown up by two locals with the combined age of three hundred and fifty. They are so strong, bendy and elegant; we feel and move like elephants.

Thai Chi works on physical and mental development. The slower you do the moves the more beneficial; it looks so easy but within ten minutes my bum muscles are beginning to hurt. No wonder all the Chinese women are so totty.

For comedy value I take a picture of Mr W. with our new best friends. The height difference is hysterical and soon others are taking pictures of the odd trio too. He is slowly but surely becoming a new tourist attraction.

Our studio really does have the most amazing view; we all arrive early as pre-broadcast jitters kick in. It is always a worry getting the first show of an outside broadcast on air, hoping there are no unexpected technical glitches, and also hoping the listeners enjoy our experience and don't think, 'It is miserable in Scotland and that pair are swanning off to the Far East.'

Denny, our guide, proves to be a natural on air and in a bit of cross-cultural exchange, Robin and Cat's language lab develops. Denny teaches me Cantonese, I reciprocate the favour by giving him lessons in Glaswegian. His first attempt at the phrase 'gonnae no dae that ya bam' ('please refrain, you scoundrel') is sensational. He likes the words so much that for the next five days he says it to everybody who speaks English. I find this hilarious, even if the recipients don't have a clue what the crazy Chinese man is trying to tell them.

Random texts this morning include:

'Can you get me Hong Kong Phooey's autograph?'
    'Happy New Year, you guys. We are still partying with Mr Ho at the Harbour Lounge Ardrossan.'

On the back of our Thai Chi wake-up session, we ask what gets you up and ready for action in the morning. The first thing you have to do before you are ready to face the world. It turns out from a huge response that most people fart. Coffee and cigarettes are also popular pick-me-ups. However, Jim from Ballieston has a slightly more interesting method: 'I put on the Australian aerobics every morning. I'm afraid I don't do it, but I DO like the big blonde at the front. Sad but true.'

The show goes without a hitch and we are mighty relieved. I scuttle back to my bedroom to finish a travel article on Hong Kong for the *Sunday Mail* magazine that has to be filed by tomorrow morning. With internet connection in the room, I can fire off my 1,500 words plus all the pictures they need in one go. Modern technology can be amazing.

It is the traditional New Year fireworks show tonight and as expected, they're absolutely breathtaking. The Chinese love fireworks and this display, over the illuminated neon skyline and choreographed to music is the loudest, brightest and most spectacular I have ever seen. We stand mesmerised for almost half an hour of dazzling light and dramatic bangs. Ironically it is the Year of the Dog; I bet any unfortunate canines nearby are still quivering behind their respective futons.

The Hong Kong tourism boss invites us for a traditional New Year celebration meal and the moment I've been dreading arrives. After a tasty appetizer of little fried white bait that I describe, much to Robin's amusement, as the crispy bits at the bottom of a fish supper, the main attraction arrived. Bubbling in a casserole dish, the spicy oyster sauce with floating shiitake mushrooms looked harmless enough, but given a good stir, the delicacies float to the top like a horror movie. Dinner tonight is chicken feet, duck feet and fish belly stew. Yum. I manage to get a plate of mushrooms with sauce, and watch as Jo from the tourism board devours a chicken foot that, as she nibbles on the tendon, is waving its bony claw at me in a defiant gesture.

We are all in party mode given the fireworks and successful first show and head out to some local bars. The drink flows as Jo ends up gambling with locals in a dice drinking game she doesn't quite understand the rules to. We manage to escape before all the radio equipment, the title deeds to our houses and Robin's kilt are lost over straight vodka and a bad throw.

Our last port of call is a karaoke bar which is full of Chinese people singing in Cantonese. With the bravado of wine and vodka combining, I am desperate to have a shot, only to be given a limited song sheet to choose from. There are nineteen English songs, all of them by the Bee Gees.

'Do you have the Beatles?' I ask.

'NO'

'Do you have Guns N' Roses?'

'NO'

'Do you have anything apart from the Bee Gees?'

'NO, only Bee Gees. You sing Bee Gees?'

'NO!'

We left and headed back to the hotel all singing in a Barry-Gibb-style falsetto: 'You can tell by the way I use my walk I'm a woman's man . . .' Oh, you had to be there . . .

Tuesday the 31st

Head hurts, and alarm goes off far too early again. This *Breakfast Show* in the afternoon lark is proving more tiring than getting up at my usual 3.30 a.m.

Today we return to Robin's spiritual home – Aberdeen Harbour. It is a fascinating mix of old and new, with boat people moored next to the famous Jumbo restaurant. I think we are both still a bit tipsy from the night before, and Robin in particular begins to fade as we arrive at Stanley market. Normally the most genial guy on the planet, his snappy barked statement, 'We need water or there is going to be a fatality' had me in stitches.

At the market, a designer rip-off paradise, I manage to pick up a splendid 'official' 2006 Scotland rugby top for £4. I also begin to fade and end up sitting on the steps of our minibus for an hour as everybody else barters with traders. Once again, my psychosomatic anti-shopping gene has shamefully denied my friends and family exotic gifts.

Robin laughs at my quality purchase on air, and we end up debating curious Scottish things spotted abroad: Irn Bru in Columbia, the *Daily Record* in Mozambique and a Forfar top in Togo rate highly. My favourite, though, was the guy who spotted a fake Celtic top in a Bangkok market, the only problem being it was BLUE and white hoops.

In a moment of sense I stay in this evening and write the script for the big *Offside* feature I am shooting tomorrow night. With radio, TV and newspaper features to contend with, my head is a bit frazzled. I order room service and suddenly feel about twelve and very naughty. I'm not sure why I can't appreciate I am actually a grown-up yet, but in moments like this, in a posh hotel abroad, genuinely doing work on a laptop in my suite ordering risotto, I feel like a total fraud. It is surely a matter of time before everyone realises I am actually not responsible enough to order posh rice dishes on a credit card.

Robin and Mr W. send texts saying they are going mental in the night market, and I'm looking forward to tomorrow when I shall inspect their gadgets. Oh, you know what I mean . . .

february

wednesday the 1st

In a shock move I actually make breakfast for the first time, and it is a gastronomic minefield. Continental, oriental, healthy and deep fried all available and all without a Scottish Slimmers check value.

I am now working on the 'If I don't know the calorific content it doesn't count' line of thought. This is similar to Euro-calories, the system I invented in Spain whereby everything eaten in the heat is comparable to the exchange rate of the pound. One KitKat in the UK equals 110 calories; eat the same biscuit abroad and it is 110 Euro-calories, making it about 85 proper ones. Obviously it doesn't work, but I then put subsequent weight gain down to bloating from the flight.

Today we have to interview the High Commissioner for Tourism. She is a lovely woman with perfect English and has the art of perfectly formed sound-bites down to a Chinese T. We have to go through about a million security checks to reach the inner sanctum of her office in the government building and yet again I have that 'daft wee lassie' giggling thing going on. Do they not know how silly we are? Would the invite have stood if they knew Scotland's principal politician has tight Bulgarian Lycra swimwear lurking in his closet because of us?

It often surprises me, but when we start recording we both switch into professional mode, making her relaxed and getting her top tips on a trip to Hong Kong. Turns out she spent a summer in the rain touring in Scotland and loved every minute of it. It just goes to show the pak choi is not always greener. We pepper clips of this interview through the show which is becoming the Robin, Cat and Denny laugh-in. He is fantastic and has now taken to flirting outrageously with Lindsey, our Glasgow-based sensible news reader.

I have butterflies in my stomach for most of the day because I am shooting my *Offside* feature tonight. I only have the crew hired from Asia Pacific TV for five hours and I have at least six locations to get to. Thankfully my Filipino cameraman, the wonderfully named Sarni Ocampo, speaks great English, even if our Cantonese driver's only recognisable phrase is 'doors please'. Sarni can't believe I am undertaking the shoot by myself and wonders why there is no production assistant, director or producer present.

One of the good aspects of being an ex-Scottish Television reporter is that financial constraints dictated that you had to learn to do everything yourself. This has actually stood me in good stead and I now prefer directing, scripting, presenting and editing my own shoots. With total control it is nobody's fault but your own if it fails to deliver. A motivating pressure if ever there was one.

I'm sure Sarni now thinks I am the daft wee lassie again, playing at being a TV presenter, but he quickly warms to me once I start sounding like I know what I am doing and calling for a variety of interesting shots.

The key to a good videotape insert package is research and I have done my homework. Through the wonder of e-mail I have befriended and arranged to meet Scott Semple who runs Hong Kong's Rangers supporters' club. He's organised a night with other ex-pats all wearing their football tops for us to film. I've also packed A4 sized photos of some of the key faces in Scottish football, after learning a few weeks ago that face readers are popular and prevalent in the night markets. So after an introductory piece to camera in Aberdeen Harbour (suck in the tummy and smile, smile, smile) it's up to the fortune tellers for their take on the future of Scottish football. Denny is my guide once again and is coming over brilliantly on camera too – this guy is a national asset, and a frustrated comedian I think.

The face reader is a young lad of about twenty but he is very intense and gives a fascinating in-depth analysis of the following stars:

Walter Smith – A good guy, he will be blessed with success eventually. He has a new challenge but a lot of people are very happy he has taken up this challenge. (Managing Scotland is certainly a challenge but good news folks – we may qualify for something someday. It is in his eyes apparently.)

Kenny Miller – He is ambitious and very talented but finds it difficult to make up his mind. I think he jumps from side to side too much. (I laugh heartily; Miller has just signed a pre-contract agreement for Celtic. Before Wolves he was at Rangers and you can't jump a bigger side to side than across the Old Firm divide.)

Du Wei – His eyes show lack of confidence, he finds himself in a job he should not be doing. For peace of mind for all, he should consider changing careers. (This is TV gold. Du Wei's short spell at Celtic was a disaster, he was rubbish and I KNOW the audience in the studio will explode when they hear this.)

The face reader did not know who any of these people were, I did not tell him and I leave mightily impressed and more than a wee bit freaked out by his talents. Naturally I sneaked a quick homer. According to my face I am highly intelligent, a good communicator, a natural leader but could be a danger to myself! This is weird beyond belief given that his breakdown was almost identical to the feng shui man. I am now scared to be left alone in case I maim myself in a bizarre act of extreme silly bastardness!

At the pub, the Scottish troops are in great form and I emerge with a better tale than I could have hoped for. It turns out that Billy Semple, the Rangers supporters' club organiser Scott Semple's dad, played for Rangers and Hong Kong Rangers in the 1970s. This I knew, but the fact that he was living with Celtic legend Danny McGrain's daughter Donna was a total bonus. They have a real laugh about their love across the great divide on camera, and I eventually get dropped off at my hotel with two digi-beta tapes' worth of footage and confident that with some creative editing and a bit of thought a very entertaining piece could emerge.

With Robin and Mr W. still up Victoria Peak for dinner, I take Denny for a late bite to eat to thank him and end up in the Hard Rock Café listening to a fairly steaming Chinese would-be rock star murdering the Red Hot Chili Peppers.

It's been a funny old day.

Thursday the 2nd

Up early to interview some posh bloke in our studio about a forthcoming cable car attraction. There is not a bloody chance this interview will make it to air, but we know how to play the game and understand the tourism board have a job to do. I almost feel sorry for the New Zealand project director who is now into the eighth minute of his first answer. Still, we smile and send him on his way happy. I'm not even sure the recorder was plugged in, but what he never knows . . .

The view from the studio today is quite spectacular, the sun is shining and the skyline is gleaming. Little boats speed across the bustling harbour avoiding each other like scurrying ants, while a couple of gigantic cruise ships glide into view majestically, hardly causing a ripple. We are both quite overwhelmed by the experience and open up the phone lines to describe our favourite views. This one is quite exceptional; I also love the view of Glasgow from the Jackie Husband stand at Firhill when the sun is setting, and sailing into Rothesay on a summer morning. Other visual favourites included:

'You can't beat coming home from a tedious business trip and flying into Glasgow from the north west. Suddenly everything seems OK.'

'My favourite view is page three of the *Sun* every morning.' Ray from Carronshore.

'I have the best view in the world. I live in Bridgeton and every morning I open my curtains to see you pair of lunatics eating big sausages on a billboard opposite my flat.' George Reilly.

'Sunset over Islay and the Paps of Jura – totally amazing.' Allan.

'I love it when you see the "Welcome to Scotland" sign when driving over the border to come home to God's own country.' Rab.

'The Forth Rail Bridge at night always gives me goose pimples.' Cathy, Dunfermline.

'The best view ever was Martin O'Neill's face on the last game of last season when Scott McDonald scored for Motherwell to make it 1–1 and the title was over.' Colin, Bellshill.

'The best view in the world is when the big lassie in Tinderbox bends down to the bottom shelf to get something. Quite superb.' Johnny, Glasgow.

After the show, Denny decided to take us all for the most traditional seafood experience he can find. We head up to a small coastal town in the New Territories where we are the only westerners. The restaurant, and I use the term in the loosest possible manner, has a huge array of tanks outside, resembling Deep Sea World. Every sea creature imaginable is swimming, squirming and pinching for its life.

Having recently watched *Finding Nemo* (and I'm still in therapy as a result) I struggled with the concept of pointing to my dinner before the waiter, in wellies, clobbers it over the head and takes it to the kitchen to be cooked. As a result of this trauma we all drink far too much and I end up in a private karaoke booth until six in the morning, working my way through a thick A–Z (including the Bee Gees) of songs to the utter disbelief of Dan the quiet engineer who is the only other member of our party to last the pace. I am invincible and feel no pain.

Friday the 3rd

AAHHH. Pain. Extreme pain, my head hurts, I am still steaming and somebody is knocking on my door shouting 'COOKING LESSON'. This is surely a trippy nightmare caused by a weird marine disease caught from some multi-tentacled sea-beastie scoffed last night when the wine made me brave.

No, it is 8.15 a.m., a whopping two hours after I arrived home, and I am due in the hotel kitchen with the main chef for a lesson in making dim sum. I somehow crawl out of bed, put on my tracky bottoms, fake Scotland top and skip cap and shuffle to the kitchens.

Hangovers are not fun at the best of times, but add clanging pots, heat and fat bubbling in a pot in front of you and suddenly staying upright becomes an issue. Robin and Mr W., who called it a night three hours before me, find this latest task hilarious, like the most warped *Generation Game* – the 'How much can we put in front of Cat before she chucks' game.

The chef places a bowl of raw king prawn and minced fish meat in front of me and my mouth starts watering but not in a good way. This is truly the worst moment of the week, the year, my life, ever. Somehow I manage to make two passable dim sum parcels before making a sharp exit to my room. I sprint to my bedroom door, time running out, and shake in frustration as the door refuses to open. I am a floor below my room and contemplate knocking the door I'm standing at and asking the resident if they'd mind terribly if I hurled in their luxury loo.

A deep breath and a gulp later I am back in lift and tearing to my correct room. Door open, LOOOUUDDD bathroom bowl-cuddling incident, face wash, ah . . . door close. So classy. I manage another hour and a half of sleep and wake up feeling brand new and ready to go again. It was handling the raw fish clearly, not the bevvy.

Today is the culmination of our week's competition and we have a trip to Hong Kong up for grabs. Denny picks a lucky envelope from a lucky tangerine tree and the woman who wins goes bonkers. I've done this show for over two years now, but it still feels amazing to give away such a cracking prize.

Sam the tailor delivers Robin's finished suit – very nice it is too – and we basically wrap up our on-air adventure having a ball at our memories, our antics and with our new pal Denny.

Tonight we go out for dinner and try to persuade the 'Adventures in Radio' people that Australia and the Carnival in Rio should be next. It's been a sensational week: the people, the culture and the hospitality has been first class. I feel very lucky and quietly count my bird-flu-free chickens.

Monday the 6th

As Soul II Soul once crooned, 'Back to life, back to reality . . .'

Today is officially going to be a struggle. Jet lag, *Breakfast Show*, monster TV edit and *Offside*. It's one of those days I wake up wishing it was time to go back to bed. A real 'pillow over the head and make it all go away' moment.

Still, as ever, the *Breakfast Show* wakes me up in minutes. It is true what they say – it's good to go away but lovely to come back. What cheers me up most this morning is the feedback from listeners about our Hong Kong trip.

I have about fifty personal e-mails from people of all ages saying how much they enjoyed our tales. Seven of these e-mails are from Chinese people living in Scotland. This makes it all worth while. We were a bit worried we would alienate people by being so far away, but it seems our mad escapades have been well received. Fingers crossed for further exotic adventures.

Talking of adventures, *The Beano* is making all the head-lines today. They have a family called 'The Neds' (Scottish word for chavs) with a son called ASBO (anti-social behaviour order). Our MSPs are again black-affronted, and demanding an inquiry. However, just like Dennis the Menace and the Bash Street Kids, it seems our youth of today love the latest scamps.

As a fully paid-up member of the Dennis the Menace fan club (I still know the secret words and somewhere have the badges with googly eyes in a special presentation wallet), I say let the Neds stay. We quickly fall into nostalgic comic chat with fans of *Look-in, Smash Hits, Twinkle, Jackie, Just 17, Victor, Commando, The Beano, The Beezer, The Topper* and *The Dandy* all getting in touch. A few texts caught my eye:

'The *Victor* comic had true hero stories from the war, my mum's uncle John O'Neill featured in one as he was awarded the VC.' James Shaw, Hamilton.

'I had a letter published in *Bunty* and got a postal order for 50p.' Gill in Kirkcaldy.

'*Jackie* comics in the 1960s were great. We got a cardboard doll shape and clothes to cut out and dress her with.' Gemma, Falkirk.

It turns out our very own Mr Suave, Bossman Jay, was actually a *Jackie* pin-up in his youth; and, never to be outdone for dodgy stories from the past, Robin finally admits he was a model in *Photo Love* in the eighties! This was one of those black and white photo stories about budding romance, with big speech bubbles coming out of the models' mouths. It turns out DJ and TV presenter Bryan Burnett was the casting director. One listener called in saying he actually remembered the story. He claimed Robin copped off with a pretty blonde, she was called Mrs G and they now have three kids. Sometimes truth is stranger than fiction . . .

Breakfast Show finished, my *Offside* persona kicks in. I spend four hours in an edit suite creating my Hong Kong package for tonight's programme. Denny stars and is as funny on camera as he is in real life. Despite the stress, I am confident the audience will like the package.

I manage to persuade the producer to let me wear the Chinese shirt I picked up for a fiver in the wee market, and then sit terrified as the 300 people in the audience watch my film. Thankfully they laugh at all the right bits and lots of other bits too, and I am buoyant and ready for some comedy banter when Tam starts questioning me about the trip.

I tell the story about our hotel receptionist in Hong Kong who is unfortunately called Fanny Pong and how the Rangers supporters' club over there are called 'The Bawdeep Loyal' . . . all a bit rude for the *Breakfast Show* but the *Offside* audience lap it up. Oh dear, bad choice of phrase given the subject matter. Sorry. I am clearly needing my bed again . . .

Tuesday the 7th

Ah, the wonders of telly. I wake up to find fourteen text messages on my mobile, nine of them asking me for a Chinese take-away. My friends are so funny.

The texts flood in from 5.00 a.m. Apparently I look like Sarah Platt from *Corrie*, Shelley from *Corrie*, a young Barbara Dickson (eh? – must be the eighties jacket) and 'Sophie Dahl – when she was fat.' Ah lovely. As I sit blotchy, make-up free, with bad hair, jeans and another oversized hoodie, I remember why I love radio so much. On radio I am a perfect size ten, and all my tops tuck in.

Today there is a great story in the *Record* about Calum Mc-Donald, a sixteen-year-old from Rutherglen who has passed his flying test before even sitting his Highers. He plans to be a commercial pilot when he turns eighteen.

'First paying jobs' become the debate of the day. I used to stick leaflets for my mum's wee gift shop on car windscreens in Milngavie car parks, but I got paid in free leg-warmers not cash. My first actual money came from renting out roller skates in the sports-drome of the Allander Sports Centre. Turns out Lindsey our newsreader used to hire them from me! Robin stacked shelves in the Star Cash and Carry in Aberdeen. The number of listeners who were paper boys/girls that roped in help from their parents with cars in the winter mornings is hilarious. Other character-building first jobs include:

'When I was eleven I had a tattie scone round in Bishopbriggs. I made eight pound a week, but sold on my business for fifty quid.'

'I started washing hair and sweeping up in a salon when I was thirteen, I now have my own salon.' Carloine in Barmulloch.

'My first job was when I was six, my aunt paid me 50p to find my uncle's cigarettes and snap them all because she hated his smoking.' Alex in Edinburgh.

Once again it was a caller who had me in floods of tears. This wee woman phoned to say she used to work in a newsagent at the age of thirteen. She explained:

'A man came in and picked a magazine from the top shelf. He gave it to me to ring up, but when you're thirteen this is the funniest thing in the world. I bent under the counter to get a brown bag but couldn't come back up for laughing. I nearly wet myself, Christine the older

shop lady, had to come over and put it in a bag and the man never came back. He was totally mortified. I'd like to apologise for my behaviour, but it serves him right!'

We all dissolve into hysterics as she laughs like a maniac on the line. Another brilliant thread from the tapestry of life!

Wednesday the 8th

It's all gone mad again at Tynecastle, home of Hearts Football Club. Lithuanian owner Vladimir Romanov is now picking the team and telling head coach Graham Rix which players to substitute and when. The players, led by club captain Steven Presley, are planning a revolt. Honestly, the goings-on at the club this year are like a crazed script from the most fantastical movie ever written. Personally, I think Romanov is like a comedy Bond baddie. Underneath Tynecastle, I reckon there are thousands of beady-eyed clones in maroon boiler suits preparing a big massive shiny rocket that, at his time of choosing, will emerge through the centre circle during an SPL match against Hibs, to the amplified sound of his evil cackle. I'm not quite sure if the possible target is Easter Road or George Burley's house, but mark my words, something is afoot.

My favourite story of the day is about Beryl and Les Lailey, a wee couple celebrating their golden wedding anniversary. For their big celebratory dinner, they opened and consumed a tin of fifty-year-old Buxton's whole chicken in jelly. It had been a wedding present in a hamper, and they served it with peas and spuds. This was four days ago and both Beryl and Les appear to be still alive and kicking.

Saving things for a special occasion is the big debate and we are inundated by responses. Robin opened the top tier of his wedding cake on his first kid's christening only to find it blue and fluffy (the cake, not his lovely wee girl . . .). Loads of listeners have managed to keep champagne from their weddings. Other interesting texts include:

'My mum got a twenty-five-year-old bottle of Chivas Regal when I was born, we opened it on my twenty-first and brayed like donkeys for days it was sooo strong!' Karen in Durban.

'I have the four pieces of umbilical cord from all of my kids. My children think it is horrific when I try to show them.' Bobby.

'I bought my mum a very expensive leather pouch with a fine brandy in it in Cyprus. I drank the brandy and filled it with cold tea. She never drinks and still cherishes it to this day.' Ali.

'I kept the top tier of my cake but when we were on our honeymoon my parents scoffed it.' Fiona in Edinburgh.

'I got married almost twenty-five years ago; I think the wife is keeping her virginity until our silver wedding. I'll let you know how I get on, it is in July.' Stu in Alloa.

'Unfortunately the only thing I have left from the wedding is the wife.' Mark in Denny.

Today is certainly a day for celebrating anniversaries. The trusty Ford Fiesta is thirty and it turns out nearly everybody who can drive has had one at some point. Again our text line went into meltdown:

'I bought a brand new Fiesta off a guy who won it the week before on *Play Your Cards Right*. I saved a grand.' Rab in Edinburgh.

'I sold my first Fiesta 950 Popular to my mate and bought a sexy 1.4 sport. Two weeks later the daftie ran into the back of me and wrote them both off. I am still gutted.' Kenny boy.

'My first car was a red XR2 it was gorgeous and I called him Freddy. He met a horrible end though when

my brother tried to take out the stereo without discon-
necting the earth and set fire to the back seat. I miss my
wee man.' Susie from Burntisland.

'I had a Fiesta that cost me £150, I kept it for six
months then sold it to Arnold Clark for £600 as a trade-
in.'

See, good old Uncle Arnold strikes again. I'm curious to
see if the salesmen will be as generous tomorrow night when
I head to Kirkcaldy for another car launch. I also wonder if
they ever made Fiestas in pink . . .

Thursday the 9th

It's great to be wee and naughty. All the papers this morning
regale us with the tale of seventeen-month-old Joshua Collins
who ran amok in the ITN news studio. He was with his mum
as part of a feature on the cost of child care but decided that
newsreader Katie Derham's knee was a much more interesting place to be and proceeded to scribble and doodle all over
her scripts. Good effort, wee man.

Robin admitted to etching 'Y-Lemon' into a lamppost
outside his house. This stood for Young Lemons, a gang of
Aberdonian would-be gangsters roaming the Granite City
and aiming water-filled Jiff squeezy lemons at any would-be
contenders. More Codfather than Godfather but, hey, he was
just a pup.

I redecorated our white porch with red rosebuds and also
scratched my brother's name into a mahogany sideboard to
get him into trouble. Unfortunately, at four years old, I didn't
realise Scott had two t's. 'Scot' did not get the blame. Ya
boo.

However, we are in good company as the confessions
unfold:

'I made my wee sister a gammon and dog food sandwich.' Jim, Cambuslang.

'When I was twelve we had to watch my brother's pal's pet mouse when he was on holiday. I wanted to take it to school so I put in my pocket but ran round the couch and banged myself off the wall. The mouse died instantly so I put it back and never told a soul.' Anony-mouse!

'My brother and I were freezing one morning so we lit a campfire in our cupboard. The smell woke up my dad before the house went up.' Neil, Kilsyth.

'On my way to Boys Brigade on Fridays my dad gave me money for his football coupon to drop off to the guy who collected the cash. My pals and I blew the £4 every week on sweets and comics. We used to shit ourselves every Saturday afternoon but thankfully his coupon never came up.' Anon.

'My twin girls emptied two beanbags into the living room when they were four and shouted, 'Look it is snowing,' when they were covered in polystyrene chips.' Bobby D.

'My son peed in the toilet display at B & Q.' Mark, Shotts.

'When we were young my sister and I used to watch the woman over the road let her fancy man in. We would wait five minutes then tie her front and back door together with washing line. Then we would knock the door and laugh as the big guy had to scamper out the side window. It worked every time.' Jim, Dunfermline.

'When I was young if I saw a button I had to press it. One day I wandered off when we were in town. My mum was mortified when she found me. I had brought down the entire till system at Burtons.' Stephen from Stirling.

Midway through the afternoon, Ewen Cameron on the sports desk breaks the story that Alex McLeish will be leaving Rangers at the end of the season. I like Big Eck very much and feel sorry for him. I once had an impromptu night out in the West End of Glasgow with him and his wife Jill.

I was in Jinty McGinty's with my pals being served by Gary Gow, another one of my buddies. Now Gary used to play in goal for Motherwell when McLeish was in charge and the two obviously got on very well. The inevitable lock-in happened, and we all got pretty tipsy. Alex and Jill left about half-three in the morning and he had training at nine o'clock. I was most surprised to see my drinking chum on telly the next night with a cracking shiner from a 'training-ground incident'. Any rumours about a spectacular comedy exit from a taxi are completely unfounded. To be honest, I never got to the bottom of it and have always been too polite to ask. Anyway, he will definitely bounce back. He's a great guy with a lot still to offer the game.

I'm heading up to Kirkcaldy tonight to compère the Arnold Clark Fiat Grande Punto launch. We have loads of listeners in Fife so I'm hoping for a lively night with lots of perfectly behaved angelic children. Ahem . . .

Friday the 10th

Ah, I could have predicted it. The Fiat Grande Punto launch last night was a great success. Mostly thanks to seven-year-old Calum Reekie from Glenrothes.

'Ten, nine, eight . . .' I decided the honour of unveiling the new car had to be shared, so I recruited young Calum who had been energetically dancing through the bubbles that the machine placed next to the glitzy new car was pumping out to create a funky atmosphere. After the big countdown, we pulled the silk cover away to a big cheer. Two minutes later the wee soul came up and tugged my sleeve in desperation. 'Caaaaaaaat. My tooth's just come out.'

In retrospect, as so often happens, I should have thought before speaking. With the wee eyes looking at me as the font of all wisdom and compassion, I blurted, 'Put it under your pillow tonight and you could wake up with the keys of a new Fiat Punto.' Not since I told Bossman Billy's daughter on air that her dad was probably buying her a pony for her birthday have I felt so guilty. However, Calum was great and said he'd actually rather get the money. Bless.

In another of our award-winning debates of intellectual magnitude, the 'going rate' of the tooth fairy, incorporating regional variations, kicked off. I never knew there was such a complex economy involved, with many people giving different rates for the size of tooth. To sum up, the tooth fairy average payment (VAT not included) list is:

- 50p–£1: Ardrossan, Corstorphine
- £1: Livingston, Whitburn, Dunfermline
- £2: Glasgow, Cumbernauld, Wishaw, Uddingston
- £3: Fauldhouse, Falkirk, Edinburgh
- £5: Coatbridge, Lanark, Rosyth.

Other notable stories include:

'We've been having a huge debate about this at the school gates. We have agreed £3 for a front tooth, £4 for a back one.' Sara, Carstairs.

'When I was on holiday with my aunt and uncle they had a puppy that was losing teeth. I thought I would chance my arm and put the teeth under my pillow. I couldn't hide my disappointment next day when I found three dog biscuits under my pillow.'

'The Kilsyth tooth fairy had no change and had to leave a bloody tenner for little Fraser.' Shona, Kilsyth.

'I knocked my two front teeth out at Hogmanay. Forget the tooth fairy, it cost me 500 quid.' Terri.

And as the show finished this final terse text filtered through: 'You do know that kids all over Scotland now have string round their teeth.' Oops. Sorry mums and dads, I'll bite my tongue next time, with a mouth full of enamel currency I hope to save for a long time yet.

Monday the 13th

Every now and then an idea comes along that makes you wonder, 'Why did I not think of that?'

Today a Finnish company is trying to introduce playground equipment for grandparents for fitness and amusement. It is absolute genius. Just last month I witnessed a sprightly octogenarian skite down a chute in a play-park in Largs, while his granddaughter sat nonchalantly on the bench playing with her woolly mittens. I'd love to do the same every now and again, but I face that over-twenty-one female trauma of getting one's ever-expanding bottom stuck in the slide. (For the record, my diet and fitness regime is shamefully on hold again – I blame Hong Kong Slimmers for poor class advertising.)

It seems our oldies are up for a bit of action:

'My dad bought himself a 650 motorbike for his seventieth birthday. My mum refuses to ride pillion. He is eighty now and still out and about.' Linda, Airdrie.

'My mother-in-law Nancy was on the roundabout in Victoria Park last week. She then insisted on taking my grandson Mathew's scooter back to the car. She is eighty-four.' Cathy Crosbie, East Kilbride.

'I watch the oldies moving like snails on sand until the bus for the bingo comes along and they are doing the 100 metres dash no problems at all.' Billy the Kelty bus driver.

'Ten years ago my granny started walking a mile every day. We have no idea where she is now.' Funtime Dave.

I feel shamed by our energetic OAPs as I head off baggy-eyed to the BBC for *Offside*.

Joyce Falconer, the actress who plays Roisin in *River City*, is on the show tonight. She used to sell pies at Aberdeen FC and was a self-confessed Dons groupie in the eighties. We have dressing rooms next to each other (I still feel like a total impostor sitting looking at the big mirror with the showbiz light bulbs around it and using a private loo with soft fluffy towels and hand cream!) so we have a right good banter in the corridor before rehearsals. It turns out her mum absolutely loved Robin on Grampian telly: 'Aye, he wis a richt hunk in his day that Robin. My mum wis totally in love wi him. She used to mak' us all shut up when he read oot birthday dedications. She called him ma wee Bugs because he had fabulous big teeth like Bugs Bunny.'

She has the best accent – like a female version of Hector Brocklebank, Robin's eccentric Peterhead lorry-driving character. The show goes without a hitch, although I know the one swear word (shite) I had to read out within the context of a limerick sent in by a viewer, will grate with Mama Harvey. Despite getting up at half-three in the morning, I do not get home until about half-eleven at night. Spookily my home phone is ringing when I turn the key. 'I didn't like your show tonight,' says my mum sternly, 'Was there any need for that?' I scuttle off to bed feeling about twelve again and very, very naughty. F***.

Tuesday the 14th

I left before the postie got there, honest. Ah, for once in my life this is finally true. Today is Valentine's Day, a day to celebrate being in love, or to hide under the pillows and hope it all goes away. Today, after fourteen months of dating, I am forced to reveal the existence of Mr Cat.

This is not because I am embarrassed about him, more the other way about really. Everybody at his work listens to the show and he doesn't want his private life to be the talk of the airwaves. I can understand this, and I quite like the mystique. I'm sure some listeners believe I still fancy my chances with José Mourinho. Actually, I do, and Johnny Depp, and Duncan from Blue . . .

Anyway, Mr Cat and I were at school together. We used to skive study classes in fourth year to walk to the Spar for Alien Spacers, the 5p crisps. He was quite hot despite the maroon bomber jacket and I recall thinking he was cool but I played too much hockey to be interesting to boys. We met again at a dinner for the first time in fifteen years and that is about it really. Oh, apart from the fact that he will also hate his new title of Mr Cat. Hee, hee.

My favourite lurve story in the papers this morning is about non-league Spartan's striker Bob Mitchell, who says he will propose to his girlfriend Jane Hamilton, IF his side beat St Mirren in tonight's Scottish Cup replay at LOVE Street. I can just imagine the poor lass sitting in the stand, hormones racing, as her man and his team draw 0–0 for ninety minutes plus extra time, only for her lifetime of happiness to be denied by a scrappy sclaffed penalty. We are inundated with people sharing their romantic stories. Kevin calls in from Edinburgh laughing his wee head off:

'Believe it or not this is a true story – I almost got arrested last night trying to be romantic. My wife Sandra is working down south this week. I went to Edinburgh Airport to tie a bow round her car and put flowers in the passenger seat. It took me a while to find it in the car park, by which time somebody had phoned the police to say there was somebody acting suspiciously. The officers were very nice when they realised I actually had keys. How embarrassing. My wife will find this hilarious.'

The *Scottish Sun* actually phone up after the show to try and track him down for a feature, but he didn't leave a surname or number.

It really is feel-good radio today. Tracy Muirhead from Glasgow e-mails in. She got all excited when she saw a card at her door this morning – unfortunately it was for a girl called Michelle Sahli. We mention this on air and within a minute,

Michelle is on the phone all excited. The secret admirer might have got the address wrong, but now we all know she has a fan.

Bossman Billy brings roses in for all the girls in Real Radio and I make a Freudian mistake in a sports bulletin. Instead of reading, 'Celtic boss Gordon Strachan is loving being at the top of the SPL,' I said, 'Celtic boss Gordon Strachan is lovely,' then fell to pieces as the magnitude of this error sank in. Still, I managed a decent recovery in the interests of fairness by declaring Rangers boss Alex McLeish to be lovely too.

Show over, and I am now flagging and totally puffed out from another late night at *Offside*. Mr Cat is cooking me tea tonight although I suspect I shall be sleeping by the main course. Ahh, who said romance was dead . . . I may even try and stay awake for the Spartans score . . .

Wednesday the 15th

It's the Brits tonight, where the cream of the UK music industry competes for a host of awards usually won inexplicably by Kate Bush. KT Tunstall from St Andrews and Franz Ferdinand are up for awards, so fingers crossed for some Scottish success.

The Brits 1989 live TV show with Sam Fox and Mick Fleetwood is in the papers today as one of the most embarrassing TV moments of all time. (The voters clearly never saw me presenting *Tartan Tenpin* from Dundee on Sky a few years back. Oh I still cringe. Even I can get strikes at ten-pin bowling and these guys were knocking them down time after time. I had to record ten one-hour-long programmes interviewing the players after every game. I think at one point I even commented, 'Nice shoes.' Awful.)

Number one on the list is Richard Madeley's impersonation of Ali G on the *This Morning* couch. His wife and co-presenter Judy looked mortified – and what about his poor teenage kids? I can imagine the hands over the eyes in exasperation thinking, 'Daaa-aad!'

Robin reckons he IS an embarrassing dad. Last week he saw his fourteen-year-old in a café with his pals. 'I had to go over, knock on the window and make a face.' He tells me with an evil grin. My dad, the increasingly famous Bobby Harvey, has always been a showman so I have been brought up with ritual humiliation. He will have to go some to beat the Glasgow Airport incident in 2001.

My mate Nichola Kane (STV reporter) and I were queuing at the departure gate with about 300 people when I hear: 'HEY TOOTS.' A quick look at the floor – he might just go away. 'TOOOOTS.' He is not going to go away. Terrified head tilt in his direction. 'TOOTS, MIND AND KEEP YIR HAUN ON YIR HA'PENNY!' Oh my god! For anyone reading this not au fait with broad Scots, this beautiful colloquialism basically means don't let anyone in your knickers. Most of the queue sniggered, Nic and I were both totally mortified and the old couple behind us (both about eighty-five) looked traumatised.

'Is that your dad?' The old fella said in a po-faced manner.

'Yes,' I whispered sheepishly. He peered intently at me over his glasses and grinned: 'Sound advice, my dear, sound advice.'

The embarrassing parent texts are brilliant:

'When I was in the fourth year at school my dad would sometimes pick me up, he used to insist we held hands and would make me skip Morecambe and Wise style down the street with my pals watching.' June, Paisley.

'My dad was breaking in a new pair of hiking boots and insisted on wearing them around the house at all times. He kept them on with just his dressing-gown when my pals were in. How embarrassing is that?' Daniel, Uddingston.

'We used to live in the highlands. In the 1970s my sister was at the village disco; my dad came to pick her up and was waiting outside in his TRACTOR. She never heard from the lad she pulled that night ever again.' Marion.

'My dad worked for a TV rental company repossessing tellies. He would pick me up from the local disco in his works van which had an iron cage in the back. Can you imagine the shame of climbing in the back of a Ford Escort Van and having the cage slammed down?' Sharry.

It seems that embarrassing your offspring is one of the joys of being a parent, and I'm in for a torrid time. My dad has already told me he plans to grow old as disgracefully as possible. I remind him: 'Guess who picks your nursing home?' We are at a happy stand-off at the moment . . .

Oh, and somewhat predictably Spartans were humped 3–0 by St Mirren. Poor Jane is still greeting into her Bovril.

Thursday the 16th

I don't believe it. My team Partick Thistle have reached the quarter-finals of the Scottish Cup and I was in my bed. Sometimes this *Breakfast Show* lark is heartbreaking. The game against Inverness Cally Thistle went to extra time and penalties which sleep-wise would have been a disaster; still, I know this will haunt me for ages.

A good night all round, though, as KT Tunstall won a Brit for being the best female artist. I've met her twice and she is a lovely lass. She came into Real Radio with her guitar strapped round her shoulder in scruffy clothes with a tambourine. All the presenters were in a meeting and Bossman Jay brought her in to give us a wee tune. She played three songs, bashing the tambourine with her foot, and she was great. The other time was at the Merchant City Festival, on a dreich Glasgow Sunday afternoon, playing in front of a crowd of about six.

Peter Andre and Darius were also on the bill. I never knew men could be so orange.

Peter Andre was actually a very nice smiley guy who was charming to all six autograph hunters, although his 'PEOPLE' were a nightmare. Darius, however, who as another Scottish success story I wanted to like very much, seemed like a bit of an arse.

Anyway, I digress. Today there is a cracking story in all the papers about Ford Keirnan and Greg Hemphill aka Jack and Victor from *Still Game*. They are filming up at the Comedy Unit in Maryhill, my other workplace, and got held up because rats were found munching through boxes of crisps from Navid's store! Instead of hitting the internet and e-mailing their pals like normal people do when killing time at work, they bought a £9.99 dinghy from Tesco and set off on an adventure down the Kelvin, a river running through the West End of Glasgow with a hue like mahogany and the consistency of treacle in parts. The boat tore on some rocks and they ended up soaking. They have been publicly reprimanded for being irresponsible by our boss Colin Gilbert, who, having being responsible for producing some of the best Scottish comedy shows ever, probably secretly applauded their marauding lunacy.

However, it seems we all have our own wee ways to conquer boredom in the workplace:

'I'm a nurse at Falkirk Royal, when we are bored we fill up new syringes and squirt each other with water.' Claire.

'My name is Colin. When I am bored at work I e-mail my friends, I surf the internet, and play games on my phone. Please don't tell my boss. He is the taxman!'

'If somebody answered the phone in the project office in the dockyard, we would tape their head to it.' Alex, Inverkeithing.

'I cut shapes out of polystyrene cups and make interesting patterns on cappuccinos with the chocolate.' Rocco.

'When I am bored I go on Google earth and visit places like the North Pole, my street and Hawaii. It is amazing.' Lianne in Leith.

And it seems bus drivers have a host of ways to alleviate boredom:

'My fiancé's uncle was a bus driver. He would stop outside charity shops, nip in and buy something even if there were passengers on board. He was nuts.' Lynne from Stepps.

'When I'm bored on my bus I sing really loudly; this is fine until someone rings the bell when I think I've been alone.' Sandy in Edinburgh.

'I'm a bus driver and I like to guess which old people are wearing wigs and what other people do for a living.'

'Big Rab here, I pick my nose, roll it in a ball and play keepie-uppie with it.'

Sometimes we get just a little too much information. Good skill though, I wonder if we could get him signed up for Thistle's impending Cup quarter-final with Hearts.

Today is the end of an era: after two and a half years on the show our producer, Mr W., is leaving to be in charge of all the presenters. We hint that somebody is leaving the show and the phones go into meltdown. One text exclaimed: 'Not since Torvill and Dean retired have I been so upset.' Ah, I'm afraid you'll have to put up with us for a wee while longer. Unless, of course, the newly promoted baldy High Heid Yin has other plans for the show. I should have made him that bloody coffee . . .

Friday the 17th

I'm a walking zombie again this morning. We had another car launch for Uncle Arnold, this time the Nissan Note, in Linwood, and got to bed far too late. These car launches are getting super-glitzy. There was a beautician, a psychic, a caricaturist (Robin looked like a pixie, I looked like Elle Macpherson, wey-hey) a magician, a pianist, a cocktail bar, a buffet, putting, my old friend the chocolate fountain and somewhere in the middle of it all was a new car, I think.

It's another pretty quiet news day. A story about a Rangers fan that had his court date for car theft changed because he is going to Spain for a European tie is grabbing the headlines. Given the way his team are playing, I'm surprised he didn't opt for enforced incarceration.

Deacon Blue singer Ricky Ross is also in the papers; it turns out he was the guy who persuaded record bosses to give Brit award star James Blunt a deal. He even wrote a track on his album *Back to Bedlam* which has sold seven million copies.

Robin was given a helping hand as a rookie at Northsound Radio by Nicky Campbell who is now one of his best mates. He says Nicky was super-helpful and went out of his way to show him the ropes.

I was given the same treatment by Hazel Irvine at the BBC. I was on work placement at BBC sport for a month and she was absolutely lovely. She took me out on stories, showed me how to interview, how to write scripts and how to edit packages together for TV. Nothing was too much trouble, she even took me to the pub with everybody (I was nineteen, it was allowed!). In fact, the producer of *Friday Sportscene* actually let me shoot, cut and voice a piece for their show and I'm told I remain the only work placement person who ever managed to achieve that accolade. Hazel is currently in Turin presenting the Winter Olympics; she looks younger than ever and is still the consummate professional and a thoroughly lovely lassie.

My first job direct from university was as a staff sports writer for the *Evening Times* in Glasgow. David Stirling, the Sport Editor, caused a bit of a stooshie with the appointment, as I was the first female full-time football writer in Scotland. I started off covering junior football in the central belt and Ayrshire, a post Kate Adie turned down on safety grounds. Russell Kyle and John Quinn were two other lovely journalists who backed me all the way and I give them a wee thank you on air, something I should have done in person to them individually years ago.

We get an amazing reaction from people who want to thank special people in their working life. Some of them are funny, some are quite emotional but all are tinged with fond memories and eternal gratitude:

'David Martin was the best boss I ever worked with but he was made redundant. However he is now doing brilliantly at his new job. We hear he's got a promotion and a much bigger salary but it couldn't happen to a nicer person. I'm still here, we all miss him and nothing has changed.' Claire in Glasgow.

'John Salton the ex-Hibs and Dunfermline player gave me a job when my life was spiralling out of control after my mum died. I am now a partner in the Dunedin Building Company. I owe him everything.'

'My mate Larry took me under his wing. Unfortunately it was B wing in the jail.' John, Broxburn.

'When I started at Weir Pumps in Cathcart I was sweeping the floors and Big John gave me a bigger brush – that is what I call a helping hand!' Big Kenny.

'I would like to thank Stella for all the wonderful times. That is Stella from Belgium. She is a lager and she's helped me lots.' Billy in Kirknewton.

Talking of which, it's FRIDAY and, despite borderline exhaustion, that FRIDAY feeling is kicking in. I have taken two tables at the Press Ball tomorrow night with twenty friends from TV, radio and newspapers. As the Kaiser Chiefs so rightly proclaim . . . I predict a riot!

Monday the 20th

Not quite a riot on Saturday night, just a fire alarm during the main course at the ball, unplanned karaoke in evening gowns in the dodgy bar across from the hotel as the men with hoses did their bit, and the fascinating case of the missing Dolina.

Dolina McFarlane is one of my pals from my STV days; she is quite simply a head-case and one of the most fun people to be around. I have no idea where she gets her energy from, but if there is a surface to dance on then Dolly is your girl. She is also rather fond of the wine; I sense somewhere there is a connection.

Anyway, 7.00 p.m. at the bar is the plan, and by twenty past, seventeen of my twenty guests are present and correct. Two other latecomers are accounted for, and then there is Dolina.

At 6.50 p.m. she sends me a text: 'Wey-hey, bring it on, in a taxi see you in five.' At 7.05 p.m. she sends me: 'At the bar, free champagne, ya beauty. See you soon.' By 7.25 p.m. she sends: 'Still at bar on glass number three, are any of you here yet? I'm talking to a nice man!'

Despite my replies telling her exactly where we are, there is still no sign of her by 7.40 p.m. when the other tables are seated. She phones all champagne giggles: 'I'm at the upstairs bar with the free booze, where are you?'

'There's no upstairs bar at the Thistle Hotel, what are you on about?' I reply. A timely silence passes.

'The Thistle Hotel . . . I'm at the Hilton. What ball am I at then?'

'I have no idea but you'd better thank them for the drink and get your ass up here.'

She retrieves her coat from the cloakroom with curious glances from the man she handed it to only an hour before, says a hasty goodbye to her new chums, and turns up in spectacular form to join us. I tell this story on air and get an e-mail from a girl from Bishopbriggs after the show. It reads: 'Is your pal Dolina McFarlane? She sounds like crazy Dolina I knew years ago. She was my bridesmaid eighteen years ago but we lost touch. I'd love to see her again and it's great to know she's not got any more sensible with age!'

I forward her details to Dolina, and they're back in touch – so a happy outcome to a crazy mix-up. I have to admit Dolly's new plan to 'wear a posh frock and turn up at hotels for free booze every weekend' has a certain creative brilliance to it.

To the *Breakfast Show* then, and there are quite incredible pictures of the Rolling Stones' latest gig in all of the papers today. Over one million fans turned out at Copacabana beach in Brazil for the golden oldies' latest show. They have the combined age of seven hundred and fifty, probably about the same amount of children, but according to all sources they still rock.

We get on to discussing our favourite gigs. I love T in the Park for the whole experience; I've camped, I get the bus, I end up dirty and smelly and revel in the whole festival ambience. Robin, on the other hand, would rather cut off his bits. I've been to hundreds of brilliant gigs but Simple Minds at the Barrowlands stands out to me for a few reasons:

1. It was the sweatiest I have ever been in my life.
2. The sprung dance floor felt like a trampoline.
3. At the time, they were a stadium band in a relatively intimate venue.
4. The intro to 'Waterfront' lasted about an hour. You know the bit that goes: 'do doom, do doom, do doom, do doom . . .'
5. I ended up wearing about fifty pints of lager courtesy of the bouncing bodies.

6. I got a snog from a handsome random.

We are swamped with tales of classic gigs. Favourites include:

- Zebade Zix at the Grand Hall Kilmarnock, '66. Jim.
- Nazareth, 1975. Ian.
- Apollo Theatre, '79, Leonard Skinner was fab. Big Alex in Hamilton.
- Back in the 1980s the late great Johnny Cash in the Edinburgh Playhouse. Jim.
- Wet Wet Wet, Pavilion 1988. I loved Marti Pellow from then on. Alison in Hardgate.
- ZZ Top Apollo, 1983. Neil from Milngavie.
- U2, Murrayfield, '87. Karen in Whitburn.
- Rolf Harris, Edinburgh Festival '05. Jules from Glasgow.
- Def Leppard, Barrowlands 2003. Lynne from Barrowfield.
- Marillion, Playhouse '95, I've seen Fish solo and the big man still puts on a great show. Mark from Dunfermline.
- Robbie Williams at Hampden 2005, it was the best night of my life. Susan.
- Runrig at Loch Lomond was a great event. John, Edinburgh.
- My girls and I went to the *X Factor* concert on Saturday. It was magic. BigTubbs.
- The Silencers, Airdrie Town Hall. Colin from Penicuik.
- The Beatles 1966, Glasgow Odeon. Diane from Bonnybridge.
- The Who, SECC 2001. John M.
- Marilyn Manson, Braehead Arena 2002. Susan in Peebles.
- Green Day, Milton Keynes, fantastic. Sophie.
- Rod Stewart at Celtic Park, Status Quo were the support. Ann Walker.
- Meatloaf, SECC, 2002. Dave in Kelty.

- Duran Duran, Ingleston '83, I took knickers to throw at John Taylor and he is still gorgeous. Laura.
- Sesame Street at the King's. Alex.
- Blondie at the Armadillo, took my man, he said it was like watching his granny gyrating in high heels. Lucy.
- Bob Marley, 1980, Apollo. Legend. Big Stu from Largs.
- Bon Jovi, Ibrox 2002. Barry.
- Slade are amazing live. Richard, Airdrie.
- Pink Floyd, Earls Court won't be beaten. Martin.
- Mydas at the QMU. Emma, Edinburgh.
- The Kylie Showgirl tour was breathtaking and it wasn't just her bum. Kevin from Lanark.

And that was just the first batch of texts. I was pleased to see Mydas, my drinking buddies, get a mention. I tried to manage them for a bit last year but ended up with too much on my plate to do them much good. I still help them out and hope to retire on their earnings eventually. They are great musically and a brilliant bunch of lads.

I also chuckled at this text: 'I've never been to a gig but I stay close to Hampden so I hope to hear some soon.'

It is great fun reminiscing, something I seem to be doing a lot of lately. Scotland really has produced some cracking bands. Visiting artists always say we are the best crowd in the world to play to (they would though, wouldn't they) and, for what it is worth, I happen to agree. You will struggle to find a better vibe anywhere than the trinity that is T in the Park, the Barrowlands and King Tut's.

It is time to jump from radio to TV mode again, and pop down the M8 to the BBC. Bumper show on *Offside* tonight: along with Johnny Watson and Tam in the studio, we are joined by pantomime regulars Grant Stott and Gerard Kelly. I've met Grant loads and he is a top bloke, but I'm quite star-struck with Gerard Kelly for no other reason than I absolutely LOVE pantomime. Oh yes I do! I've always wanted to be one of the ugly sisters, the naughty wee boy with a heart of gold that throws the sweets or the fluorescent skeletons that dance and remove their bones until they disappear.

Anyway, Gerard tells us a belting story about performing Cinderella at the King's this year. He said: 'As Buttons, I used to always get the sympathy vote from the children when I didn't get the girl. I would ham it up a bit and pretend to cry and they would shout, "But we love you, Buttons." This year I made the mistake of catching eyes with a wee eight-year-old kid in the second row. I was wiping away my fake tears when he growled, "Ach, get over it!"'

A group of guys hang back in the studio after the show and I can tell they want to chat. 'Hey Cat, my wee pal wants to meet you,' says the loud one. Eventually, a reluctant wee guy steps forward and introduces himself as 'Peter the wee sweeper', one of our lovely regular *Breakfast Show* callers, who drives a wee street-sweeping machine in Cumbernauld. 'No way!' I exclaim in excitement before smothering the wee fella with a bear hug. Turns out I was right. The wee guy blushed then added sheepishly: 'Well no, I'm actually Peter the wee taxi driver from Coatbridge, but he's much more famous than me.' My chipmunk cheeks hurt laughing, and I go home into the night wondering if the good people of Cumbernauld know how lucky they are to have such a highly regarded ambassador . . .

Tuesday the 21st

The feng shui man in Hong Kong said I needed to add colour to my wardrobe and on last night's TV show the wardrobe lady had me in fuchsia pink. I nearly fainted when I tried the top on, but it was big and baggy and covered the bumps so I went with it anyway.

I woke up this morning with nine text messages: nobody commented on the show, which I thought was a funny one, just my pink top. My fashion guru TV mate Nichola, who can identify the cost and make of every single garment and accessory in a Christmas party with 500 people, said simply: 'Oh my God – a colour!' My cheeks now match the top. I really must try harder, but black is so easy. And baggy hooded tops are much more comfy than blouses, and jeans are hardwearing and trainers are good for your feet or something.

Anyway, a cracking wee yarn in the *Scottish Sun* today about Kamran Quasim from Pollokshields who tried to buy a birthday cake and party poppers but was asked for ID. The pensions worker is twenty-six! Apparently you have to be sixteen to buy party poppers and toy caps these days. He laughed it off and was allowed to make his purchase after flashing his bank card with his thirteen-year-old nephew in hysterics in the aisle.

I shamefully confess that my pal Rhona and I, despite running a supporters' bus, still went through the under-sixteen gate at football games until we were at least twenty-four.

Robin admits he was arrested for under-age drinking in Aberdeen and his dad still doesn't know, while Lindsey our newsgirl reveals she was always the one sent to the bar because she was tall. Predictably the nation springs to life:

'Years ago when I was 18, I used to buy my carry-out at the Spar. I was asked for ID so often I took my passport. One night there was a new girl on and asked me again, the manager shouted over, 'She's the wee lassie with the passport.' The name stuck for years.' Alison.

'A daft pal of mine had been drinking at the local miners' welfare for a few years and decided to hold her eighteenth birthday party there. She had a great night and was then barred for her previous under-age exploits.' Heather in Dalkeith.

'I'm twenty-nine and get asked all the time. The worst was a few weeks ago in Sainsburys buying a 12 DVD. Ironically, it was called *13 Going On 30*!' Donna, Glasgow.

'When I was twenty-two and six months pregnant I asked for a full fare on the bus. The conductress did not believe me and would only take a half. She nearly fell off the bus when I got up to leave.' Sandra, Livingston.

'We were in Florida and were refused beer because we had no ID; my mum was with us who is sixty-four!' John the bus driver.

'I got barred from a pub at the age of fifteen because they said I was too OLD. It was an under-eighteen night I wanted to go to with my pals.' Tom in Fife.

'My dad took me to the Parry Lamp in Livingston for my first legal pint and he was very proud of me and telling everybody. The manager heard and banned me on the spot. I'd been going for a few years and was even on their pool team.' Mick from Livvy.

'I was twenty-one and was asked for ID trying to buy beer in a shop. I was asked for ID and the only thing I had on me was my Special Constable's warrant card. The cashier looked mortified.' Rob in Kilmarnock.

This reminds me of the time Rhona and I tried to have our first drink at the football at the age of fifteen. The venue was the Norseman Bar in Greenock; Thistle were away to Morton. We changed into suit jackets and heels pinched from our respective mums' wardrobes, put on lip gloss and strutted to the door.

When the bouncer asked for our date of birth, Rhona panicked and added three years instead of subtracting them. Her speedy reply obviously flummoxed him, and he let two girls who had just told him they were twelve into the bar. We shared a brandy and lemonade (the only drink I could think of because my mum drank it on rare occasions), we both felt a bit sick and then went to the game for a pie, some proper juice and half a Mars bar.

Today, I decide to tackle my demons and re-join fat class and the gym. I have deliberately avoided both since leaving for Hong Kong and have perfected the ostrich approach to fitness by sticking my head in the sand and hoping I'll emerge a neat size ten. This charity run is edging closer and I still haven't managed to run on my gammy knee yet. If only you had to have ID proving you were sixty before being allowed to buy chocolate, curry and pickled onion Monster Munch, my life would be so much easier . . .

Wednesday the 22nd

It hurts to sit down, it hurts to move and it hurts to sit still. Yes, I finally returned to the gym yesterday and have strained muscles I didn't even know I had. Still, I managed to run for the first time in a year, a whole whopping eight minutes. Paula Radcliffe will be bricking it. On second thoughts, I maybe shouldn't encourage her with her past trackside record.

It is gloom and misery all the way in the papers this morning. Six thousand sex slaves in Scotland, liver disease is up, plus more stories about murders, Iraq, and drugs. We always mention the big stories in the newspaper review section of our show, but generally choose to stay away from the big heavyweight issues. It's difficult enough for people to get up and out to work in a freezing February morning without depressing them further.

Mick Jagger is in the news again. He turned up at his little boy Lucas's school in Brazil and caused major commotion. It got us on to the subject of famous people at school, or who visited our schools. Celtic and Scotland legend Murdo McLeod used to go to my school, Douglas Academy, Milngavie, and came back for a question and answer session in my second-year English class. The actress Natalie Robb from *High Road* was in the year below me and that is about my only claim to school fame. Oh, apart from the girl who worked in Colpi's ice-cream shop who was the cousin of the singer from the Supernaturals apparently.

Baz, our new producer (the producer formerly known as Golden Baz – a nickname that has been deemed too rude for a family show by those in suits. Boo!), had school visits by 911 and Peter Andre, while former Dons legend Martin Buchan handed out the prizes at Robin's school.

Our first call is from Eric who claims to have snogged *Chewin' the Fat* star Karen Dunbar in the bike sheds at primary school. The fact that she is now a prominent Scottish lesbian makes this revelation hilarious. Other claims to fame include:

'I was at St Ambrose in Coatbridge with Pat and Greg Kane from Hue and Cry and Scotland player Tom Boyd. Bob Crampsey was our headmaster.' Steven, Motherwell.

'I was at school in Aberdeen with Robin and he had lovely big teeth then too.' Helen Ryan.

'I was at Beath High in Cowdenbeath, full of stars. Stuart Adamson from Big Country was the year below me, Jim Leishman the Dunfermline manager was the year above.' Mike from Kinghorn.

'I was at Morrison's Academy with Ewan McGregor and the Queen came to visit. She was a hackit-faced old cow.' Nic.

'I was at school with Lulu and she punched me in the face.' Joyce.

'Jimmy Savile came to Carstairs Primary in 1977. I still have the photo.' Cooky in the big green parcel machine.

'I was at school with Jackie Bird and she had BROWN hair!' Elaine.

'I went to Portobello High, the same school as Gail Porter. In fact her name was scribbled on my exam desk.' Sarah.

'Alan Rankine the guitarist with The Associates was at Linlithgow High with me. He was a prefect!' Liz.

'Big Bird from *Sesame Street* came to Sighthill Primary 17 years ago.' Scott the taxi driver.

'I was at Hunter High in East Kilbride with *Taggart* star Blythe Duff and Ally McCoist. In fact I was in the *Wizard of Oz* with Blythe, she was the witch and I was the scarecrow.' Anne from Tollcross.

'In the 1970s I went to St Stephen's High in Port Glasgow. Christian and Midge Ure, before he was in Ultravox, played our school dance. They were brilliant.'

'Gail Robbins, whose dad owned Hercules the bear, was at my school for a few weeks when they were touring, does that count?' Kay.

'Stephen Hendry came to my sports day and he was really grumpy.' Mary from Renfrew.

'Hollywood star Alan Cumming was at my school, Woodlands High in Falkirk. He was a total nerd and into James Bond and the X-men.' Tam from Bankrigg.

'John Hannah was in my maths class, he was nice.' Derek in Strathaven.

'My boyfriend went to school with the Chuckle Brothers' children and the blonde one from *Two Pints of Lager and a Packet of Crisps*.' Beth in Stirling.

And finally a current classic: 'I am driving a taxi at the moment with Killie and ex-Hearts star Gary Locke's granny in the back. Not a school story but not bad, eh?' Tommi.

Tonight, Rangers face Villarreal at Ibrox. They are the first Scottish team to make it into the last sixteen of the Champions League and I have managed to persuade Robin to come out on a school night to go to the pub to watch the match. We don't get out much during the week and I feel naughty. I suspect I've had a psychological allergic reaction to the gym which can be fixed only by a trip to the boozer. Oh, and I never went to fat class yesterday. One cellulite-laden step at a time, methinks . . .

Thursday the 23rd

The secret is out boys. You are the guilty secret shoppers in Scotland. It's in the *Daily Record* today so it must be true.

In turns out that men in the UK smuggle £17 million worth of goods past their partners every week. The average man buys £336 worth of gadgets, sports equipment and clothes that he hides from his better half every year. Women, on the other hand, only squander £227 on secret shopping. A bargain (and clearly fibs).

Now, I am notoriously rubbish at shopping and the only thing I actually hide is a secret tub of mini Mars bars for emergencies. Robin, however, has a daily arrival of secret packages delivered to the radio station from his ever-increasing eBay habit. Mrs G is blissfully unaware that the Postie is becoming his best pal.

John from Glasgow called. He has just swapped his people carrier for a Mercedes and his wife won't find out until March. Stuart Carey bought a motorbike without informing his girlfriend, while a guy from Penicuik admits trading in his wife's car. She got the last laugh, though, and bought a new house for them when he was working away. Nice work lady.

It seems we like our little secret sprees:

'My husband bought an Xbox 360 and hid it in a cupboard. I found it the other day and you should have heard his excuses for having it – priceless.' Shirley from Gullane.

'My sisters and I from Xmas to summertime would always say, "I bought that with the money Gran gave me for Christmas." I bought trainers, CDs, concert tickets and shoes and all from twenty quid.' Wilma, Moira, Lorraine and Heather, East Kilbride.

'I've spent over ten grand modifying my car. If the wife finds out I'll have to sell the motor and look for a flat of my own!' Shaun in Glasgow.

'I am always finding shirts in the wardrobe. My husband says he's had them for ages but the creases are still in them from the packaging.' Donna.

This made me laugh out loud: 'Cat, I think women are most definitely the better secret shoppers because we are not daft enough to tell you and Robin about it and get caught.' A text, I should point out, that was signed by Audrey in Mayfield!

It's always nice to get out and about, and after the show we popped over to the Ruchill Family Centre to present NCH Scotland with a cheque for £75,000 from our 'Bring a pound to work' day campaign. The play area outside the centre has been upgraded using some of this cash and now boasts a fantastic bouncy surface for the kids. Stupidly, I decided to entertain the children by having a shot on the world's smallest space-hopper, sort of like a Mitre size-five football with two handles. Despite two visits to the gym this week and my first run in over a year, I only managed two bounces before the 'incident'. I felt a warm sensation in my left knee and then a pop as the ligament I originally knackered on an inflatable assault course was once again twanged by an inflatable bouncy thing. I am an arse. There is nothing else to say on the matter.

For the record, Rangers drew 2–2 against Villarreal last night and are still in with a chance of reaching the last eight. I wonder how many men will conveniently be on secret 'work trips' a week on Tuesday for the replay . . .

Friday the 24th

My knee is now the size of a melon and I'm seeing the evil orange face from my childhood space hopper taunting me in my dreams. I am destined, as the feng shui man said, to be destructive to myself in ridiculously silly ways. A space hopper! A bloody space hopper, I am shaking my head in rueful disbelief as I write this.

Anyway, it is Friday and that cheers me up no end. I have a cracking weekend ahead of me and that is mostly down to the fact that Partick Thistle are in the quarter-finals of the Tennent's Scottish Cup and we're playing Hearts at Tynecastle.

I've covered football for a living for over ten years now and have been lucky enough to work trackside at internationals, European games and even the Champions League Final at Hampden. I was the only TV interviewer on the pitch with Martin O'Neill when he won his first title with Celtic, and I was in the tunnel with a half-naked Lorenzo Amoruso as Rangers reclaimed it.

That said, there is NOTHING like going to see your own team in a game they are expected to get thrashed in, but with that little sense of anticipation. The 'What if', the 'Get it right up ye', the 'We have to stay out and party until Monday if we win' feeling. Magic.

Robin, on the other hand is really looking forward to a curry tonight. Bossman Jay and his lovely wife Dawn stayed with him last Friday and didn't want Indian food. He is now craving it badly and is genuinely very excited at the prospect.

We decide to make things easy for our lovely listeners and get a fantastic glimpse at Scottish life. The task: complete the sentence, 'I'm looking forward to the weekend because . . .'

'It is my Christmas night out tomorrow!'
'My son Dave Anderson is in a piping competition after winning the *Young Musician of the Year* zone final at

Heriot-Watt University this week.' From Neil, the proudest dad ever.

'I'm going to see my god-daughter Tina's new baby.' Sandra.

'I'm going to cheer on the rugby boys taking on England at Murrayfield.' Katie in Alloa.

'It's my mate Kaz's twenty-fifth birthday and we are going out in the Fire Engine limousine, anything for a laugh really.' Fe fee.

'It's the World Clootie Dumpling Championships at Avonbridge.'

'I'm just looking forward to my girlfriend coming back from her holiday in Tenerife.' Chris.

'It's the psychic fair at the Antonine Hotel in Falkirk.' Alex

'I can't wait. Tonight's the Stenhousemuir Rangers supporters club sportsman's dinner at the Plough Hotel.'

'I'm buying my wedding dress this Saturday.' Carol

'It's my wee sister's gangster themed hen-night tomorrow in Glasgow and we are going to go mental. Watch out boys.' From Top Dog and Mother Hen.

'I'm looking forward to Hearts gubbing that wee pub team.' Heather.

Fraser the Jambo from Stirling offers to run naked through Gorgie if Thistle do beat his side and I take a note of his mobile number. He will not get away with this one. Finally Franny in Cleland added simply: 'I'm looking forward to the weekend for ma hole.' An interesting sentiment, but a 2–0 Thistle win would be MUCH more satisfying.

Monday the 27th

It is combusting celebrities grabbing all of the headlines this morning. George Michael has blown it again. He was found slumped over the wheel of his car as high as a kite and with dodgy substances in his possession. The media treat this latest indiscretion with respectful sensitivity. 'Wake me up before you blow blow' and 'Careless spliffer' are two of the better front pages. And it turns out, surprise surprise, that Vince Vaughn is getting rather annoyed with Jennifer Aniston for not being able to get over Brad Pitt. That's something I'd quite like to do. Get over Brad Pitt, and under and beside him for that matter.

However, the biggest story in Scotland is the rugby team's sensational 18–12 victory over England at Murrayfield to win the Calcutta Cup. Once again national pride comes to the fore. It seems everyone and their granny got caught up in the moment. Texts include:

'At the end of the game I stood up and shouted, "Oh, ya f****** dancer." Unfortunately my two-year-old daughter is now running around repeating it.' Shamed dad.

'I was out partying until 7.30 a.m. because of the result; when I got home there was a note from my girlfriend chucking me for staying out again. Still, great result.' Callum from Cumbernauld.

'I was at a party down south with twenty-seven England fans, how much fun did I have?' Maureen in Edinburgh.

'The girls and I were at One Spa in our robes, looked out the window and the team were outside practising throws before the game. We nearly gave them a flash for luck.' Lorna, Edinburgh.

'I'm at Edinburgh University and it seems 95% of people there are English rugby fans. I can't wait to go in today!' Robbie from Tranent.

'Does that mean we are World Champions?' Wullie in Fife. [The answer is 'YES', Wullie, and I told you it was everybody AND their granny.]

'My granny goes mental at rugby games with Scotland playing. I have never heard language like it on Saturday. She is ninety-three for goodness' sake and she was standing on the couch shouting.' Gaynor in Whitburn.

It's this kind of fighting spirit that got us a result. The guest on *Offside* tonight is Sanjeev Kohli, better known as Navid the ageing Asian shopkeeper in *Still Game*. In real life Sanjeev is only about thirty and it's funny to see a few mannerisms of his elderly alter-ego when we are chatting in the green room. He tells a cracking story about Jane McCarry who plays Isa, the busybody old wifie in the show. She is also in her thirties. 'Jane was breastfeeding a few months ago and had to go into a chemist for something to help with the process, I'm not sure what, but we were filming in Clydebank and she was in costume. The woman's face just looked shocked when she told her she was breastfeeding. She disappeared behind the screen and three people popped their heads out to have a look at the crazy old lady with the imaginary child.'

I finally get home and go to bed at eleven. I am sensing my crazy weekend in Edinburgh has taken its toll. Thistle lost 2–1 to Hearts, by the way, but rugby is the only sport I'm interested in anyway. Well, at least for today . . .

Tuesday the 28th

It's such a dull freezing cold morning in Scotland, making the pictures of the Carnival in Rio on Sky telly look all the more vibrant and exotic. Both Robin and I have always talked about trying to wangle a trip out there somehow as we've always wanted to witness the spectacle. I love the samba music and pulsating parade but I suspect the stunning girls wearing not

much but a handful of strategically placed sequins may be a factor in his interest.

We end up discussing things we'd like to do before the end of the year. *Heat* magazine suggests we should all try a personal shopper, have a cookery lesson from a celebrity chef, go to the casino, and gatecrash a famous party. I just want Thistle to go up and my weight to go down.

Moira from Wishaw calls in and makes my day with her enthusiasm. 'I wrote a list of things to do before I was fifty and I've not done any of them. However, I have decided to change it to things to before I am sixty. Number one on my list is to learn how to tap dance. I have always fancied it and I've decided to go for it. So if anybody out there wants to teach a slightly unfit Wishaw lady how to tap dance please get in touch.'

It appears we all have our own wee agendas:

'I can't sing or dance but I'd love to be in a West End musical.' John, Edinburgh.

'I hope to DJ in the Arches this year, hopefully Ibiza by 2007.' Alan in Alloa.

'This may sound odd but I'd love to own a bird of prey. I love these birds.' Cathy in Armadale.

'I'd like my girlfriend to get divorced so I can propose to her.' Scott.

'I'd like a one hour meeting with Jack McConnell. I am a social worker with young people and I'd like to chat about things.' Mary.

'I'd like to walk the Inca trail this year.' Zoë in Motherwell.

'This year I'd like to lose two stone, but I say that every bloody year.' Sandra, East Kilbride.

'My wife always wanted to see the Pyramids so we are going this year for our twenty-fifth anniversary.' Ally and Pam from Ratho.

'This year I want Slade to reform.' Donnie, Kirkintilloch.

Not a Noddy Holder in sight, but this afternoon the Sugababes pop into the studio for a wee chat and they look a bit tired of the whole media merry-go-round sessions they have to attend to promote their latest single and forthcoming tour. However, it turns out the girls were at an awards dinner in London last night so I forgive them and envy their youthful ability to look so fresh after a night on the batter.

I really like a lot of their music; I've seen them live at T in the Park and was very impressed with their vocal talents. Heidi the blonde is by far the nicest, with a Scouse accent as strong as Steven Gerrard. Keisha, who is reputedly the bossy one, IS the bossy one, while Amelle, the new girl who looks identical to Muyta, the one she replaced, says not very much at all. Keisha has been in the band since she was twelve and admits she gave up her childhood for fame. 'I'm a total perfectionist,' she says without a hint of a smile and the other two look on expectantly waiting for her to indicate what they should do and say next. I think there is a nice girl trying to get out somewhere, but she seems so driven by her career it's almost like she is not allowing herself to enjoy life.

I leave the studio feeling quite glad I'm not a pop star; I also feel massive. The wee souls were about seven stone apiece. It is with a heavy heart and bum and thighs and bingo wings that I leave Real Radio and head towards fat class. Or do I . . .

march

wednesday the 1st

Two pounds off! Not too bad considering I haven't been for weeks and I've been to Hong Kong, the Press Ball and had a lost weekend in Edinburgh. Chips are obviously good for me after all.

The big news today in Robin and Cat land is the return to our TV screens of the children's show *Rainbow*. Nick Jr, a kiddies' satellite station, has decided to broadcast all the episodes from 1982 onwards, but at night-time. This is clearly for the adults who should know better but like to indulge in a bit of retro entertainment with Geoffrey, Bungle, George and Zippy. I remember the show well from my school lunch days. We used to get the bus home, have fifteen minutes for a cheese or ham piece with a cup of water, catch a bit of *Rainbow* (hopefully not the Rod, Jane and Freddie sing-along bit) or *Pipkins*, then run for the bus back.

School lunch break memories flood back:

'I used to go to my auntie's house every lunchtime. She would make me listen to her Shirley Bassey album and I loved it.' George, Wishaw.

'I used to love *Let's Pretend* and *Button Moon* with Mr Spoon.' Lisa, Grangemouth.

'My pal and I stole Echo margarine from the cookery room and sold it for 2p a slice to go on the boggin potatoes. We both got belted by the headmaster for our efforts.' Cathy in Armadale.

'I went to my granny's for lunch every day. My abiding memory is her ladle being completely yellow because it was never out of a pot of chicken noodle soup. She also watched *The Sullivans*.' Gwen, Coatbridge.

'I watched *Pigeon Street* at lunchtime and knew it was time to leave when *Pebble Mill* came on.' Lorraine, Hamilton.

'I loved the *One O'Olock Gang*.' Mary in Alloa.

'I loved *The Clangers* so much I married a soup dragon!'

'I watched *Tales of the Riverbank* with Johhny Morris.' Jen.

'I went home every lunch-time for a wee snooze. I lived right next door to the school so the bell to go back woke me up.' Steven McMurdo, Edinburgh.

Dawn from Blantyre called in: 'I had insider information at school because my mum was the dinner lady. She would tell me the day before what was going to be on the menu and I could decide if I wanted to go home or not. The best thing about it was she used to bring left-over trays of caramel slices home, you know the ones like millionaire's shortbread without the chocolate, just chocolate sprinkles. It was fantastic.'

Great tales from a really up-beat show and I feel happy heading off to my next appointment. Happy and hungry, that is, and quite possibly prepared to kill for a fix of that caramel cake.

After a three-hour meeting at the Comedy Unit, I popped out to see my parents and discovered Bobby Harvey has created ANOTHER embarrassing dad moment. We were just talking about the Jags game when he piped up: 'I sent John Lambie a letter yesterday.' Lambie is no longer manager at Thistle although he is still involved at the club. I've interviewed him loads and he is a legend, a right down-to-earth guy who swears for Scotland and is obsessed with his bloody pigeons.

'What is it about?' I asked fearing the worst.

'I read a nice wee story about an Aberdonian who wanted to take up pigeon racing and I thought he would like it.'

'Do you know John Lambie?'

'No, but it was a nice wee story about pigeons.'

Now had this been a unique happening I may have forgiven him, but about thirteen years ago he sent Ivan Golac, the then Dundee United manager, a column I had written about him in the *Evening Times*. I never knew this until I found a letter from Yugoslavia inviting our family over to stay with his. Mortified, I enquired how the former United boss happened to be in correspondence with Faither. 'I sent him that thing you wrote about him with one of my ceilidh CDs and we've been in touch since. He's a nice man if a wee bit mental.' HELLO! POT, KETTLE, BLACK!

Anyway, as far as I am aware he is not in any other pen-friend relationships with international footballers. It's a bit of a shame really. I think he would get on great with the divine José Mourinho . . .

Thursday the 2nd

I'm quite stiff this morning. Not from another fabulous workout at the gym, but because I blitzed my flat last night attacking a clothes mountain and monster dish pile-up. I can coordinate three or four media assignments on the go at one time but I am really rubbish at keeping myself in order. My mum calls it being 'a clatty wee midden'; I prefer 'artistically disorganised.' It is therefore hugely ironic that reports this morning list the UK's most hated domestic chores. In reverse order:

8. Cleaning the kitchen – my kitchen is roughly a metre by two metres and the floor is a powerful magnet for food.

7. Making the bed – the *Daily Mail* said bedbugs breed if you pull your duvet up and keep them warm. Not making the bed is therefore the healthy option.
6. Vacuuming – this sucks.
5. Cleaning the loo – yuck. But I'm not too bad at this. Flash wipes rock.
4. Washing up – I have recently developed an inexplicable love for the smell from Persil washing-up liquid. I also love the smell of petrol (don't try this at home, kids) so take no notice. I do have a dishwasher, but my pal Rhona stood on the door to reach a bottle of Miller on top of a cupboard a year and a half ago and I've, erm, not had time to get it fixed.
3. Dusting – I give this the brush off.
2. Ironing – never. I refuse. I deliberately buy clothes that don't need ironing. The only time the iron comes out of the box is when Nichola comes to stay, and even then she has to iron on a bath towel on the floor.
And the worst of all, according to the survey:
1. Cleaning windows – I get up in the middle of the night so there is no point really. I actually love watching window cleaners. Not in a pervy way, but the whole soapy window squeegee thing is hypnotic. The tight boiler suits are good too, right enough . . .
Other reviled chores include:

'Getting gloss paint out of brushes is murder. I did it once, now I just throw them away. Costs me a fortune but keeps my sanity.' Kevin Rafferty, Edinburgh.

'I don't mind hanging washing on a line but I hate bringing it in.' Ann in Motherwell.

'Cutting up turnip should be on that list. It is a nightmare.' Sandra.

'I use paper plates and plastic cutlery, saves me having to wash up.' Andy in Glasgow.

'I hate emptying the Hoover and cleaning the deep-fat fryer, I would chuck them out if I could.' Jackie in Denny.

'Hand peeling tatties drives me nuts.' Bob in Livingston.

'Grocery shopping is a nightmare; you buy the stuff, it gets eaten in no time and you have to do it all again!' John in Falkirk.

[And Stevie in Edinburgh concluded our moans with a hair-raising subject:]

'The worst chore ever is cleaning the bath after the missus has been shaving her bits.'

This horror hairy chat is quite weird actually because I had a very real dream last night which I've been discussing with the troops. I was sitting in the make-up lady's chair at *Offside* and she was putting heated rollers in my waist-length black shiny beard! I've checked on the internet for the meaning of this dream and it says the masculine side of my personality is trying to shine through. I am also, according to the guide, subconsciously trying to be more assertive and controlling. The feng shui man was right. I am the HUSBAND in our working relationship. As such, I DEMAND Robin shifts his pretty wee ass round to my flat immediately and cleans the kitchen . . .

Friday the 3rd

A factory has blown up in Irvine, an Edinburgh man has kept his dead wife in a freezer for over a week and the Scottish Parliament is falling down, or at least one beam has. It is also National Doodle Day. I doodle all the time, during songs, links, adverts, you name it, I doodle though it and on it. I am also one of those really infuriating pests that love to scribble on newspapers and magazines. Maybe it is another subconscious identity issue but there is nothing finer than defacing Naomi

Campbell or Kate Moss by giving them a stubbly beard, cross eyes and a gangster-sized facial scar.

There appears to be a day for everything, for example, this week from Monday onwards has been National Wild Flower Day, Pancake Day, National Self-Injury Awareness Day, National Book Day and now National Doodle Day. We open the floor to new suggestions. My favourites that I think should be upheld are:

'National Be Nice To Everyone Day.' Mo, Livingston
'National No Telesales Day.' Stewart, Cambuslang.
'National Swally Day.' The workie boys.
'National Chicken Pakora Day.' Fe, Glasgow.
'National Use Your Indicators Day.' Al the fed-up trucker.
'National Nookie day.' Wendy, East Kilbride.
'National Tell Your Boss What You Think Of Him Without Getting Into Trouble Day.' Brian, Falkirk.
'National Duvet Day.' Charlie, St Andrews.
'National Scotland Wins A Friendly Match Day.' Tam.
'"National Naked Day" so I can show off.' Alex, Erskine.
[And ones that don't make the grade:]
'National NO FAT BURDS Day.'
'National Wash Your Underpants Day.' Chunk in Hamilton.
'"National Swap Your Bird With Your Mate's Girlfriend Day." My pal Tony is going out with a stoatir.' Simon, Kirkcaldy.
[And the final anonymous offering:]
'National Admit It's Your Fart Day'

Today is the climax to one of our favourite competitions – win £7,000 with the Dunfermline Building Society. We've had ten winners in the past fortnight who all have to guess the answer to a tie-break question. The question was, 'To the nearest £10,000 what was the largest residential mortgage granted by the Dunfermline Building Society this year.'

Now these competitions are nervy enough for the contestants but Robin and I are jumpy wrecks because there is so much that could go wrong. Like what to do if two contestants are the same amount away from the correct answer, which incidentally was £1,570,000. (I sit poised with a fluttering heart, shaky hands, a scribbled list of all sorts of numerical connotations, and a calculator just in case.) However, thankfully only one winner gets close, and with a cracking guess of £1.5 million Darren Doak from Blantyre ends up a very happy lad.

It's always brilliant when we get a good winner on a competition but Darren is in a different class. He screams, he is emotional, but he sounds like such a cracking down-to-earth bloke. His fiancée Paula is going bonkers in the background as he tearfully tells us: 'You don't know what a difference this will make to our lives. We can now bring forward our wedding. We can afford to get married!'

Robin asks him to propose again to Paula, he gets down on one knee (I know it is radio but he tells us he is doing so and I believe him!) and asks, 'Paula, will you please marry me ahead of schedule! I love you very much.' She yelps in delight and there is not a dry eye in the studio or the cars and buses travelling to work. He is a REAL WINNER and we all leave for the weekend feeling bloody fantastic!

Monday the 6th

Sometimes you can't buy class. Deputy Prime Minister John Prescott, feeling peckish at parliament, ordered vegetable curry. Not content with his lot, he disgusted his fellow dignitaries (and the chef) by asking for a big dollop of Heinz beans on the top.

Food is one of our favourite topics of a morning and we jump on the chance to ramble more about what technically should be horrible combinations. Health-conscious Robin actually has a penchant for salty crisps with plain chocolate, while I love a big splodge of Heinz salad cream on ANYTHING. I've also developed a craving for turnip with everything. Chicken kebab and turnip is my latest favourite despite the odd looks. It seems we all enjoy repulsing our mates with extreme kitchen creativity:

'I know this sounds minging but I have to dip my chips from McDonald's into my strawberry milkshake.' Jason, Seton Sands.

'I spread butter on my Weetabix and eat them like biscuits. It gives my partner Gordon the boak.' Elaine, Bo'ness.

'I can't eat curry without tomato sauce on the side.' Dave, Carntyne.

'I'm currently eating sardines and peanut butter on toast. I'm not pregnant or a student.' Des, Isle of Bute.

'I love fried rice and curry sauce mashed together on top of pizza.' Brian.

'People think I am weird, but I love Primula cheese spread on my chocolate digestive biscuits.' Colin.

'My mum used to give me slices of orange with milk chocolate in a roll.' Eddie, Livvy.

'I eat square sausage on a roll with banana and get pelters for it!' Billy.

'Dipping Rich Tea biscuits in Heinz tomato soup is a must.' Graeme, Rosyth.

[And the one which perhaps explains why Scottish people have the worst hearts in the universe:]

'My favourite snack is a roll and square sausage with a big doughnut in it.' Stu, Kirkintilloch.

Surprise of the day comes courtesy of the good people at Lexus, Glasgow – an Arnold Clark garage – they've dropped off the biggest, shiniest car I have ever seen. An 'IS 250' for those in the know, with plush cream leather interiors and more buttons to play with than the cockpit of a 747. I have the car for a few weeks to test drive for them and I am shitting myself. I have never driven a big car before and with my skip cap, hooded top, jeans and trainers on I look one of three things:

1. A wee daft lassie that's pinched Daddy's car;
2. A bad wee lassie that's knocked it;
3. The valet girl that's taken a client's car for a spin.

The carpets on the floor are thick and velvety and made of the palest cream material you could imagine. I'm sure the guys at the BBC think I am some sort of drug dealer. I turn up every week for *Offside* in a different car.

Tonight's guest on the show is my old pal, Scotland's First Minister Jack McConnell, who I haven't seen since our shameful Christmas party exploits. I emerge from make-up and find the green room filled with Comedy Unit executives, Jack and a group of luxurious-suited advisers all engaging in very polite if somewhat nervous chit-chat ahead of the show.

'CAT!' Screams our First Minister as he leaps to his feet with a massive grin. 'I'VE STILL GOT THEM – BUT I'VE NOT GOT THEM ON TONIGHT!' Concerned looks all round, not helped, I may add, by my giggling explanation: 'Oh, I gave him a pair of Speedos when I came back from holiday once.' It certainly broke the ice, I can tell you.

The show goes well, Jack survives relatively unscathed; we learn he pretends to support Stirling Albion but actually goes to Parkhead and that his wife was mortified when she saw 'THAT KILT' in the papers. For the record, and this I believe is important, he had one coffee and a white bread cheese piece. No beans on the side or anything!

Tuesday the 7th

Tragic news for culture lovers today: the famous North Pier Theatre on Blackpool Pier is closing down. After over 100 years of good old family seaside entertainment the curtain will fall for the final time this summer. Acts like Russ Abbot, Les Dennis, Freddie Starr, Joe Longthorne and The Krankies will no longer play for laughs. A multi-million pound casino complex is hoped to get the green light to regenerate the town, with acts like A-list global stars Celine Dion and Shirley Bassey tipped for runs. Aye, right.

I haven't been to Blackpool since I was twelve, possibly because it rained all week and it's where my near-death experience took place. I can still close my eyes and see the tram coming at me in *Coronation Street*'s Alan Bradley style. My dad grabbed my shoulder and whisked me to safety but it was a very close encounter. My other abiding memory of Blackpool is being up the tower and looking down at the wee dots walking along the prom. My dad told me the apocryphal tale about the penny. 'Drop one from here and you will kill somebody. It goes straight through their head and they die instantly.' In retrospect I've had better holidays!

However, I can see that there ARE fun elements to the resort and we are bombarded with texts and call from people defending their favourite location:

'I had my first holiday there without my parents when I was sixteen and I've been there every year since.' Robert.

'Our pool team goes to Blackpool every year, although we've never actually played any pool yet.' Big Jock.

'My mum and dad go every year, they took me when I was a baby and I am now forty-four. They now take my daughter who is twenty-two. My honeymoon was also there and we saw the 'Mr and Mrs' show with Derek Batey, twenty-six years ago.' Mo, Ballieston.

'I went to the haunted house on the prom and nearly shat myself when a guy jumped out of a coffin.' Big John.

'My mate and I got up at 6.00 a.m. on Saturday, drove down, had six hours on the Pleasure Beach and drove back. It was a great day.' Lee and Robert.

'I took my dad on the Grand National horse race rollercoaster thing at the Pleasure Beach after he had one too many. His terrified face as he clung on for dear life will live with me for ever.' Craig, Edinburgh.

[And it seems alcohol-fuelled bravado has a lot to answer for:]

'I got my first tattoo in Blackpool. It was a love heart with Glen loves Alison. I haven't seen her since that weekend!' Glen Roberts from Wishawhill.

'Big Del from Hamilton is the only person in the world with a green crest on his Rangers tattoo. He got it in Blackpool.'

As Jack McConnell has been on the *Breakfast Show* and is in an odd way responsible for this book, I tell Robin of our latest meeting and in fact of his latest whisper to me – what the First Minister actually does on a Saturday night. Without soliciting for texts we receive the following suggestions:

'He phones fake taxis and curries for Tony Blair.'

'I think he builds model ships.' Fiona.

'He plays his PS2.' James.

'He goes down the park with a bottle of Buckie.' Mick.

'He rings bells and runs away.' Kenny, Edinburgh.

'He gets rat-arsed.' Ron from the pub he actually drinks in!

'He dresses up in *Rocky Horror* gear wearing Speedos.'

'He moisturizes with St Tropez.' Wendy, Wishaw.

The real answer is great for us at Real Radio – he listens to the *Saturday Night Breakfast Show with Robin and Cat*, the show where we talk even more nonsense than we get away with in the morning. 'You're a bit naughty on that one aren't you?' The man who owns Scotland's most famous Speedos beams. And, thinking back to one particular link at the weekend, when we basically accused Andy Horn our technical operative of sitting in a room playing with his 'mockit pocket rocket' all evening, I had to smile in agreement.

It's just as well this diary is about our Monday to Friday antics or the Bargain Books bucket would have to go up a ladder to a top shelf somewhere near you.

Wednesday the 8th

Woof. We go barking mad this morning. Turns out Glaswegian dogs are the most pampered in the whole country. From doggy clothes to grooming, our west coast Westies are more likely to be treated to designer gifts from Poochie than Hound-stretchers. In a spectacular quirk of fate, sorry, exemplary forward planning, Crufts starts tomorrow. (Hey, if you can't be good, be lucky.)

I used to love watching the agility section where athletic canines weaved between poles, ducked through tunnels and careered down zip wires. OK, so I made the last bit up but it IS brilliant. Robin's camp Shih Tzu, Casper (pedigree name Lexicon Stepper of Naveroke, no less) sits for hours in front of the box when Crufts is on, and it seems the wee fellow is not alone:

'Crufts is fabulous. It is a wonderful experience showing the dogs on the green carpet and meeting people from all over the world and the dogs love it.' Lucy, Lanark.

'Talking of pedigree names, my Dalmatian's granny's name is Crystal Black Jobie, I kid you not.' Nat and Alan, Bellshill.

'My dog's pedigree name is Rum on the Rocks.' Gus.

'I love to watch Crufts but my wee Lakeland terrier prefers to watch *Deal or no Deal* with Noel Edmonds.' Elaine.

'Crufts is great. Me and my pals watch it and take our own bets on the best of breed.' Deborah, Rosyth.

'I try to watch Crufts but usually just catch the TAIL end.' Gordon.

My disastrous trip to fat class yesterday is revealed to the nation when Robin reads out the confidential text I sent him at 1.27 p.m. It reads: 'Walked to bloody fat class in the rain without a bra for weighing purposes. I missed it by ten minutes, heading home for pizza.' He finds it incredible that I actually took the effort to remove a bra for the big weigh-in. I, however, have a host of rituals that will make me lighter on the scales:

- I must wear exactly the same clothes (the lightest I own without being nightwear).
- I must pop to the loo for a wee streamie before joining the weigh-in queue.
- I never eat lunch on weigh-in day.
- Hair should be tied back in a plain band (clasps can be SO heavy).
- Socks must go.
- No make-up.

While even I can see this seems a bit ridiculous, my fellow female dieters spring (like the sylph-like gazelles we shall all become) to my defence:

'Yes Cat we all do it! Jewellery has to go and the lightest clothes possible go on.' Lesley, Bathgate.

'I only wear enough clothes to cover my dignity.' Lynn, Newmains.

'I go to Scottish Slimmers too and I pull my hair off my face into a pony tail, it makes me feel thinner!' Mary, Falkirk.

'Depending on what you're wearing you could be three pounds heavier.' Annie.

'I had a really good week once and only lost half a pound. I was so annoyed I took my jeans off, stood on the scales in my pants and lost two pounds. Oh, and I am not telling anyone my name.'

[And an ingenious tip from Gillian:]

'The best thing to do is to wear really heavy items to your first weigh-in so every week afterwards you do quite well.'

With this new-found knowledge I plan to let my hair down, pile on the bling, find an old-fashioned diving suit, slip into ski boots and join a new fat class . . .

Thursday the 9th

Read all about it – snowballs to be banned shocker. Honestly, are we turning into wimps or what? A school headmaster in Devon has banned snowball fights in the playground – UNLESS the victim has consented. Pupils are being asked for written permission to be pelted.

At my secondary school British bulldogs, gobstoppers and make-up were banned, while at primary sliding on ice was banned (remember crouching down and doing a 'wee man' with slippy shoes on?) due to my big brother Scott. He selfishly fell and split his head open during playtime, an act that made Mr Shirkie our janny get out the big grit bucket and spade in jig time. Boo. He recovered in two days but the ban lasted.

We always get a fantastic reaction when we ramble down memory lane, and other prohibited acts flood in:

'We were not allowed to wear our Mohicans spiked up or tuck our sta-press trousers into our Doc Martin boots.' Johnny Christie, Bo'ness.

'They banned smoking and magic mushrooms at Cowdenbeath High, life got a bit dull after that!' Craig, Cowdenbeath.

'Grey Olympus tracky bottoms and Campri ski jackets were banned in my school in 1984.' Lenny, Motherwell.

'Segs on shoes were forbidden in my school.' Stevie, Wishy.

'Our school banned the girls from wearing black patent shoes in case the boys could see up our skirts!' Liz, West Kilbride.

'Superglue was banned in our school; we kept gluing coins to the floor and laughing at teachers trying to pick them up.' Calum.

'I went to Shotts School and rebelled by putting whisky in the fish tank and letting the locusts loose because they banned us from going to the snack van in a bid to increase school dinners.' Davy, Harthill.

'I got expelled from school in 1980 for throwing snowballs, if only I had got permission from my targets!' Big Wullie, Airdrie.

'My son's primary has just banned "The Boys Chase the Girls".' Shona.

'I was banned from breaking wind downstairs! Honestly, I had to get a line from the doctor explaining my flatulence problem which incidentally I still have.' Robert, Glasgow.

'Kiss, cuddle and torture was banned because the girls kept ending up black and blue for refusing our kisses.' Paul, Bellshill.

'Clackers were banned after Jamie McPherson broke his left wrist.' Danny, Motherwell.

'Scud books were banned at my school, don't understand why. We all thought we were learning biology.' Stuart, Ardrossan.

[And Rod from Bridge of Allan had a unique tale of prohibition:]

'I went to school in Kenya and we were banned from cross-country running. This was because leopards kept picking off pupils in the forest!'

Hmm, makes needing a letter for snowballs seem a bit tame really.

Another wee tale I like today is about hapless ex-Scotland manager Berti Vogts who has opened a restaurant in western Germany called the Pina Colada Lounge. Poor Berti seems jinxed – on the opening night he dropped coffee on himself and badly scalded his arm. He reminds me of the lost one-eyed three-legged dog that answers to the name of Lucky.

Busy old day, prizewinners Darren Doak and Paula from Blantyre pop in to pick up their £7,200 cheque today. They are a lovely couple and totally hyper about getting the Real Radio tour and that vital bit of paper.

I'm reluctantly heading off, on the threatening command of Sam the *Offside* make-up lady, to get my highlights done. 'PLEASE, just get them done – we shall pick up the tab!' RIGHT, time for a funky new look, in a designer salon with a senior stylist and five colours in my hair . . .

Friday the 10th

My new hair ('Erm, just tidy up the ends and same again please') is so sensational nobody notices. One day I shall surprise everybody and even myself by taking the plunge. I think my fear of change comes from my childhood. I remember being about eight when my dad, a barber by trade, decided, after a large quantity of Glenmorangie, to give me a 'number one' fringe for easy-keeping purposes. This not only looked ridiculous with my shoulder-length hair, but proceeded to stick up, unassisted, in spikes for the best part of six months. Then I had the repugnant bowl cut, the pineapple, and finally the 'do' I've had for the past ten years, give or take a layer or two.

Anyway, heavy snow is predicted for the weekend and Robin slips into 'Weather Boy' mode with lots of excited links about preparing for blizzards etc. While he's fantastic at his wind-ups and anchoring the show, his weather is generally about as useful as an ice sun-umbrella. 'Expect mild temperatures that could drop to being chilly, high winds that may die down, scattered showers with possibly some sunshine and patchy cloud which could clear later.' I think it is called covering all eventualities; however, he does his best from whatever forecasting website he subscribes too, but like my sport, you lovely lot LOVE it when we get things wrong. Last weekend, Robin had us all stock-piling soup, tea-lights, torches and blankets. It was a nice but chilly weekend so we all take his latest ramblings with a pinch of 'put it on your path before it freezes' salt.

My favourite story today is about a wee woman from Tranent, Mrs Mack, who has worked at the primary school for forty-five years. For her leaving gift, staff gave her a blow-up male doll, dressed in snooker gear, with a photo-copied picture of her hero Stephen Hendry pasted on. While most people would prefer the golden clock or a nice wee whip-round, Mrs Mack is delighted. 'I love Stephen because he is a great ambassador for Scotland. Every time he is on the telly I sit with my tartan rug on and cheer him on.'

We get on to the subject of leaving dos. I've only had one, a night of extreme carnage in the City Merchant function suite with lots of journalists from the *Evening Times*. I woke up the next day with no coat, no bag and a bruise the size of Africa on my bum (a spectacular slip whilst high-kicking to 'New York, New York', so I am told . . .).

When I left STV they had basically binned the entire sports department after not getting the football rights. We found out courtesy of the front page of the *Daily Record* and we all slipped out under the cloak of darkness. It was quite sad, actually, because we'd had some fantastic times. There were, naturally, other great leaving memories:

'I worked in the maternity ward at Wishaw General; when I was leaving they carried me and dumped me in the birthing pool.' Linda McDonald, Motherwell.

'I used to sing for a living. On my last night the folk I worked with gave me a chocolate microphone. The announcer said, "It will either melt or he will eat it." Somebody in the crowd shouted, "Who cares, just as long as he doesn't bloody well sing again."' Big John.

'I worked in newspaper advertising; a girl called Helen was leaving to become a farmer's wife. In her speech she said, "It won't be so different to what I am doing now, up to my neck in shit all day and working with cows!" We certainly remembered that leaving do.' Gill, Falkirk.

'I was a chef for fifteen years; when I left they gave me a cook book.' Paul, Uddingston.

'I got the usual condensed milk, syrup, chocolate, coconut, eggs and flour thrown over me on my way home. The moral of this story is don't leave a chocolate factory!' Marc.

[And finally a text about the lovely wee wifie herself:]

'I went to Tranent school and Mrs Mack was tops. She always made me smile and was a great laugh. I'm not going to say my name though or all my mates will slag me.'

She sounds just like Mrs McCaskill who was my primary one teacher. She was a big friendly woman, with clickity-clackity Scholl sandals, who was always there and always smiling. Mrs Mack, I hope you enjoy your retirement and spend many happy nights watching the snooker with your new inflatable friend and tartan blanket.

Monday the 13th

Oh my! Robin was right. Scotland is covered in the thickest snow in years, eight inches of perfect snowman and sledging snow in the central belt. Yesterday was the best fun ever in terms of winter frolics, but today it is messy on the roads as the slush freezes and outlying streets are impassable.

I was out on Saturday night when it fell, and Glasgow was absolute bedlam.

11.00 p.m.– No snow, freezing.

11.15 p.m. – A wee flurry starts.

11.20 p.m. – Horizontal sheets of snow.

2.00 a.m. – Complete whiteout. (This is when I leave the research club at Glasgow University where we have somehow managed to gate-crash a French bloke's thirtieth birthday party.)

There are at least six to eight inches lying and it is still falling heavily, a bit like my pal Michelle who is wearing her finest pointy-heeled 'slut boots', her words not mine. We had to totter back to my flat because there was not a sign of a taxi. The woman in the office said she had gone from 750 cabs to fewer than 300. They all must have been hiding at a big snack van somewhere.

The papers today are full of tales similar to our trek home. In fact over 3,000 clubbers were stranded in Glasgow because there was no public transport or taxis on the roads. The police had to ask the Garage nightclub in Sauchiehall Street to re-open to let people shelter; Buchanan Bus Station and the

Central Hotel reception area were also commandeered for emergency accommodation.

However, as I mentioned, yesterday was hilarious. I took a walk through Kelvingrove Park where there were snowboarders, skiers, at least 1,000 snowmen, women, rabbits, cats, dogs and even a Loch Ness monster. My favourite bit was watching the two maniacs in bright orange canoes, complete with paddles, zoom from Park Circus down the slopes to the river. That said, the four lads in the bath tub looked as if they were having a ball too. It seems we all had a lot of fun:

'I had to stagger home four miles in a T-shirt, but we had the best snowball fight in years.' Frank, Bellshill.

'On Saturday night the Fire Brigade made a bonfire outside the taxi queue at Hamilton Palace to keep everybody warm.' Jackie, Hamilton.

'I took my daughter out on my old wooden sledge to Barshaw Park. It's not been used since the early eighties but we had a great time.' Tam, Glasgow.

'The last time we had snow like this was 13 January 1993. I know this because my eldest daughter was born then.' Dave, Dunfermline.

'My partner Evan and I took my wee boy out on our new sledge, it is like a rubber ring. Great fun, but I am STILL trying to thaw out my bum.'

'There is a cracking wee snowman in the middle of the M8 roadworks.' Jim, Linwood.

'The worst year I remember was 1982; the field out the back of my house was so hard-packed with ice we could actually skate on it.' Joyce, Armadale.

'I work in Marks and Spencer's in Hamilton, and a woman came in with a sledge under her arm to do her shopping. I think it was to carry her stuff home.' Lorraine, Hamilton.

I have another bumper Monday, and given the weather it is trains and taxis all the way. After the show I head up to the *Offside* edit to cut a cheeky little feature on insults. Tam always likes the last word, so I'm basically having a wee pop back.

I interviewed Robin for my package because he is the wind-up king. It was a very odd experience, though; I was in sensible TV director mode telling him what to do for set-up shots. I ask him if he's ever been insulted back: 'I was once going on a bit on the show when a text came in that said, "SHUT UP YOU ANNOYING WEE FART OF A MAN." I think that is quite straight and to the point. "You're talking crap, you short, fake-tanned Aberdonian arsehole!" is another favourite.' I also recruit Baz to be a 'Ned' for the shoot and mid-morning presenter Dougie Jackson does a bit of voice-over for it too. A REAL joint venture you may say.

The show goes really well tonight, which is a miracle given that Tam was ill and pouring from both ends prior to filming. He warned the audience there may have to be an emergency dash at any time in the proceedings; I think they thought he was kidding. When we stopped mid-shoot and he groaned, 'I think I have followed through,' I was the only one to believe him. Thankfully, on this occasion he was talking shit, quite literally, although he will count tonight as his least pleasurable show of all time. Oh, apart from the one 'comedian' Roy Walker was on. He was as funny as a week in the jail, and as for catchphrase? 'You're murder' would have been apt.

I get to bed at 11.00 p.m., a whopping nineteen and a half hours after getting up. Still, at least I don't have the skitters . . .

Tuesday the 14th

Celtic and Scotland legend Jinky Johnstone passed away yesterday, and today every paper is cover-to-cover with tributes to one of the finest players Scotland has ever produced. Jinky was loved by both sides of the Old Firm and every football fan in the country for being an amazing player and a real character. His long battle with motor neurone disease has been well-documented; he campaigned tirelessly for stem cell treatment and remained an inspiration until the very end.

I've interviewed Jinky a few times at Celtic functions and he was always a right wee live wire, great fun and full of mischief. He achieved glory in the Lisbon Lions squad that won the European Cup in 1967, but my favourite tale is the rowing boat incident in Largs.

The Scotland team were on a training camp at Largs ahead of a game against England; Jinky was out with the players, he'd a few too many and decided to take a rowing boat out for a wee hurl on the way home. The boat had no oars, the coastguard were involved and the rest is the stuff of legend. He was slated in the press, played a blinder in the match and gave the journalists a slightly cheeky hand gesture after skipping his way gracefully past another dazed opponent. Good lad. Today our phones ring off the hook with listeners hoping to share their 'Jinky' tales:

Lily Paterson was first on. 'I worked in the kitchen in a pub in Glasgow. Jinky came in one day for his dinner and I asked him for an autograph for my son who is a Rangers fan. He was happy to oblige and wrote on a napkin: "To William, wish you were one of us!! Love Jinky x." And he meant it in a humorous way, he was a fantastic guy, never without a smile.'

Davie Martin from Maryhill was next: 'I have always looked like Jinky and my mates have called me that for years. I was in the loo at Hampden during a boxing match recently and my pal shouted, "See you outside, Jinky." I came out the cubicle to find Jonathan Woodgate, the Real Madrid star. He'd overheard my mate and said he'd always been a fan and that it was a total honour to meet me. I said, "Nice to meet you too, son," and went back to my seat laughing. At the end of the bout we were walking down the stairs and Woodgate was with a bunch of premiership players all shouting, "Jinky, Jinky, give us a wave." It just shows how highly he was thought of by people outside Scotland as well. Oh, and I used to work with Jinky at Lafferty's and know he would have found this whole episode absolutely hilarious. He was a wonderful man.'

Texts included:

'Jinky was a legend with Rangers and Celtic fans. What a player and an amazing man.' Harry, Larkhall.

'About twenty years ago Jinky used to jump on my school bus when he was out running. We wondered if someone was timing him. He also used to come into Angels pub in Uddingston and serenade the girls with Bon Jovi songs. He was a total character and will be sadly missed.'

'I only saw Jinky play once at the last game before they closed the Jungle. He had the ball, ran past the Jungle, raised his arms in salute to the crowd and in true gallus style chipped the Man. Utd keeper from about thirty yards. If that was Jinky retired I can only imagine what he was like in his prime.' Thomas, Milton.

[And a final anonymous message with a beautifully poignant mental image I reckon must have brought a wee smile to everyone listening:]

'Do you think when the big man opened the pearly gates yesterday the wee man ran past him with the ball?'

There is nothing more I can add. A legend.

Wednesday the 15th

The name is Bond – James Bond. And nobody likes me because I'm new, I'm blonde, I'm a bit of a minger and I can't drive my nice fancy car unless it's an automatic. Poor Daniel Craig, the knives, lasers and plutonium-filled missiles are well and truly out for the latest 007 who is pictured everywhere this morning on set of *Casino Royale* in tight swim shorts looking quite hot – from the neck down.

Martin Campbell, the new director, describes him as 'by far the best Bond ever,' insinuating his acting talents will take the character to a new level. Personally, Sean Connery and Pierce Brosnan are my favourites. And we are passionate about our number one secret agent:

'Sean Connery was best without a doubt; those eyes, I would pay money just to look at them.' Alison, Airdrie.

'Pierce Brosnan is suave, he had everything. I have every Bond DVD and every matchbox car they released. Girls do not like Bond.' Iain, Larkhall.

'My favourite Bond was Pierce until I saw him choking on a big fat prawn in the film *Mrs Doubtfire*.' Elaine.

[This show is certainly an education:]

'The best thing in any Bond film is the end credits where Cecilia Cowdenbeath is mentioned.'

[And some funny bloke calls in with a tale that I believe to start with:]

'I stayed in a hotel down south last year and I thought I was in a room next to James Bond. All I could hear through the wall is "Roger MORE, Roger MORE."'

Oh dear. I can see Bossman Jay having another one of his road-swerving moments as he heads in to the station. Still, it WAS funny.

It's all about entertainment this morning. *The Muppets* are fifty this year and Robin suggests we bring them back on a weekly basis. I have to agree, I thought they were magic as a kid and loved every minute from the opening sing-along titles to the big final low note from the slightly spaced-looking Muppet saxophonist.

We open the forum on special guests, basically discussing which celebrities would we like to see on the show and with which Muppet. (Can you believe I have two university degrees?) I would like to see Vanessa Feltz with Miss Piggy, while Robin wants Gordon Ramsay and the Swedish chef to meet over a hot stove. The calls and texts are brilliant:

'Mick McCarthy and the Bald Eagle, you couldn't tell them apart.' Billy, Hampden Cars.

'Statler and Waldorf ARE Ewen and Roughie from the *Football Phone In*.' Harry, St Andrews.

'Jools Holland and Rolf the big shaggy piano-playing dog could duet.' Angela, Glassford.

'Donatella Versace and the long-faced girl in the Muppet band are like twins.' Carol, Clydebank.

'I'd like to see the mad professor with Celtic player Stephen Pearson – let's face it, he is Beaker's double.'

'It has to be Frank McAvennie with Big Bird.' Rab.

Ah, they made me chuckle.

For the record, I have not been to fat class for over two weeks. (Worst thing about this diary lark is I now have written proof of my failings.) In a bid to make myself feel better I make a pot of 'no check soup' big enough to dunk a small country in. No check soup, for the non-diet-obsessed, is basically a big pot of vegetables that tastes OK but leaves you craving pineapple pizza about twenty minutes later. I eat about a gallon of the stuff and an hour later my tummy is like Bond's Martini – shaken but not stirred!

Thursday the 16th

It's a hair-raising show this morning. The perm is 100 years old today. First invented by some mad mental German crimper, its place in history has become etched in all of our minds, and usually in a pained 'Why oh why did I do that to myself' kind of way. Robin, it turns out, was inspired by Scotland's most famous curly-heid, Alan Rough, whose 1978 World Cup 'do' is possibly the most famous haircut ever, and predictably the *Scottish Sun* has a massive picture of Partick Thistle's finest with his glorious locks.

I had a demi-wave once when I was about eight, which was a horrendous half-head of curls. I hated it so much I cried my eyes out, the lassie panicked and one hour and a lot of neutraliser later my hair was straight again and my unfathomable fear of change began. And it seems we all have a love–hate relationship with the perm:

'My brother Danny had the mullet with a perm at the back – it was absolutely hideous. He also used to wear his jeans above his waistline and tucked into leather boots.' Lee, Glasgow.

'I had my hair permed before a holiday in Cyprus. I put lemon juice on it for that golden glow; the result was like straw hanging oot a midden!' Karen, Stonehouse.

'I had mine done before a primary school prize ceremony. I had never been to a salon before and thought I was getting a wee 'set'. I looked like a wee woolly lamb and it took forever to grow out.' Carol.

'I've always had a tight perm and couldn't imagine life without one.' Jimmy, East Lothian.

'I had a perm in 1979, I washed it and went out for the bus, and by the time it arrived I had a head full of icicles.' Donna, Shotts.

'I have had the perm and moustache since the seventies and don't know what I would look like without it now. My mates call me 'Porn Star' and despite looking like Rudi Völler I have done not too badly on that front.' Stevie the Porn Star, East Lothian.

Tonight I have an invite to the launch of *No. 1* magazine, 'Scotland's top celebrity read'. I'm afraid to admit I usually avoid these glamour nights for several reasons:

- I have nothing to wear;
- They are always on school nights;

- They can be full of complete tossers.

However, for *Breakfast Show* research purposes I shall force myself to drink free champagne and mingle with the glitterati. I hear it is to be a 'star studded' event and we start speculating on the line up. I reckon every cast member of *River City* will be there along with the omnipresent Justin and Colin. Robin opts for Carol Smillie (again!) and Sarah Heaney. We decide, with the help of our lovely listeners, to write a list of likely celebrities for me to try and spot:

- Jackie Bird
- Peter Lovenkrands
- Jack and Victor from *Still Game*
- The *Taggart* cast
- Jimmy Krankie (keep her away from the plants)
- Lorraine Kelly
- Shareen Nanjiani
- Martin Compston
- Lulu
- *Sunday Mail* columnist Alison Craig
- Eadie McReadie from *Balamory*
- Billy Connolly
- John Amabile (that wee designer guy in the kilt who is bloody everywhere).

In a vain bid to detox before a weekend of madness, I've had 'no check soup' for breakfast, lunch and tea. I suspect even one glass of champagne could send me into mental mode this evening. So assuming I'm not arrested and in jail, I look forward to dishing the designer dirt tomorrow . . .

Friday the 17th

Top of the morning to you. St Patrick's Day today, and I've had four hours' sleep. The reason I hardly ever go out on school nights any more is my complete inability to go home at a sensible time.

The *No. 1* magazine bash was a big glitzy affair with loads of people I've not seen for ages, models painted orange dancing on podiums in skimpy bikinis, top DJ entertainment but possibly the most alluring draw – a FREE BAR. Two little words causing so much pleasure. The drinks on offer were vodka cocktails with fresh crushed raspberries, so healthy too, in a way.

The problem with getting up at 3.30 a.m. and being on a silly diet is that after a few wee tipples you become a giggling idiot. With my celebrity list in pocket, I went for a wee tour of the room hoping to tick off our likely candidates. Poor turn-out from the regulars, I'm afraid. NO John Amabile or Justin and Colin; however Anna Ryder Richardson was there flying the flag for MDF wholesalers everywhere. NO cast members of *Taggart*, although *River City* did have a healthy turnout, including my new pal Joyce Falconer who plays Roisin, and NO Alison Craig, Sarah Heaney or Peter Lovenkrands.

However, we did have Arthur Numan, Gordon Smith, Murdo McLeod, and Federico from *Big Brother*. I can't believe we missed him from the original list. He was a certainty, and boy, what an attitude that lad has. If he was a raspberry cocktail he would drink himself in one!

My pal Angela who lives in Germany arrived at my flat out of the blue half an hour before the event started and, despite coming in for 'just a coffee', ended up at the bash (full of supermodels in tiny frocks with lots of silicone on show) wearing jeans, a woolly polo-neck and her mum's finest snow boots. I packed her on the last train to Polmont with a designer goodie bag, assuring her that my life is not like this every night of the week.

Today we are celebrating Scotland's two Commonwealth gold swimming medals as every paper features Caitlin McLatchie and David Carry looking mighty chuffed. My athletic claim to fame is winning the Open Sack Race at the Island of Seil highland games. Robin got ninety-eight per cent in his cycling proficiency test and won a Mr Muscles competition in Stonehaven at the age of ten. Posing in Speedos, it seems, has been a lifetime talent.

With our swimmers leading us in a feeling of national euphoria, tales of remarkable victory emerge:

'I won a Miss Wet T-shirt competition on holiday. I only entered because nobody knew me, turns out my boss's son was in the crowd and took pictures.' Karen, Stirling.

'I won six points and a £250 fine for driving along the Stepps bypass at 82mph.' Scott, Falkirk.

'I won Mr Glaxo Junior Muscles in 1983; in 1984 I wanted to defend my title but was too old. Ten years later I won Best Male in the Montrose Pantomime Group.' John, Edinburgh.

'I was given an award for being the best litter-picker-upper in school. I am thirty-two now and still have it.' Cat, yes I'm Cat too . . .

'My partner was given an award for being the referees' worst nightmare at junior football. His name is Rab Smith.'

'In June 1976 I won the donkey derby at Butlins on the world's smelliest donkey. I still have the red rosette.' Billy, Wishaw.

'I used to win pool competitions, take the food prize home and sell it to my mum for money to go out again at night-time.' Tumshie, Falkirk.

'My man and I won champagne and T-shirts for winning a swap your clothes competition on holiday. We had to exchange everything including pants.' Cheryl, Kirkcaldy.

'I won a plastic plant at a charity bingo night. It still has pride of place in my loft!' Avril, Airdrie.

'I got first prize for singing at Glen Michael's travelling cavalcade show in Dalmarnock, aged ten. It has been downhill ever since.' Jan Melvin, Rutherglen.

'I won an impressive gardening set two years ago. I stay in a top floor flat.' Jim.

'I've just won fifty points on my Nectar card at the BP garage in Glasgow.' Steve.

'I won the World Stone-Skimming Championship on the Island of Seil. The sack race is next!' Ian from Luing.

'About twenty years ago I won two awards; I won Star Carrier for being the best paperboy and Best Ice cream Scooper.' Daryl.

'I won best bum of the day on a train to Plymouth as voted for by a bunch of army guys on the same journey. That was twenty years ago and it is a bit bigger now.' Lorna, Cairneyhill.

O'Neill's, the Irish bar in Albion Street, Glasgow, somehow must know I am beginning to flag about 8.00 a.m. and send a delivery of two full breakfasts. Choosing to ignore the mental Scottish Slimmers' check count of about six hundred, I tuck in and feel much better. They also leave Guinness hats and shamrock beely-boppers. These will be useful for me tonight as my pal Mini-Me (Laura McKay) is having a St Patrick's Day bash for her thirtieth birthday.

Mini-Me was christened so by Radio Clyde commentator Peter Martin who worked with both of us at STV. As a quiet wee young thing she arrived all fresh faced and eager to please. On her first night out with the troops she became a silly-drink-downing maniac, full of fun, laughter and nonsense. Within an hour she had exploded out of her shell and was demanding to murder cheesy tunes on a karaoke. Peter looked at me, then Laura, then me, then Laura and uttered the immortal line: 'F*** me, its Mini-Me.'

The name has stuck. She still works at STV where she's still known as Mini-Me despite the fact I left five years ago. For the record, she is an absolute diamond, and I am very proud to be her Big-Me. I would also like to put it on record that we do differ in some aspects, though; I have never followed through after a night out.

Back to the story, well, Mini-Me comes from the Murphy family, who are all massive Celtic fans. I'm sure Terry, her dad, made her mum push extra hard to deliver her on this particular day. Anyway, the theme for her party is Green. Everybody MUST wear green. This is particularly amusing given that Garry her husband is a rampant Bluenose, as are most of his pals.

In our final link Robin says, 'Well have a great time tonight, I bet you'll look great in your leprechaun outfit.' The outfit I had assembled as a big surprise! My shocked look that said 'YOU FANNY' made him fluster as it dawned on him the Cat was quite literally out of the party shop bag. Still, it's about time the little people had some recognition on the radio.

The streets of Glasgow are at a standstill today as Jimmy Johnstone is laid to rest. Thousands of people line the route from Uddingston right up to Celtic Park where the funeral cortège weaves a slow-moving final journey. It is very rare that one player can unite the great divide so spectacularly. Jinky has managed this. The live TV pictures are remarkable, showing how one man can mean so much to so many. Up until now the national media paid little attention to the Wee Man's passing. Today the whole of the UK is left in no doubt just how special he was, with scenes similar to George Best's recent funeral in Belfast. We say goodbye to a legend. When shall we see his like again . . .

Monday the 20th

It is a grim day. It's my birthday and I keep getting older and older. Today I am officially showbiz twenty-six. Apparently there is an unwritten rule for females in the media that you can't ever go over thirty, so when you DO you simply start going backwards. I'm now thirty-four, I still feel about twenty-five, so showbiz twenty-six is not too bad at all.

It's been an odd week too. For the first time ever I found myself alone in my flat shouting at swimming on the telly. The Scottish team have done tremendously well in the Commonwealth Games, although I never thought I had it in me to shout at some lad in trunks doing the backstroke. Shouting at some lad in trunks – yes, but actually swimming?

Robin shouts at and I quote, my friends, 'thick people on *Who Wants to be a Millionaire*'. Personally, I think they should start the show at £1,000 but I know what he means. And it's not just sport that gets us hot under the collar:

'My wife shouts at idiots on *Question Time*, you should hear her language, it is choice.' Malcolm, Dalkeith.

'I shout when ITV split a good film with the news. It never feels the same after a half-hour break.' Brenda, Moodiesburn.

'I have started shouting at *Deal or No Deal* which is bad because I can feel myself turning into my mum!' John.

'I shout at Heather with the weather, she gets on my nerves.' Janice, Dunfermline.

'I shout at actors in scary movies being so stupid. They always go down dark lanes alone and into the cellar with no lights.' Clair.

'English commentators on the telly make me mad. The can never accept it if their team lose, and don't start me on 1966!' Boab.

'Ainsley Harriot on *Ready Steady Cook* asks ridiculous questions like why should we wear oven gloves? He also does a full body wiggle when adding salt and pepper to things. Arrrrgh.' Angry, East Kilbride.

'My mother-in-law makes me shout at the telly. She comes to our house, takes the remotes and watches rubbish all day. She nods off holding them, but if I try to take

MARCH

them away from her she wakes up and denies she was sleeping.' Eddie, Yoker.

It's the second-last *Offside* of the run tonight and we are still finding our feet. Tam is so funny and sharp with the one-liners, I have to be on my toes to fight back. Tonight I am feeling the effects of a heavy weekend and a three-thirty alarm call, my ad-libs are average and I feel like I'm not on top of my game. Tam on the other hand is in electric form and I endure a friendly pasting. That said, I love my wee slot in studio. My TV trousers are now fitting better than they did on week one and I'm still in a job where being sensible is not allowed.

At the end of the show, a few people are hanging about waiting to chat to me. Grant from Ballieston is patiently waiting behind a camera. 'Cat, my wee boy absolutely loves you and will be so jealous when he finds out I've met you. Would you please sign something for him? It would totally make his day.' I blush as I always do when people ask for autographs (which is not very often, I have to add) and rip a page off my script to give him a wee note to take to his son. I draw my wee cartoon cat face and his lights up. 'He will be absolutely over the moon with this by the way. He will put this straight up on his wall next to his autograph from Jinky.' I am absolutely mortified. Jinky is a legend. He should be on people's walls. I, on the other hand, am fortunate enough to be paid to talk for a living.

I never really appreciate that we DO cheer people up and entertain them, and never 'feel famous' because I firmly believe we are only as good as the listeners we have. I have to confess I am extremely uncomfortable with the whole 'celebrity' thing that sometimes comes from presenting such a massive show, but I shall now never lose sight of the fact that some wee boy thinks I am important and to an eleven-year-old that can be a huge thing. I'm sure his tastes will improve with age, but for the moment I feel like a humbled showbiz

121

twenty-six-year-old who's done not too badly for her tender years . . .

Tuesday the 21st

Sleep, sleep, I need sleep. Three hours again last night and I am really beginning to look quite ill. I've got sunken eyes, and a grey pallor which is now beginning to look ghostlike. I'm meeting my mum and dad tonight for a belated birthday tea and know I'll have to trowel on the slap to avoid the 'Why you can't look after yourself properly?' inquisition.

Insomnia is one of the most frustrating aspects of this show. I suffer quite badly and generally need to read for at least an hour before nodding off into some fitful slumber. But for the past few weeks I've had the full blown works. That awful state when you are so physically tired you're unable to function, yet the brain keeps tick tick ticking away with ideas, anxieties and thoughts that have no place in a weary head that simply needs to switch off.

On that happy note, I come into work with as much sparkle as a bottle of supermarket discount coke that's been left open in the heat for a fortnight. Still it is amazing how the banter can wake me up. No matter how tired or lethargic we feel, when the red light is on we have to come alive. And somehow it IS much easier to perk up with texts and calls from the listeners who are all struggling to wake up in their own wee ways.

Anyway, not much in the news today; Belfast Airport is going to be renamed the George Best Airport. I suspect it will now have to build the biggest duty free in the world. It's what he would have wanted.

I'm instantly drawn to the *Daily Mail*'s page three (no, not some posh bird with Versace skants on); it is a story about the cast of *Dallas* and what they are up to now. The American soap which ran from 1978 to 1991 was a personal favourite of my mum's, and I got hooked when I was old enough to stay up past eight o'clock.

I remember being given a task at primary school where the class had to write about our ambitions. I can clearly recall the epic in my 'NEWS' jotter stating that my main ambition was to attend either the Oil Barons' Ball, or the Ewing Barbecue at Southfork. Bizarrely, managing Aberdeen FC, being a professional showjumper and owning a chocolate factory were others. Subconsciously, I obviously wanted to work for charities and help those less fortunate than me.

Some of the cast of *Dallas* have had colourful lives away from the set. For example, JR's nemesis Cliff Barnes, played by Ken Kercheval, is a recovering seventy-year-old alcoholic with SEVEN children from THREE different women and he has just left his SECOND wife for a younger woman. How many cliff-hangers is that in a lifetime? Hollywood executives are currently casting for *Dallas the Movie* with John Travolta rumoured to be JR, and the eternally glamorous J-Lo as his quivery-mouthed booze-fuelled wife Sue Ellen. Our listeners think the following casting would be better:

- Jock – Roughie
- JR – Ewen Cameron, Jack Nicholson or Gordon Ramsay
- Bobby – Ewan McGregor or Dougie Jackson from our drive-time show ('He sounds like a nice wee man with fine morals like Bobby,' says Mary from Motherwell)
- Lucy – Britney Spears ('Now that she's been eating all the cakes,' says Jim from Govan)
- Pam – Victoria Beckham ('Before she had her ridiculous boob job,' says Liz in Falkirk)

Despite rarely going out on school nights any more, I am slightly worryingly cast as Sue Ellen. That said, it might not be the worst idea I have ever heard – think of the sleep I'd get with all that brandy . . .

Wednesday the 22nd

It's odd how going off on a tangent can lead to some of our best banter. Robin and I are beginning to specialise in tangents, much to the disapproval of Mr W. who is now being super-efficient in his new role as head of presentation. He makes us listen back to links where we have clearly been all over the place. There is something odd about hearing your own voice; I should be used to it by now, but sitting in a room, listening back to rambling chunks of previous shows can be a very odd and sometimes disconcerting experience.

I think breakfast radio should be totally spontaneous and off the cuff. To me, adverts and talk-ups, where we have to give out information about forthcoming events or competitions, get in the way of having a laugh and speaking to more people. But I know that, fundamentally, this is how commercial radio exists. The radio experts also seem to think breakfast radio should sound spontaneous but ultimately be planned and controlled. I think we sit somewhere in the middle. Room for improvement AND room for more badness! Hee, hee.

Today is a fine example. The newspaper story I pick this morning is about an unfortunate woman who has a serious phobia about peas. Garden peas, frozen peas, marrowfat peas, you name it. She can't walk down the pea aisle in the supermarket and goes all mushy if she sees peas in a restaurant.

I think the plan was to go down the 'irrational phobias' route, but I suddenly remembered my one and only pea story. Mince and peas was the second dish I ever made in home economics at school. I recall this vividly because the lid of the Tupperware tub I carried it home in fell off in the crush for the bus home and I spilled the lot down my good Tammy Girl skirt and the trouser leg of the guy in front (all that good gravy!). Robin jumps on the home eccie chat with glee. His dish *de jour* was 'sausage plate'. Basically a home-made sausage roll with tomato purée as a topping. My début dish, however, was cheese and toast and a cup of tea. Lindsey, our newshound, was tested to the limit with making a strawberry Nesquik milkshake and taking a digestive biscuit out of a packet.

Without us even saying our phone number, the board is full and every line flashing. As I said, I like tangy tangents. It is always great when an expert calls in, and first on is Mrs Donaldson, a very chirpy home economics teacher. She informs us her fourth years are sitting an exam today with chilli con carne, spaghetti Bolognaise and crème roulade on the menu. However, she also concedes that powdered milk-shake and a biscuit remain lesson one for first years.

Once again, pushing the reminiscing button does the trick:

'The first thing we made was Welsh rarebit, it was disgusting and to this day I shall never forget the taste.' Andy, Lanark.

'I remember we made cheese and toast but the teacher gave it some la de da French name. We may have been in the first year but at the end of the day we knew it was just cheese and toast!'

'My first meal was cheese and toast too, but we grated apple through it which was lovely. It cost me 50p to make and that was in 1982.' Calum, Stirling.

'We made jam roly-poly pudding. My pal Tracy and I liked it so much we made it every day for about a year. I am surprised we never turned into roly-polys ourselves. I couldn't even tell you how to begin one now.' Louise.

'My old food and nut. teacher used to insist on sampling ALL of the food. She was massive.' Tam the cone worker.

'We had a crazy teacher called Mrs Wyness who used to try and scrub love bites off our necks with white spirit. I remember one day the gorgeous replacement science teacher came in to borrow an egg. By the time he left she had cut his hair with kitchen scissors and chastised him for being a hippy.' Jayne.

'We had a home economics teacher in the 1980s called Miss Drake. She was a page three stunner and all the guys could think about was putting a bun in HER oven.' Mick the Livvy taxi driver.

[And it turns out Miss Drake the cooking teacher ironically caused a bit of a stir. Five minutes after reading out the last text, this arrived:]

'WOW, Miss Drake, I forgot about her. She taught at Whitburn Academy as well and I agree with the last bloke, she was sensational.' Kev.

So, if the good men folk in Whitburn and Livingston can't boil an egg or make strawberry milkshake, we now know who to blame. Miss Drake you have a lot to answer for . . .

Meanwhile, it has all kicked off at Tynecastle once again. Vladimir Romanov has sacked head coach Graham Rix and director of football Jim Duffy. I am now convinced it is only time before I am proven correct. He is up to something. Get Daniel Craig to Gorgie now. Minger or no minger, the good people of Edinburgh need to know!

Thursday the 23rd

Oh dear, it is almost too coincidental. An anonymous teacher is front page of the *Daily Record* this morning after her mobile phone was stolen in class and hot video footage of the lady in question, erm, entertaining herself in the nude is now doing the rounds at her school. Pupils are delighted (and dilated no doubt), mums are calling for her head as are dads, but I won't go there. Tayside police are currently investigating the incident – I bet they are – but I can assure you they have confirmed the lovely Miss Drake is not in the frame.

This reminds me of a blonde art teacher at my school who was allegedly in a *Playboy* magazine. It was never proven if she actually did the spread (what an awful term) or not, but the very thought of it helped every schoolboy make the leap from boy to man at Douglas Academy.

My top story today is about a set of TEMPORARY traffic lights in Ardlui, next to Loch Lomond. Today they have been there for THIRTY YEARS and the locals are having a tongue-in-cheek party for them. We initiate the 'roadwork rant-line' and 'pot watch' to name and shame potholes of gargantuan proportions. And I'm pleased to say we are inundated with one of my favourite traffic gags. OK, my only traffic gag: 'There is a massive pothole in Glasgow city centre; police are looking into it.' Boom Boom. These also caught my eye:

'The reason there are so many potholes is that the council seem to put all their materials into making bloody speed bumps everywhere.' Colin, Springburn.

'The potholes on the A800 are like the Grand Canyon but not as pretty.' Darren, Dunfermline.

'I've been in Glasgow fifteen years now and I've never seen the Kingston Bridge free of roadworks.' Angry, Pollok.

'Robertson Street in Glasgow has so many potholes Chris Rea wrote a song about it – road from hell.' Miriam.

With the Budget taking up most of the news headlines, it's great to see we still have a cheeky sense of humour. Step forward the Motherwell prankster. Somebody at, or at least near, the football club has been swapping number plates on the players' cars without them noticing.

Now, poor midfielder Kevin McBride was first to feel the real impact of this jest as he was stopped by cops with a professionally made 'SHAGGER' plate on his Audi TT. Thankfully the policeman saw the funny side of things when it became evident the driver had no idea it had been done. Another player has been driving about with 'BAWBAG' on his car, while manager Terry Butcher has had saltire plates with 'MCBUTCHER' added.

The *Scottish Sun* has added some other examples: 'P45' – the plate they suggest for Graham Rix, 'GR8 TAN' for sun-bed-loving Dons boss Jimmy Calderwood, and 'RICH B' for Celtic skipper Neil Lennon who's been in trouble all week for boasting about his wealth during the CIS Cup final against Dunfermline.

There's also an interesting survey out today in *AutoTrader* listing the Lexus I am currently driving as one of the top three cars in the world. The Fiat Punto is the most hated, as voted for by their owners! In yet another quirk of serendipitous fate, a young lad called Derek arrives unannounced from Arnold Clark at lunchtime to pick up my Lexus; he shows me the new car I have for two weeks – yes, a Fiat Punto. You couldn't make it up . . .

Friday the 24th

'Hearts boss fired from Russian submarine.' Without doubt the finest sports line I have written ever. My 'Romanov is Bond baddie' theory must now have some credence.

The *Record* today has a cracking tale about Vladimir and how he decided Graham Rix had to go, when he was on the deck of a Russian nuclear submarine. As a former sailor, he was meeting his ex-Admiral on board for a reunion, and that is when he decided it was time to torpedo the Hearts management team again. Robin adds a cannon noise, 'BOOM', then a 'WHEEEEEE', and submarine sound effects to the bulletin. The whole Hearts saga is now so bloody bonkers it is brilliant.

We are puffed out this morning on many levels. The smoking ban comes into force in Scotland this Sunday and people are just beginning to realise the impact this will make on daily life. As a non-smoker I can't wait for public places to be smoke free, but I can understand how lifelong smokers will struggle to cope with such a massive change to their daily routine. Pubs, clubs, restaurants, public transport, work-places, and pretty much every enclosed space will be smoke free. Enforcers will be out looking for puffing perpetrators, issuing £50 on-the-spot fines.

We are bombarded with calls on the subject, particularly from irate lorry drivers who are now no longer allowed to light up in their cabs. Response to the ban is mixed; we don't often discuss serious subjects but I must confess I love get-ting my smoke-stain-free teeth into the burning issues. Texts included:

'On Monday I am getting a new kitchen fitted and ap-parently I have to stop smoking in my own house before the men arrive. This is ridiculous, what about my rights?' Ashley, Coatbridge.

'I'm a nurse at Paisley and we do tests called broncho-scopies every Tuesday. I see smoking-related cancers every week. I hate this part of my job as I am diagnosing people's deaths. Please quit while you can.' June.

'I drive fifteen hours a day in my OWN lorry; they will have to catch me to stop me. It is nonsense.' Stevie, Motherwell.

'A lot of companies are banning smoking outside too now. Why don't they just burn us all at the stake? However I am looking forward to the SMATING. In Ireland smokers keep meeting and getting together outside the pubs which could be fun.' Jacqueline, Glasgow.

'Are you playing requests? Can I get "Smoke gets in your eyes" please?' Hazel, Glasgow.

'I am a smoker but I think it is great, I also make health and safety signs for a living.' Iain, Perth.

'I used to drive buses in Edinburgh. We had cameras up the stairs where smoking was banned but I don't think anyone has ever been charged. This could be difficult to implement.' Stevie Shanks, Tranent.

'I'm pregnant and the thought of my baby being born in a smoke-free country is brilliant.' Jools.

'Delighted at the ban, it means we won't all smell after a night out, apart from the lager-flavoured bottom burps that is.' H, Lanarkshire.

'The ban is my big push to quit. My wee boy Jackson is only twelve weeks old; I want to smell baby smell and not cigarettes all the time.' Tommy.

'Stuff the ban and give me my rights, I drive a big artic-ashtray!' Davie, Bathgate.

Robin and I are also puffed out after a four-hour intense meeting with Australian radio guru Phil Dowse. He is a gruff Aussie paid a bucket of cash to annihilate breakfast shows all over the world. Feared by many as he is, I actually quite enjoy our sessions since he is frank and clearly knows his subject inside out. If he thinks something is shit he says so, and does so frequently, but equally he points out areas to focus on and improve.

After four hours of tearing us apart, he told us he actually believes we are one of the top FIVE breakfast shows in the WORLD. Now I'm not sure how much Real Radio splashes out on this guy, but quite frankly it's not enough. Robin and I both clocked the look of surprise from Bossman Jay, Mr W. and John Simons, our super-important chief cheese from down south at this historic comment. When we do something wrong on air we are always told: 'Phil Dowse says you should . . .' When it comes to contract negotiations WE shall now be saying, 'Phil Dowse says . . .'

As the bloke in the film *The Mask* once said – SMOKIN'!

Monday the 27th

Slightly demob happy today. It is the last *Offside* tonight and I have tomorrow off. I applied for it in back in December when I found out the TV run dates. It is very difficult to get individual days off at a radio station with continuity issues and the like, but I called their bluff and offered to take the full week and was miraculously allowed the day. Ha, my furtive advance plotting for a good night out knows no bounds. I have my mad head on and am quite looking forward to a right good bender this evening. I sense an evening of excessive drink and dancing and chips covered in full fat cheese on the way home.

The *Breakfast Show* flies by as we debate everything from how the smoking ban has affected our weekend to the number of working fish vans in central Scotland, a 'smokie' theme I suppose.

Now, I've known for a few weeks that my humble journal will actually be published into a proper book and I audaciously find myself evaluating situations to make the tome more interesting. The glitzy *No. 1* magazine party launch for instance, not my thing but I forced myself to the free bar for editorial purposes, honestly. I have also started getting photographed with the pop stars I meet in a vain bid to make my life appear a smidgen more showbiz than the reality of it (see the photo section for those who make the grade).

It is only as I write this I accept how calculated my recent behaviour has become. It actually took the visit this morning of Journey South, the brothers from the *X Factor* who finished third, to make me realise this. The lovely sales girls are all gushy over the boys and scream and yelp in delight as they get pictured with them.

'Cat, do you want your photo taken with Journey South?' shouted Stephanie, our super-efficient programming assistant.

'Erm, No.' They seem like nice lads who can sing and play a bit, but to be honest they remind me of banjo players from Alabama and the whole *Pop Idol, X Factor* thing is beginning to annoy me a lot.

Robin and Baz come to *Offside* tonight which is weird. I feel more nervous presenting in front of the two of them than the 300 others in the audience and the half million or so watching on telly. The show feels like a good one, Tam and I bouncing off each other well. Johnny Watson is made up like Justice Minister Cathy Jamieson and I find myself in hysterics when he comes on at the end for a bow and sticks his fake breasts in my face. They're a great bunch to work with and I feel quite fortunate to be involved.

I drink a bit too much wine and decide to purchase most of my TV clothes from the series including the bright pink outfit. That bloody car is still having an effect . . .

Tuesday the 28th

Today is all about those three little words that mean the world to me – a long lie. I wake up at half-ten in the morning which is something of a record. OK, so I went clubbing until 2.00 a.m. but, as a paid-up member of the insomniac association, this is a fantastic achievement. Booze is great, but possibly the wrong way to cure sleep deprivation on a regular basis.

My phone has eleven text messages, universally implying Robin has been a twat and may possibly be out the door. I leave him for one morning and carnage! There is also a concerned voice message from my dad, the ever-popular Bobby Harvey. 'Toots, he's gone too far this time. I think he's for the chop. Bossman Jay is making an announcement at two.' It would've helped if at least one of the informants had given me a tiny clue as to his misdemeanour. I phone him but his mobile is off.

It turns out that in a moment of, I think, total lunacy, he's decided to rant about today's strike where 200,000 council workers protested about proposed pension changes. The station is bombarded with angry callers and for some part of the morning it is unclear if Real Radio is planning to reprimand him for his outburst.

At two Jay comes on and informs us Robin has gone AWOL. I try his phone again and it is still off. By half-two he has shown up and is on air sounding awful. He says his views are HIS views alone and NOT the views of the station. You can tell the proverbial gun is at the head. However, support begins to flood in for him and the right of free speech. I am convinced once again his wind-up gene has taken over his brain.

All I wanted was a peaceful day off and I'm getting hassled from all sides. I am now anticipating a heated show tomorrow and seriously consider going back on the bevvy . . .

Wednesday the 29th

I have two hundred and thirty-four e-mails, all regarding Robin's outburst. My mail box is too full to receive any more, so who knows how many more are floating about cyberspace? It is 4.31 a.m. and I'm not sure I can cope with the intricacies of public sector strikes this early. Sometimes 'Do they still make Cremola Foam' chats can be a much nicer way to start one's morning.

Robin always starts each hour of the show with the weather and I can tell from the nature and plenitude of text messages it is going to be frosty all day. He has really pissed people off. We strike (oops bad choice of word) a fine balance this morning. Robin has dismounted from his high horse but is humbly defiant, an oxymoron if ever there was one. I accept his right to free speech but question his stance on the strike. Personally, I can't help feeling he mouthed off to deliberately create the rammy it did.

It turns out Robin left the studio after yesterday's show and went for a two-hour drive with his phone off to clear his head. When I am angry or upset I batter out tunes on my piano with an aggression best used in the boxing ring. I also lock myself in the loo and have a good greet every now and then, particularly when PMT kicks in and intravenous Galaxy is my only true friend.

We are inundated with texts about stress relief and Robin's current plight. To beat stress:

'I go fly-fishing for a few hours, brilliant.' Frank, Edinburgh.

'Boxercise is great for stress, a mix of punching and circuit training.' Darren, Tranent.

'Swingball is great for stress, just batter the tennis ball as hard as possible.' Jeanie, Drumchapel.

'Ten pin bowling is great, a couple of strikes feels amazing.' Gus (who said the banned 'S' word).

'I visit my favourite men when I am stressed. Jack Daniels, Johnny Walker red and Johnny Walker black.' Kim.

[And I appreciated this refreshingly honest answer from a man who takes matters into his own hands:]

'If I'm stressed I just give my boaby a good bashing. It works wonders every time.' Jimmy.

Robin's rant provoked the following response:

'Tell Tory boy to stop digging a bigger hole for himself. He has damaged his reputation and that of the station.' Joe, Twechar.

'I didn't agree with your thoughts, but I agree with your right to air them.' Charlie, Lanark.

'Hi Robin, thought you were talking mince yesterday but I won't be changing stations because the rest are rubbish.' Andy, Clydebank.

'There is no real freedom of speech in this country which is just as well or I would get the jail for telling

Robin what I thought of his outburst.' Big Ray, Grange-mouth.

'There is no such thing as a wrong opinion. An opinion is a personal view. Well done for saying what you feel.' Kirsty, East Kilbride.

'Good on you Robin, in this PC-mad world it is great to hear someone speaking their mind. I am furious you got slapped across the wrists. Carry on mate.' Chris, Edinburgh.

'Great to hear you Robin, you had us worried yesterday.' Fiona, Cambuslang.

We come off air mentally drained and the sales girls are downstairs looking lip-glossed and gorgeous in a haze of hairspray and perfume. This can only mean one thing – a guest. True to form, Shayne Ward, the winner of *X Factor*, appears to promote his new song. He is quite like Justin Timberlake and is the hot young sensation Sharon Osbourne fancied. He is actually a very nice lad, exceptionally grounded and obviously loving every minute of his musical journey. My anti-reality-TV-part-time pop star stance has lasted a whopping two days. He is STUNNING and I am over getting my picture taken (hug me tighter, oh that's it, closer now, and another one . . .) before you can say one-hit wonder. This job is great.

Thursday the 30th

The reason Robin looks so ridiculously young for his tender forty-four years is in the *Daily Record* today. Research from Denmark reveals that the secret to looking young is getting married and having kids. Married women with kids look on average TWO years younger than their single friends of the same age. (It's the booze-free pregnancies I think . . .) And men with THREE kids (e.g. Robin) look the youngest of all.

This does not explain his persistence in dressing like a teenager, though.

In another delightful tale of Galloway fatherhood, he reveals today how he found his youngest boy in front of the mirror at the weekend wearing jeans and a vest top with hair gelled back and dancing the full routine to the 'Macarena'. Personally, I reckon walking into a young boy's room and finding him ONLY doing the 'Macarena' is quite a result. However, these 'life stands still' moments will haunt both father and son for years to come.

But we've all been embarrassing kids:

'When I was twelve I used to take the net curtain from our kitchen and put it in my hair pretending to be a bride when the milk boy I fancied came round to collect the money. It makes me cringe to even think about it.' Siobhan.

'I used to flash my bare bum anytime I got the chance including my primary one nativity play. My mum was totally mortified but I still remember the feeling of sheer naughtiness.' Lucy.

'My mum borrowed our neighbour's brand new Hoover and nagged me to do chores. I was eight and sucked the water out of the loo because I thought it was dirty. The Hoover broke and I lied about what I had been up to.' Dougie, Edinburgh.

'My big daft brother painted his eyelids with nail varnish and had to go to hospital to get his eyelids released. He is still embarrassed about the incident.' Ali, Glasgow.

'My cousin Daneka went to meet her mum at the airport when she was five. Her mum was delighted to see her and asked her if anything had been happening. She shouted out enthusiastically 'YES I HAVE NITS!' We still laugh at the memory.'

'When I was at Strathblane Primary in the 1970s the guy in front of me was boasting about his new Rangers badge. As a Celtic fan I grabbed it off him and decided it needed a bit of green. I tried to stick it up my nose to cover it in snotters but it got stuck. The teacher and head-mistress tried to get it but they had to call my mum and I got taken to Yorkhill hospital to get it removed. She still ribs me about it all these years on.' Mark, Livingston.

'My daughter Caitlin Butcher drew a man with big hair and waving hands on my car bonnet with a stone. It cost £350 to repair nine years ago. She remembers it as clear as day.'

[My favourite tale, though, was from Davy from Kirkintilloch who called in with this:]

'When I was four I kept seeing the Hare Krishnas who kept shouting "Gouranga" in the street. I thought they were really cool so decided to hack my hair off. My mum went mental but my aunt has a brilliant picture of me with the Hare Krishna hair holding a real monkey down the Barras. Your embarrassing kids chat has brought the memories flooding back.'

On a sadder note today, Celtic and Scotland legend Tommy Burns has skin cancer. He is in hospital for an operation to remove a lymph node and I wish him well. Tommy can come across as being quite serious sometimes but he is one of the funniest men in football. I've shared many a wee swally with him after *Scotsport* Champions League games and he's had me in tears with his hilarious stories. And on this rare occasion, despite the 'head first into a taxi' story being a cracker, my lips are sealed . . . Get well soon, Tommy.

Friday the 31st

Ah, the day before April Fool's Day and we feel a bit cheated. It's generally great fun broadcasting on the first to see what we can get away with. A few years ago we convinced people The Proclaimers weren't related. We broke the news that the twins, Charlie and Craig Reid, had never met before their record company decided to manufacture a band with their look and sound. Charlie was supposedly a Hearts fan whose family disowned him when he was told to support Hibs for PR purposes. We had both the lads on the show apologising for hoodwinking fans for so long, and they played along brilliantly.

A survey has shown the *Panorama* TV spoof about spaghetti growing on trees is still regarded as the best April Fool's hoax ever. Burger King's 'left-handed whoppers', and Tesco's sale of 'whistling carrots' also made the top three. I also liked these ones:

'I'm a nurse and sent my trainee colleague to the gynaecology ward for a set of fallopian tubes and she went.' Claire.

'The *East Kilbride News* ran a story last year about the Whirlies roundabout changing its name to the Magic Roundabout with a statue of Dougal planned for the middle. My sister told everybody she knew and only found out the truth when she was telling a local taxi driver.' :)

'In 1983 I worked in Fine Fare in Anniesland; two of the young lads swapped the signs on the ladies' and gents' toilets and hid behind boxes to watch the carnage.' Elsie.

'I worked for an estate agent and we advertised the Scott Monument for sale, stating it could be broken down and shipped abroad. The Scottish public were fantastic and rose to the defence of it, saying we had no right to remove part of our history. We had several interested parties from abroad, but got so much stick we never did anything on April Fool's Day ever again.' Brian, Penicuik.

This morning we also catch up with Wendy and Alan, the parents of wee six-year-old Ivan from Rosyth who has a part of his brain missing. They're still in Florida where Ivan is receiving dolphin therapy treatment thanks to the £12,000 the good people of Scotland raised on our show in one morning, and his progress has been amazing.

Wendy tells us how he has been learning signs. She also says he cried for the first time in his life when leaving the dolphins and he has tried to say his first word. He has said 'Da-da' to his dad and the pair of them are ecstatic. She sobbed, 'I can't thank Real Radio enough, the therapy has been amazing. We couldn't imagine how much of a difference it has made in such a short time. The treatment seems to be unlocking my little boy's world.' It's really emotional radio and we are inundated with texts and calls from people crying on their way to work. Again, everything seems put into perspective. Natalie from Fife calls to say: 'I was having a really rubbish day on my way to work and I've just listened to Wendy and her story. I feel ashamed for moaning about nothing really. We should all be grateful for what we have. Thank you so much for keeping us up to date with the family. I'm sure the whole of Scotland wishes them well.'

I am becoming an emotional wreck and nip to the loo for another wee mini-sob. It really can be quite overwhelming at times.

Tonight I head to the *Sunday Mail* Young Scot awards in Glasgow where nominated youngsters are rewarded for their achievements in various activities like fundraising, community service, volunteering, sport and music. I am surrounded by teenagers who spend their spare time making a difference to others and it is really quite awe-inspiring.

My old pal Jack the First Minister is there (without the Speedos) along with the entire cast of *River City*, Elaine C. Smith, and Cameron and Federico from *Big Brother* (the latter really does seem rather fond of himself). Sitting on the next table down from me are the super-famous design gurus Justin and Colin. Now, I know I shall have to say hello because we've met several times before. However, I can't remember which one is which. I text my pals Nichola and Michelle with:

'HELP – showbiz dilemma about to unfold. Is Justin or Colin the dark-haired one?'

Michelle replies: 'Definitely Colin, he is lovely!'

Five minutes later Nichola replies: 'Justin, a hundred per cent certain.'

Turns out the wee jobbies are in cahoots, they are out together scudding back cocktails and no doubt creasing themselves at their contrived replies.

After a while, Justin (the blonde) comes over and says, 'Colin is at the bar . . .' Ah, sorted. They are amazing to watch working the room, getting photographed with every nominee, guest and waiter within a mile. They are quite simply FABULOUS in real life and I am pleased to report they called me 'DARLING' with dramatic gusto about twenty times in a five-minute chat. They're as camp as an Elton John PVC party, but a nice touch of welcome glamour to a pretty exhausting day.

I also log in my scientific journal: two glasses of pink champagne and a pint of free screw-top wine EQUALS seven hours' sleep . . .

april

Monday the 3rd

Shhhhh. Time for a secret. Today we launch the 'Secret Song', an infuriating competition where people try and name a song from a ridiculously short snippet of the intro. The prize starts at £5,000 and goes up and up until it is won. It is a simple competition with a lot at stake.

Debbie Wilkinson from Grangemouth is first on. Robin plays the clip, then plays the tension-building low-drone and gives her the big intro. 'So Debbie (PAUSE) what is (BIGGER THEATRICAL PAUSE – THIS LADDIE IS GOOD) the secret song?'

'Eh? I havenae got a clue!' she says indignantly. I am wetting myself. This is hardly the text book execution the big bosses who are all listening in are expecting, but infinitely funnier.

'Just give us a song title,' Robin pleads.

'Eh, I cannae think of one,' she replies. My cheeks are hurting. I am expecting her to say, 'Have I got the wrong number, is this not the doctor's surgery?' or something. Anyway, she finally settles with:

'What about the new one that is at number one, what is it called again?'

We help out with, '"Crazy" by Gnarls Barkley,' which is the wrong answer, but I suspect she is not too fussed anyway.

She was so wonderfully laid back she was horizontal. Hilarious.

So the secret song remains a secret, which gets us chatting about secrets we were told when we were wee (constant regressing, I think we ARE having mid-life issues). Robin's mum told him their house had barley water on tap but not to tell, she put the cordial in the cup without him knowing and filled up from the tap. He was about twelve when he discovered the truth. My charming brother Scott told me I was found in a Templeton's poly bag outside the front door. He also told me they wanted to hand me in but felt obliged to keep me. But we were all hoodwinked at times, it seems:

> 'My mum and dad told me they saved up tokens from the breakfast packets to send away for me.'
>
> 'My uncle told me chewing gum was made from rats' tails. I find myself telling my wee girl the same thing.' Martin, Clydebank.
>
> 'I was told the tooth fairy needed teeth to make furniture. I used to be terrified in case she burst her couch and I would wake up all gumsy.' Elaine, Glasgow.
>
> 'My grandpa told me if I put my finger in my belly button and turned, my bum would fall off. I believed him for years.' Ross McLeod, Fife.
>
> 'My partner told her daughter, when the ice-cream van plays music that means there is nothing left.' Ian.
>
> 'My parents told me the crosses on the roadworks where they're levelling the ground were the burial sites of dead workmen. I believed them for years.' Christine, Glenrothes.

I bump into former Rangers and England star Trevor Steven in town this afternoon and have a great wee catch up. I've not seen him since the great 'STV CIS CUP CRISIS NIGHT' at Aberdeen in the year 2000. The game was Aberdeen v. Rangers in the CIS Cup semi-final and it was a night the word STRESS was invented for.

Minutes into the game our satellite feed packed in and the powers that be hadn't ordered a back-up because it was deemed too costly. Thankfully Setanta Sports (who nobody had heard of at the time) were broadcasting the game from a wee van back to a few pubs in Ireland. We piggy-backed their feed and the game was shown to the nation.

I was working trackside at the match, Trevor was in the studio as our guest, with Jim Delahunt presenting. This was an evening where the frailties of working within the ITV network came to the fore. Quite simply we were told the game was 'NOT ALLOWED' to go to penalties. *Coronation Street* had to start at 10.00 p.m. no questions asked. Now as is so often the case, the 1000:1 scenario began to unfold. Both halves ran over, the teams were late out at half time and it was 0–0 with two minutes of extra time remaining. Since the whistle at 90 minutes, the gallery had been scrapping with STV presentation in Glasgow and ultimately ITV in London.

'You have until 10.00 p.m. and *Coronation Street* goes out. That is it.'

We knew, doing the sums, that if the game went to penalties we would be cut off and the production team on site were quite rightly going mental. Can you imagine watching 120 minutes' worth of a cup semi-final between Aberdeen and Rangers only for Mike Baldwin to pop up when the final penalty-kick is about to be taken? Total career suicide and we all knew it.

Archie MacPherson was doing well to keep calm commentating, while pressing the talk-back button and threatening to resign at every moment there was a gap in play. Jim Delahunt was unpinning his mike and preparing to head for the door as well if the game was to end after ET and we were not allowed to show the penalties.

Well, in a quirky twist of fate, Andy Dow scored for the Dons with about twenty seconds to go, the final whistle blew,

Jim managed to say, 'So Aberdeen go through 1–0, good night,' and that was that. A collective sigh of relief, but we all knew we had only just got away with it.

Looking back, part of me wishes the shit had hit the arm-chair fan, and the penny-pinchers and schedulers got their just desserts. However, we all ended up in some vomit-splattered nightclub near the beach power-drinking to calm the frazzled nerves. I remember Trevor ordering tomato soup from the night porter at about four in the morning in the foyer of the hotel and being served a bowl of heated up ragu sauce.

As I've mentioned before, TV is not as glamorous as it is cracked up to be. He didn't even get a roll and butter for goodness' sake . . .

Tuesday the 4th

An interesting moral dilemma has arisen this morning. A posh letter had arrived at Real Radio and I've been invited to present prizes at the Duke of Edinburgh award scheme's fiftieth anniversary at Holyrood Palace. The invite is on royal embossed paper and says I shall be presented personally to the Duke of Edinburgh on the day.

The award scheme is a fantastic programme getting kids out and about helping in the community, but also learning new skills and keeping fit through a variety of options. I completed my bronze and silver awards at Girls' Brigade, and completed about seventy per cent of my gold before discovering booze, bands and boys.

Now, here is the problem. The awards are great, but I think he is a complete fanny. (Please accept my apologies for the extreme choice of word but I've pondered long and hard about it, even consulting the tattered thesaurus I've not used since university, and couldn't find a more suitable one.) I know, I know, throw me in the tower and take my bronze and silver awards off me for being disrespectful, but I do. It's not just his numerous indiscretions and his lack of sympathy for foreign cultures, he just annoys me. He appears so cold and calculating and personally speaking, having a conspiracy theorist father, I obviously have doubts in my mind about greater issues. My probable opening gambit of, 'Nice to meet you Your Highness, did you kill Diana?' I'm guessing is not the right tone for the celebratory nature of the event.

That aside, the kids do so well to get the awards, as a holder, it is flattering to be asked. I am allowed to take a guest and there is only one person I can think of, Mrs Anne Goodlet, my old Girls' Brigade leader. I've not seen her for over fifteen years, but she was an absolute superstar to a whole group of my pals, trekking weekend upon weekend away from her family to put us through our paces, always with a smile on her face, and always with a kind word. Despite rain lashing down in horrendous mountain-top conditions, she would still find time to pop behind a tree to apply her lippy, much to our amusement. And on the day four of my pals and I almost met our end, she was an emotional wreck.

We were fourteen or fifteen and on Arran walking for our gold expedition. We had camped overnight in the back of beyond after day one, when we set off into the hills. Mrs Goodlet had two groups of girls on Arran to supervise (you had to walk alone on the gold) and was petrified when the fog descended, making conditions treacherous. She had been catching up with the other bunch and realised we were expected to be heading over the trickiest sections of the entire route at the height of the bad weather.

We couldn't see two feet in front of us so my pals Rhona, Lynn, Denise, Debbie and I weighed up the pros of continuing – our gold award, a year's worth of training completed – and then considered the cons – likely death. So we came off the hill, followed our maps to a farm track and then ambled down the main road towards civilisation munching Mars bars and generally lamenting the end of our Duke of Edinburgh awards achievements. About an hour later her little clapped-out cream Lada put-putted into view and she ran out in tears of relief that 'HER GIRLS' had shown such superb leadership skills.

Only when we returned did we realise the extent of her anguish. The freezing fog had completely covered the glen we were meant to be out on and mountain rescue teams had been scrambled and were currently out searching for Army cadets who hadn't been so wise. So for Mrs Goodlet, her lipstick and her admirable attempts to keep my motley crew on the straight and narrow, I think I shall accept. Hey, if nothing else we get a free dinner and a photo for the book . . .

Wednesday the 5th

According to a new survey out today women nag men more about their failure to listen than any other subject. Second on the ear-bashing list is not completing household tasks and watching too much sport on the telly.

Robin reckons Mrs G complains too much about his ever-increasing love affair with his lap-top and I reckon she has a point. He takes it everywhere with him including meetings and seminars, checks e-mails every ten minutes, and even takes it to the loo in Real Radio to surf Google earth whilst squeezing out a big one. What happened to the papers or the *Oor Wullie* book?

Funnily enough we are swamped with texts with men claiming women have a built-in nagging gene, while our lovely lasses reckon men are the grumpy ones

'She keeps nagging me to do DIY and I keep telling her I am not a plumber, joiner or painter. She usually replies, 'Aye, an am no a chef so get yir ain bloody dinner.' Alex the trucker.

'Men are the nags, my husband Mal is always on at me because I spend money on clothes and you can get shoes in Asda for a fiver.' Elle.

'I used to nag my ex about putting the loo seat down, but he reckons because I don't put it UP for him he shouldn't have to put it DOWN for me. My son is now trained to put it down so any future wife should thank me!' Liz.

'My missus isny happy unless she is nagging or spending money; when she starts I just go to give her a big sloppy kiss and that soon shuts her up.' John.

'My wife nags me for spending £15 a week on cans of lager when she spends £30 on make-up. She says it is to make her look good, I told her that's what the cans were for too.' Cammy, Easterhouse,

'There is only one thing worse than a nagging wife and that is a nagging ex-wife.' Alex, Glenrothes.

In the mornings we have Press Association access to a variety of international stories as well, and I laugh out loud at this absolute cracker from Austria. The article reads:

Burglars served free beers to a drunk until he passed out after he walked into a pub while they were robbing the safe. They were clearing out a pub in Amstetten, Austria, during the night when drunk Hermann Bendt, 47, stumbled in, sat at the bar and ordered a beer. The duo served him three pints 'on the house' and chatted to him before Bendt fell asleep across the bar. The burglars then emptied the safe and took all the valuables, including expensive stereo equipment, from the pub. The sleeping guest was later woken up by police. He could only describe the men as 'one big bloke and one smaller one'.

Well, he was only following the last orders of the law.

On a sporting front it's quite amusing today as Rangers fans everywhere are hoping Celtic beat Hearts tonight to win the SPL title. It's not often you hear Gers fans mutter, 'I want

Celtic to win tonight,' but with a European place at stake it's vital for the Ibrox side that Hearts don't get any points.

I text myself a message to remind me to turn my phone off this evening, nothing worse than phone calls from half-cut celebrating pals when you get up at half-three. As a passionate Partick Thistle fan, I'm just jealous I don't get to make those calls too often – not that I'm nagging the players or anything . . .

Thursday the 6th

Grim news this morning: bird flu has been confirmed in Fife – it seems Frank McAvennie's clubbing nights in Dunfermline are cancelled for the time being. Seriously, though, this is scary and the coastal village of Cellardyke has been cordoned off while scientists wait for results on the strain of the virus. Satellite trucks from broadcasters from all over the UK are heading there and the news could have horrendous ramifications for everyone. Robin highlights the severity of the situation by playing a cuckoo with a cough sound throughout the show. Ah, humour in our darkest hours.

In other news, Gordon Strachan may have wee legs, but he's got the biggest smile in Scotland. Celtic beat Hearts 1–0 to become the new SPL champions, sitting twenty points clear with loads of games left to play. When asked if it was a dream come true to win the title he replied: 'It is just a dream come true to stay in a job!'

There is a story this morning about football mad Eddie Duk, who made a 12,000 mile trip from Tokyo to see his beloved Inverness Cally Thistle play Aberdeen. The adventure cost £7,500 for the weekend and his side lost 1–0. 'I enjoyed a cheap pint, though,' he said reflectively.

I went to Metz in France once to watch Partick Thistle's wacky Intertoto Cup experience in a bus that broke down as often as it stopped in lay-bys to let the boys do their thing. Yuck. (I did find my self staring every time, though.) Golden

Shy and retiring even as a four-year-old

Posing with my now infamous pink pussy

Even as a three-year-old ice cream was a big part of my life

There's no business like show business. Debbie, me, Denise, Jane and Claire put on a show

The adventurers. Rhona, Mrs Goodlet, Lynn, Denise, me and Debbie
prepared for the great outdoors

Rhona and I not taking our Graduation seriously enough with our Thistle colours

Turns out my mum is off her heid too.
Christmas in the Harvey House

My wee pal Starsky meets the demure
Bobby Harvey

The night that started it all . . . who is that with Robin and Cat?

THAT car

Louise, Carol and Scott from Arnold Clark
are given the message

Hong Kong Denny and the magic tree

The Real Robin and Cat

Spot the dragon?

Robin and I take our jobs very seriously

Fun in the sun in Torremolinos

Ewen and Roughy wear Alan Rough t-shirts in case he forgets he's a Scotland legend

The Real car wash

Robin and Baz explore their feminine sides

The Breakfast team support Trinidad and Tobago in the World Cup

Princess the Pony visits Real Radio

Mrs Goodlet – my Girls' Brigade leader and a legend

Officially the back end of a bus

The troops – back row from left to right: mini-me, Janis, sleepy Lynn, Michelle.
Front row from left to right: Dolina, Alyson, me, Kaza, Nichola

Loose Women – Kaye Adams, Shareeen Nanjiani and I cheering on the boys at France 98

Celebrating 'New Year' with Franz Ferdinand

Sweet talking the Sugababes

Lee Ryan from Blue, not a minger after all!

Is this the way to Big in Falkirk? Janis and I meet Tony Christie

Sandi Thom, number one in the charts and wondering who the strange lassie next to her is

Can Orsen tell I've been at the free bar?

If I was . . . next to Midge Ure, I'd copy his rock star sun glasses on the head routine

Shayne Ward – he clearly wants me

Champions League Extra with Mark Hateley

The *Offside* team

Two Amorusos, there's only two Amorusos

Small and fiery – and so is Gordon Strachan

Horny – having fun with the management!
Bossman Billy and Sales Guru Gavin Bruce lead me astray in Norway

Mark Roberts, manager Dick Campbell and Derek Young, help Alyson and I raise funds for NCH

Tinkercat

Mrs Slocombe slips into the Peter Pan line-up

Happy in the best job in the world

Baz once went to Skye for a fish supper, and it seems we're a determined lot who stop at nothing in pursuit of our dreams.

James Robertson is first on the phone with this cracker: 'My mate and I drove to Blackpool for a phone call! My step-mother Christine kept slagging off my clapped-out car so we drove to Blackpool and phoned her in Stepps just to prove it could make it. We made it home too.'

Texts include:

'I went to New York for a special edition Gucci bag and shoes I couldn't get in Scotland. I was there for a day and flew home. It was a VERY expensive venture.' Ellie.

'I came home from work one night and decided to drive to Inveraray for chips, when I got there the chippy had closed for refurbishment.' Elaine, Glasgow.

'We went to Spain to watch Rangers – in the pub!' D.J., Kilmaurs.

'I was living in southern Ireland and came home for a roll and square sausage.' Wendy.

'I went to the Ukraine for women.' Anon

'I went from Stenhousemuir to Guardbridge for a venison steak.' Jimmy.

'I went to Sydney in Australia for the day. My pal works for Virgin Atlantic and I went with her. The trip was two nights in Hong Kong, one in Sydney and two in Hong Kong again. It cost me £100 and I had a ball.' Donna, Glasgow.

[And finally:]

'I took a girl to Wales once, to Bangor.' Jim, Craigend.

As Gordon Strachan, with a team full of ageing players, might concur, sometimes the old ones are the best . . .

Friday the 7th

Bird flu is dominating the headlines. The sleepy wee fishing village of Cellardyke has become media central after the deadly H5N1 strain of the virus was found in the dead swan in the harbour and restrictions are now in place. Reports today suggest T in the Park may be in jeopardy as the site at Balado is next to a massive poultry farm. Experts reckon there is only a minimal risk to people, but it's quite a development and more than a little bit scary.

My mum has a rare autoimmune disease called polymyositis which is a muscle-wasting disorder that also leaves her vulnerable to any bugs at all. I have to admit any health scare terrifies me because of what it could do to her. Even flu or a bad cold could be life threatening. I don't even visit if I have an upset tummy. There are only a handful of people in the UK with the disorder, which attacks the immune system as well. She is now in her seventies and after today's news I have decided to ban her from T in the Park just in case. Shame really, I'm sure she would LOVE the dance tent.

It's the Grand National tomorrow and we take a quick look through the field in one of the newspapers' cut-out sweepstakes. There's a horse called The Real Bandit, which should be backed by everyone who works at the station. Risk Assessor should be the horse for Bossman Billy as he battles to balance the books, Baron Windrush is the one for Robin the vegetarian, while Baz reckons Just in Debt is the perfect cuddy for him and then rants for forty minutes about the 'evil bastards' from the student loans company. I'm happy with any horse in red and yellow colours but decide if I was to own one I could call it Sitting Second for no other reason than to cause commentary chaos: 'Sitting Second at the rear, and Sitting Second is now sitting fourth and Sitting Second has finished first.'

The names our listeners would pick come in thick and fast:

- Last Slice – he's a big outsider
- Robin's Dobbin
- Askit – 'What's yir horse called pal?' 'Askit'
- McDonald's – that's where it would end up if it lost
- Fell at the First – then any offspring would be Fell at the Second etc.
- Sofa King Good – because he would be unbeatable
- Hfir – as in H fir horse
- Dusty Carpet – he'd never get beaten
- Horsed again – as it probably would be
- Diarrhoea – it is still running.

And just imagine a race with the following participants: Cupid Stunt, Norfolk Enchants, Mary Hinge, Mabozza Ritchie, Bun ya Rastard and not forgetting the inseparable pair of stable mates Hoof Hearted and Ice Melted. Finally, Colin called with this tale:

'Just a wee story about the National, remember when it was cancelled a few years back because of a bomb scare, well a guy in our footy team had a few bets on and asked who had won. My mate replied it was a bomb scare and he said, oh right but who was second. He never lived it down.'

I'm off island hopping next week, but not to Greece, the Caribbean or the Balearics – nope, I'm heading up the west coast to Oban, Mull and Skye for some healthy outdoor adventures. However, the weather forecast, so Robin (who is heading for the sunshine) tells me gleefully, is for gales, rain, sleet and snow showers. I suspect I may return two stone heavier and an expert in malt whisky. I shall return to fat class soon. I promise.

Tuesday the 18th

Easter break over and back to work, bruised, saturated and at least half a stone heavier. Hill-walking holidays are evil. Well, ones to Oban, Mull and Skye where fried B & B breakfasts are the only way to start the day are.

Mr Cat and I had a pretty good time away considering it poured for four days, but in a bid to get slim and fit I even climbed the Old Man of Storr in Skye in the wettest day I have ever endured. Apart from two bizarre evenings I was relatively well behaved all week.

The first evening was a night out in the pubs of Oban; I attract loonies like you wouldn't believe. I'd just grabbed a seat in the Oban Inn when Hans, a sixty-year-old Swede started chatting to me with his bearded friend smiling away in the corner. Hans, it turns out, was on a whisky trail of Scotland for his birthday. I suspect Hans and his pal had managed to complete a few laps of the trail by the time we met them. He tells me, with a glint in his eye, he is a highly respected photographer. I tell him that the west coast can be lovely at this time of year.

'I'm not that kind of photographer, I prefer other lovely things.' He smiled knowingly. Yes, folks, in a bar with fifteen people in it I plonk myself down next to a professional PORN snapper who was clearly looking for a new Rubenesque model. Time for a polite but sharp exit.

On Sunday night I ended up having another bizarre night out with my crazy pal Kaza who knows more famous people than Elton John. She's been pals with Tony the keyboard player from The Charlatans for years and when the band comes to town they hook up for a drink. I've met the guys a few times before and they've always been great crack. Well, a crowd of the girls are out in the West End when he texts saying they are having drinks in the Radisson Hotel after a gig and that we should pop in.

APRIL

Cue Rock and Roll mayhem. Alyson, who is a massive fan, was all excited to be chatting to the band while Jon the drummer insisted I engaged in a game of 'COCK' with him. Now bear with me please, for this is not half as bad as it sounds. It involves shouting the word 'COCK' louder than the person before you. In my day it was called 'JOBBY' while Dick and Dom, on Kid's TV, resurrected it as 'BOGIE'. Anyway, according to Jon, the acoustics in the hotel foyer were perfect for a game, and despite it being half one in the morning I found myself shouting 'COCK' at the top of my voice much to the amusement of one the UK's most successful rock bands, as the poor bar staff looked on helplessly.

I would like to apologise for any offence I may have caused. I am not proud of my vodka-influenced behaviour and am gutted to admit I lost the game after laughing so much I had to run to the loo before a wee streamie accident occurred. So no telly-smashing, drugs or orgies with groupies to report, just a right funny night and a happy wee trip to the chips and cheese shop on the way home for the girls.

Anyway, back to work then. I actually quite like coming back to catch up on the gossip and to feel part of something again. I shall never tell him, but I actually quite miss Robin when we are apart. Not in a dodgy way or anything, we just spend so much time together it is weird being apart. Still, the Dubai–Oban text service worked just fine.

It appears that in our absence our A-list celebrities are continuing to amaze with their opulent stupidity. Today we learn that David Beckham paid for chefs from London to fly to Madrid to cook Posh Spice her thirty-second birthday dinner. Waste of money really, given that she eats about three raisins a week. He also bought thirty-two white roses and, wait for it, an £8 million Bulgari necklace. EIGHT MILLION POUNDS? I would expect a small country, with a Wonka-sized chocolate factory, for that. I hope it turns her neck green.

Money doesn't buy you happiness, and this lot were more than happy with their celebratory treats:

'I spent my thirty-fifth with rolls and spam and a flask of Heinz tomato soup with my missus on the banks of Loch Lomond. Who needs fancy chefs when you can enjoy a moment like that?' Jamie, Greenock.

'I spent my big five-oh in an Indian river washing an elephant!' Gerry, Allanton.

'I got a helicopter ride over Stirling one year, the following year I swam with sharks at Deep Sea World and this year the family are sending me up in a microlight. I'm not sure they like me!' Andrew, Larkhall.

'My wife treated me to a trip to New York and Vegas. Beat that Becks.' Doug.

[Finally Jim added:]

'Japanese chefs and an £8 million pound necklace, what rubbish. I got my wife a Chinese take-away and then gave her a pearl necklace and she was more than pleased!'

Quite.

Next time, Becks should treat his missus to a hill-walking trip up the West Highlands – at least the sausage, eggs and black pudding would put some meat on her scrawny bones, and who knows, the increasingly vain couple might run into Hans for that ultimate family snap . . .

Wednesday the 19th

I had another ridiculously clear dream last night and woke up this morning wondering if it had happened or not. I was at the Cowal games in Dunoon sitting on the grass with Nichola, Nicola Sturgeon SNP MSP (who I have never met) and Alex Kapranos from Franz Ferdinand. We were drinking wine and laughing. Alex had been snogging me (which was quite nice, as I recall) when Jack McConnell started ranting at the ice-cream van. He was trying to buy us all a tub of raspberry ripple ice cream and his Switch card had been declined. He was shouting, 'Do you not know who I am?' as the ice cream started melting, and then I woke up.

Robin takes great delight in making me recount this weird scenario and asks for dream interpretation from the listeners. Views ranged from, 'She eats too much cheese' and, 'Stay away from drugs,' to, 'She wants her hole from that rock bloke'. I feel slightly embarrassed that my inner thoughts are being dissected. However, I'm slightly reassured that at least I wasn't kissing Nicola Sturgeon and that MY Switch card is still in operation.

I am struggling to get back into work mode this week given that I am only back for three days before jetting off to Spain with the rest of the radio station. After a week in the solitude of the Scottish hills I am right in the mood for a good shindig.

The Queen is eighty this week and the *Daily Record* have an interesting feature today about memorabilia that could be worth thousands or could be complete tat. I have a Glasgow Garden Festival mug which could be worth, oh, at least a fiver in about 2,000 years' time. The *Antiques Roadshow* should head to the central belt to analyse these classics:

'I've got the tambourine Freddie Mercury chucked into the crowd at the Apollo.' Graham, Law village.

'I have a bottle of limited edition Coca-Cola from the 1978 World Cup unopened.' Peter, Airdrie.

'I have a 1978 World Cup mug with Roughie's face on it. Any offers?' Edinburgh.

'I have an original Babycham glass with the little deer on it; surely it must be worth a fortune.' Katrina, Stirling.

'I have a Charles and Diana wedding day coin that I found on my way to primary school years ago. I'd love to know if it was worth anything because if it is I'd punt it. It's rubbish and I'm skint.' Kelly, Wishaw.

I wonder if they will sell commemorative mugs and tea towels in Dunoon when the bloke from Franz Ferdinand and I eventually cop off together . . .

Thursday the 20th

The latest survey commissioned by HP sauce (no, I never knew they were great survey commissioners either!) says that the demise of the traditional café is imminent. Local establishments, with chipped Formica tables and rotund sixty-year-old waitresses with smiles, banter and fag-stained fingers are, it seems, a dying breed (clogged arteries possibly).

Continental coffee shops and trendy bistros are now the norm, with all hot beverages apparently having to end in 'iccino' before we part with our cash to sup. This is devastating news and I for one shall be signing the petition to 'SAVE OUR CAFÉS'.

Jaconelli's in Maryhill is a treasure. I don't think it has changed décor, staff or stock since 1960. It has a proper juke box, great ice cream and booths where people have to share and chat to each other as they eat their chosen delicacies.

Robin points out that the one thing that reminds him most of traditional cafés is the waitresses delivering endless rounds of white buttered bread. For me it has to be mugs of tea (spoon still in) or extra-pink milkshakes in slightly scratched ice-cream glasses.

We are rightfully fond of our cafés and fond of the following:

'There has to be a wee man doing a crossword in the corner.' Margaret.

'There must be a tomato sauce bottle shaped like a tomato and clogged up with crusty bits at the hole.' Kay.

'Ice cream drinks that foam when a blob is plonked in fizzy juice is a café delight.' Gav, Glasgow.

APRIL

'A coffee machine that goes SCCCCHHHHHHHHHH.'
Alan, Airdrie.

'A real café has scones not muffins!' Tommy, Greenock.

'In a proper café the plates are so big you have to turn
them around to get to bits of your dinner.' Billy.

'There is always a table for staff in the corner with
their papers, fags and coffee, and one will always get up
slowly when they have to serve.' Jackie.

I have to admit I would much rather have a cold juice
and a roll and sausage from a wee café than a frappacino
and char-grilled brie brioche which is basically just a rip-off
cheese toastie. That said, not all of Scotland's cafés get full
marks for friendly service and electric banter. Nichola and I
were in one in Dunoon a few years ago after we'd returned
from a holiday in Florida (fear not, no politicians or rock stars
this time).

The waiters in the States were so in your face with faux
friendliness we actually had to ask one guy, who had plonked
himself down next to us in a booth, to GO AWAY. The fact
that he'd got to the point in his story explaining why he was
a waiter and not at college that involved the line, 'I didn't
mean to shoot him but I ended up in the detention centre for
three years . . .' didn't help either.

Anyway, back to Dunoon where our surly teen waitress
was moping behind the glass cake stand studying her finger-
nails and wishing she was talking about boys with her pals
instead of picking up her £3 an hour in the service industry.
Nic pointed at the solitary fruit scone in the cabinet and the
following dazzling dialogue unfolded.

Nic: 'Can I have a scone please?'
Teen grump: 'Wha-aat?'
Nic: 'Can I have a scone please?'
Teen grump: 'It's the last one.'
Nic: 'OK, can I have it please?'

157

Teen grump: 'But then I'll have none left.'

I'll save you the next five minutes' worth of chat, but Nic eventually got her scone and the stroppy one huffed and puffed until we left. I'm sure it was just a phase.

All this talk of cafés, scones and roll and sausages has made me very hungry and I'm shamed to admit it is 10:58 a.m. and I've already eaten an entire Smarties Easter egg, a plate of Special K (to drop a dress size), a roll and square sausage and half the chicken sandwich I brought for lunch. I haven't so much fallen off my Scottish Slimmers' diet, I have plummeted from a great height. Any dieters will know that one small lapse can often lead to a complete binge. Personally I think I have an intestinal worm, and at the moment my worm is a greedy wee shit making my life a misery.

Still, the Real Radio trip to Spain beckons and a weekend of oh so healthy living . . .

Friday the 21st

Yee-hah! It is party time, folks. Thirty-seven employees from Real Radio are heading to Torremolinos for some team bonding and cultural enlightenment. Check-in is at four in the morning. Ha – welcome to my world everybody.

In typical *Football Phone In* style Ewen, Roughie and their producer Victoria have not been to bed since a wee night out after their show and arrive at the airport in tremendous form. All of them are wearing T-shirts with Roughie's face emblazoned on them, with 'SCOTLAND LEGEND – ALAN ROUGH' written below. If nothing else, it could prove useful for the Scotland keeper when he tries to remember who he is later on!

I'm standing in the queue to check in when a girl I've never met before runs over enthusiastically shouting: 'Cat, what about you snogging the guy from Franz Ferdinand!' Red-faced note to self: quirky pop stars are fine, but never admit to kissing a minger in a dream on air . . .

After a relatively pain-free flight (I only cried at take-off, not landing) we arrived to glorious sunshine. Within an hour we had checked in to our lovely hotel and were pool side to enjoy an afternoon of sun, sangria and sizzling banter.

Most of the girls at Real Radio are blessed with stunning bodies and lay out in bikinis chatting for most of the afternoon. Wearing swimwear in front of colleagues is right up there with pulling John Prescott in my list of things to do. So my three-quarter length trousers (black), vest top (black) and over shirt (black) made me look like a shapeless goth at the pool. Still, my face was bright red, so the feng shui man would be happy with the mix of colours. Anyway, Shareen, Hayley and I got into the sangria and my horrific body image problems slowly but surely disappeared. In fact by midnight I was Elle Macpherson, albeit only in my own head.

The evening's activity was a five-hour meal at La Mancha tapas bar, with Maggi, our esteemed trip organiser, making sure all the (slightly tipsy) bigwigs made it. This, it turns out, was because John Myers, the biggest chief from down south made a 'surprise' appearance with his wife. It must have been like walking into a zoo. It was total carnage, with most people now at least eight hours into the unscripted alcoholic endurance test. In fairness, they seemed to have quite a laugh at us all, and sat in astonishment as the Real sing-a-thon started.

Bossman Billy was called upon first, so he rose to his feet (quite steadily which was impressive) and belted out 'Living on a Prayer', his party piece. Bossman Jay was next up with a slightly ropey rendition of 'Brown Sugar', his speciality, while Steve McKenna belted out 'I Owe You Nothing' by Bros. Sensational. Somewhat predictably all eyes turned to me, as calls for 'Sweet Child of Mine' rang out. I am useless at this without a piano or karaoke backing so took the bold decision to alter my repertoire.

I asked for everybody to stand up and broke into one of the best versions of 'Heads and Shoulders, Knees and Toes' the world has ever seen/heard. Twice through, and then a final time but at twice the speed, everybody joined in, and it was absolutely hilarious. John Myers gave me that look which I interpreted as, 'You are clearly a nutcase, but that was actually quite funny.' I'm so glad I was in good form, the first time I ever met him I threw a chicken wing at the back of his head and called Simo, our other big programming boss, a 'cock'. I blame wine. In fairness to Simo he always greets me with the welcoming line, 'Alright Cat, it's not the same when you are not swearing and talking dirty at me!' Forgiven, but definitely on probation I think . . .

Next up, we found a karaoke bar and took it over. Robin became crooner of the evening with some pretty good, if truth be told, Frank Sinatra renditions. I murdered Dolly Parton's 'Nine to Five' with Lyndsey from sales, and a jolly good time was had by all.

Shareen, Hayley and I, the sangria trio from earlier, tried to continue the musical theme of the evening when we found a baby grand piano in the lobby of our hotel; however, it seems the security guard does not appreciate the finer intricacies of classic Guns N' Roses at 5.00 a.m. Either that or he wasn't best pleased with Hayley's magnificent Michelle Pfeifferesque sprawl over the piano lid. Suitably chastised, it was off to bed to prepare for round two . . .

Saturday the 22nd

Oh my! Wake up feeling horrific as the sun shines through the window. Ewen and Roughie both appear in our room at 10.00 a.m. to chat to Victoria, the *Football Phone In* producer and my party girl room-mate on trips away, about their afternoon show. I am under the covers wearing a skanky T-shirt and baggy pants, desperate for the loo but unable to get up to go until they leave. I finally surface at two, unable to eat solids or sit in direct sunlight, Betty Ford ahoy!

The *Football Phone In* and *Breakfast Show* crews decide to track down the Hibs v. Hearts game on the telly and set off on a splendid adventure. After walking for about three miles and visiting every Irish/British pub *en route*, Roughie decides enough is enough, it is time for food and a small refreshment. We plonk ourselves down in a beach-front café and stay for five hours. The banter is hilarious and we hear several un-printable tales about how players wind each other up. There are some crackers, and I shall never look at Derek Whyte in the same light again!

Eventually the time comes for Ewen, Roughie and Victoria to head back to do their show. Robin, Golden Baz and I decide to remain for 'one for the road.' Well, that road turned out to be the M8 and we get back when it is dark. Our evening ends up in Benalmadena, the next resort up where we take over a bar and the shameful scenes unfold.

The wee Chinese man selling cheap toys and an assort-ment of ridiculous lighty-up things must have thought it was Christmas. We had light sabres, flashing tiaras and wands and Robin could not be parted from his duck glove puppet with extending tongue which he soon sussed could put out candles and splash pints of lager.

For some unknown reason Ewen and I decide to start pole dancing around one of those patio heater things. In my head I am Demi Moore in *Striptease*; I have now seen the video and I am more Patrick Moore in need of medical assistance. Ewen gets totally carried away with the music and lovingly caresses the pole so much both he and it end up on the floor. A nice move, if only really appreciated by the Real Radio crew.

So, taxi home at half-four to give myself a whopping three hours' sleep before check-out. This team-bonding lark is hard work . . .

Sunday the 23rd

The itinerary states CHECK OUT – 9.00 a.m. I have never seen such a sight in my life. Thirty-seven battle weary bodies ranging from the pale-faced and bleary-eyed to the still completely steaming. I have never worked anywhere before in my life that 'having a good time' is part of the contract.

Just as the bus arrives I remember I don't have a presenters' photo for my *Sunday Mail* travel feature. I assemble the troops and the snap is taken, although it is not until it is published a week from now, that I comprehend quite how rough everybody looks. The flight passes without incident, which is good given our past experiences, namely the flight home from Benidorm when Roughie suffered extreme 'wind' issues.

We had a hilarious call into the show, after our return last year, from a Paisley taxi driver. He phoned to say he took two girls home who had been on our flight and all they could talk about was how the whole plane 'reeked of Roughie's farts'. At least we leave an impression . . .

Mr Cat picks me up at the airport and I can tell from his face I look like the stinky wee bedraggled midden I feel. I am trying to put to the back of my throbbing head the fact that tonight it is the Scottish football writers' Player of the Year dinner. My body is screaming STOP, NO MORE! I vow to have a quiet evening with mineral water and be home for ten. I have work tomorrow and I am a professional.

Monday the 24th

One hour and twenty-five minutes' sleep. I am way too old for this!

My inability to leave a good bash early is well known and last night's football writers' dinner proved to be a hoot with hundreds of famous faces from Scottish football past and present gathering in the Thistle Hotel for an end of season rammy.

I was invited to my pal Michelle's table along with Craig Hinchcliffe, Chris Smith, Ian Maxwell, John Potter and Simon Lappin from St Mirren, Jim Mercer from Stenny and my mates Janis, Alyson and Graeme Brown who is now at Alloa. Broony, a footballing lawyer would-be rock star, and I actually met at the SPFA dinner five years ago when he played for Cowdenbeath and have been best mates ever since. Anyway, we had a ball and the chat was hilarious. I thought I would just have a quiet one, but with this bunch of maniacs it was never going to happen.

Gordon Strachan won Manager of the Year and paid tribute to 'big spotty pasty face' – his pet name for Alex McLeish. Craig Gordon won the Player of the Year award and gave an impressive speech. However, as is often the case, the best fun comes at the bar once the official business is over.

As I don't report on football every week now, I don't get to see all the faces I used to see on a weekly basis, so it was great to catch up with guys like Jim Duffy, Mark Hately, Alan McGraw, Billy McNeill and Billy Dodds. I presented *Champions League Extra* on STV with Mark for two seasons, he's a funny guy and we've had some cracking nights out. The one I always recall is the great headstand stand-off. There were a crowd of us in the residents' bar of the Thistle after a big live match, we somehow got on to party pieces and I admitted (apart from kicking my height) that I could headstand anywhere without a wall for any length of time. 'So what, I can do that too,' challenged the Monaco, Rangers and England legend. I'm not sure who suggested it, although I suspect it may have been pesky wee Stuart McCall, but we had a competition on the tile floor of the bar at 2.00 a.m.

The bar was full of about 200 people from the trade union conference who clapped and cheered as we stood on our heads for what seemed like hours. I could see him from my upside down position, and he could see me and neither of us wanted to lose. Despite the fact I should've had a better centre of gravity being a short-arse, I eventually lost concentration due to my 'is my top covering my lumpy tummy' anxieties and made a fatal wobble. I toppled. He got the big cheer and the headstand title, and I got a headache for my efforts. Still, I beat him at badminton once after another stupid bet – so one each on the old athletic front me thinks.

However, getting back to the dinner, my dream team of maniacs remain the 'singing posse' who bonded at John Lambie's testimonial dinner a few years ago. Gerry McCabe, Dick Campbell, Jimmy Bone, Jimmy Calderwood and Jimmy Nichol were the main party animals on that night and were all in splendid form last night too. Dick Campbell and I enjoyed a short blast of 'King of the Road' while Gerry McCabe, who knows I like a wee impromptu singsong, made me an offer I might not be able to refuse: 'Come and join our Monday club, we meet in Carrigans in Hamilton every Monday afternoon from two until six and everybody has to sing. My mum who is in her eighties gets up and sings too, you will have a ball.'

Sounds like a hoot.

My other great offer came from the Two Jimmies (Calderwood and Nicol), now the management team of Aberdeen. They are a pair of nutters on a night out in the best possible way. They were delighted to see my buddy Jane Lewis and me, and lamented the fact we never go to visit them any more (Aberdeen being way too far out of our transmission area). Jimmy Nic clearly thought he was in for another cracking sing-along, and was gutted when I told him I was working and we both had to leave soon. It was quite nice to be missed, actually, and I had a wee warm glow at how many friends I've made in football.

I mentioned to him I'd just returned from Spain with work, and he said they were going there in a fortnight. Jimmy Calderwood then came up with the booze-inspired bright idea that Jane and I should go with them and, I hasten to add, the entire Aberdeen backroom staff for the trip. This grew arms and legs, and within twenty minutes we were actually agreeing to a boozy adventure with the Dons.

I must stress to any of the morality police getting uneasy, that there was NOTHING dodgy at all in the invite it was just 2.00 a.m. long-lost camaraderie madness. They are a pair of crackers and I miss their chat.

Anyway, today's show is all about the juicy bits from our trip to Torremolinos. We agree to answer any questions from listeners with the truth, the whole truth and nothing but the truth. The internal studio line flashes instantly and we answer off air to hear Bossman Billy say the immortal line: 'The absolute truth jeopardises contracts!' before hanging up. Class. The show goes without a hitch and without too many careers or relationships being ruined.

I am now totally exhausted and have to go home before I pass out. Given that I took three attempts to spell my name correctly to log on this morning at half past four, I am fairly proud of my flawless on air performance. That said, I now smell and look like a hobo, enough is enough . . .

Tuesday the 25th

Ah, I feel so much better today, probably something to do with sleeping for six hours during the day yesterday and not being half cut!

The *Daily Record* has a great feature today about innovative new ways to find a partner. Forget blind dating or copping off down the pub, in London 'lock and key' parties are all the rage. Funny that – I thought Frank Bough held these years ago. Anyway, turns out these are innocent nights where girls wear necklaces with lockets round their necks like mini padlocks. Men are given keys and spend the evening tracking down whoever has the corresponding lock. The aim is not to pull but to enjoy meeting various people without the embarrassment of saying they fancy them.

'Motorflirting' is another new phenomenon. It is for people who catch eyes with a hottie at the traffic lights and don't have time to chat. Simply log on to motorflirt.com, type in the registration number of your target and see if they have logged on to leave you a message. It turns out 30,000 people are members already.

I've already mentioned Mr Cat was at school with me, and we didn't end up together until fifteen years later. But I loved these weird and wonderful examples of the unpredictability of when cupid's arrow can strike:

> Brendan O'Conner called in to say he met his wife Sylvia at the BULL market in Perth. He was working on a catering stall, but people still laugh when he explains they really did meet in a cattle market.
>
> 'My parents met while they were training to be nurses over twenty-five years ago. My dad loves telling people how they met in the psychiatric ward, which is true!' Simon, East Kilbride.
>
> 'I bumped into my husband in the swimming pool, he actually knocked me out cold. We are still together after twenty-five years.' Anne, Glasgow.
>
> 'I met my girlfriend by crashing into her by mistake. We swapped details for insurance purposes and are still going strong after ten years.' Big Kev.
>
> 'I met my lovely wife Jane at the dentists she worked in when I was getting a full set of false teeth. She said she even fancied me with my old rotten teeth as well, now that IS love.' Kenny, Cambuslang.

There is no love in the air in the office when a sleazy freelance reporter calls our press office trying to find out, 'Which footballer is Cat going abroad with from the DUNDEE team?' Apparently he heard about it from a 'source'. If it wasn't so sad it would be funny. It's not much of an exclusive when I have already told the story myself ON AIR to over

150,000 people, and to then get the bloody team wrong, give me strength . . . which is what I would need in abundance to keep up with the Two Jimmies if I actually ever did take them up in their kind offer.

Today the *Record* printed a last gasp get fit for the 'Race for Life' plan. It is now just over six weeks to go and I still can't run for more than ten minutes. However, I am going to follow this to the letter and day one inexplicably says 'REST' so that is what I intend to do. This training lark is a skoosh . . .

Wednesday the 26th

I had an interesting journey to work this morning thanks to the four young men walking home at 4.20 a.m. along Woodlands Road in Glasgow. I stopped at the traffic lights as two of them started play fighting in a twelve-pint boy kind of way, wobbling all over the pavement.

They spotted I was a female in a car, or possibly they just spotted the car and promptly straightened up, wheeched down their breeks and waggled their bums until the light turned to green. I'm not sure if I was disgusted at their shameful loutish behaviour or at myself for laughing the whole way along the M8. The one on the left looked quite fit actually.

My tale of getting to work fits in with my chosen paper review story this morning, about a bloke in the west coast of Scotland who knocked back a new works car in favour of a canoe. He now paddles eight miles to work every day and loves it.

Len the janitor at Headwell School gets in touch. He leaves for work at 6.00 a.m. but his elderly neighbour Bob always stands at his window to wave him off – it makes his day. While Pauline in Edinburgh walks four miles to get to work and says the baby daffodils are currently putting 'a cheeky wee smile on [her] face'. Ah, the joys of spring.

I'm meeting my mate Sosij for lunch today for some running tips. Ironic, really, meeting for food to discuss getting fit. Sosij – Greg McEwan from Cardenden in Fife – used to run middle distances for Scotland and on Sunday, while I was recovering from a Torremolinos hangover, he completed the London marathon in four hours, four minutes. I worked with him at STV when he was a young pup and given his nickname. He used to come in all keen and eager to please, and offer to get coffee and rolls from the canteen for everyone in the sports department. 'Dis anywin waant a so-sij?' he would say in his Fife twang, and so it stuck. When he was still competing he became the 'Flying Sosij' in our office. Then he found drink and girls and now does it just for fun, the running that is.

Today's quest, in the *Daily Record*'s cut-out-and-keep guide to preparing for the race, is run one minute, walk one minute and do it ten times. I sense even I may cope with this one.

The front pages today are filled with the news that Hollywood star Kevin Costner was the man who took a rub quite literally into his own hands at a posh hotel in St Andrews. The shocked masseur was given money to settle out of court and the news he was actually on his honeymoon at the time of the incident has the nation sniggering into their porridge. The *Scottish Sun*'s headline of 'Rubbing Hood' is quite simply genius.

Story of the day has to go to Golden Baz who admits to the funniest seduction story I have ever heard. He once took a girl for a luxury break to Turnberry Hotel. At £200 a night, oor Baz, a poor student, had to think laterally about his budget. I'm sure the lovely lady managed to hide her surprise when our bold hero took a George Foreman grill out of his bag and offered her salmon or steak. To make this escapade even funnier, it turns out he then had the audacity to phone room service for chips. My sides are sore laughing, and it is not difficult to work out why she is now an ex-girlfriend.

Talking of romance, I am gutted to report that, funnily enough, my alleged elopement with a Dundonian football hunk has not made it to any newspaper; shame, really, I could do with the money from the out-of-court settlement. Isotonic Lucozade Sport is expensive you know . . .

Thursday the 27th

I am not sore at all today. Probably to do with the fact my lunch lasted four hours, I ate too much sticky toffee pudding with ice cream, walked home and promptly fell asleep on the couch. I woke up at half-seven covered in dribble and without the desire to find my trainers and go running. The running guide says there should be four rest days in week one; well, I have had four in a row and now feel great.

In the world of football the insanity continues at Tynecastle where it transpires a female Lithuanian faith healer called Rima has been brought in to hit players with a big golden stick to see if they're fit enough to play. You really can't make this stuff up, bonkers.

There's a funny feature in the *Sun* today with former pupils of Jack McConnell dishing the dirt. Apparently he was very strict, quite scary and a bit of a looker!

I had a teacher called Numph at school who was terrifying. His name was Mr Galbraith, he taught music and hated first years. He had a bit of plastic tubing he called his 'hollow head tester' which he bopped over unruly pupils to shame them into silence.

I was one of just five people who took higher music, and I remember the day I was the only person in the class.

'YOU GIRL,' he bellowed.

'GO TO MY DESK.' I did, petrified.

'OPEN THE DRAWER.' I did, now quite concerned.

'TAKE A SWEETIE. NOW EAT IT.' Phew. He was actually a great teacher, but his methods certainly made a lasting impression. So did these guys:

'Mrs Scott the French teacher at Camelon High was very popular. In the 1970s the guys used to trip on the staircase because it was rumoured she didn't wear knickers.'

'We had a teacher called Chibber who had loads of Rangers tickets on his wall, he used to give us something to do and then put his feet up and play his guitar, he was mental. He also drove a big motorbike, he used to let the older boys call him by his first name. One day I tried to call him John and he nearly ripped my head off. He was cool though.'

'We had a nutty science teacher called Mr Caler who painted a big target on the wall and played darts with three sink plungers. His classes were great.' Mick, Torrance.

'We had a teacher called Peep! One day he made the mistake of saying 'if I hear one more peep out of you lot . . .' Wullie from Carluke.

'We had a geography teacher with a really bad lishp. We used to be in fits when he shpoke about the glashiated swish alpsh.' Nicky in Falkirk.

I have just returned to my computer after a two-hour presenters' meeting about Big in Falkirk and Jay has just sprung a secret lunch on everybody. He has booked a table in Da Luciano in Bothwell and I am sensing my training routine may be postponed for yet another day. I wonder if Paula Radcliffe had to conquer such obstacles . . .

Friday the 28th

It is too bright. Everything is too loud and every part of me hurts. Correct, you've guessed it, I didn't run anywhere, wine was consumed and both Robin and I are suffering from the hangover guilt. That horrible anxious feeling when you simply KNOW you've been a twat.

After the lunch, everybody returned to Real Radio apart from us. We left at seven fifteen after four bottles of wine and an incident that nearly involved the police. Da Luciano in Bothwell was the venue and I am convinced we are now banned. The trouble, as ever, began when I decided to treat the bar (two old wifies about eighty having coffee and cakes) to 'Sweet Child of Mine' on the piano. The po-faced manager told me off (acceptable), but I returned five minutes later offering to play a (oh the shame) 'nice wee medley for the old dears'. Mr Po told me off again, fast forward half an hour and we try again.

'Right, if you touch the piano one more time I am calling the police.'

It gets worse.

We then, stupidly, returned to Real Radio and barged in on the *Football Phone In*. I got stuck in the door, Robin was giggling like a nutter and when Ewen asked me who my SPL striker of the year was I shouted 'Johnny Lambie'. Even now, I have no idea where that one came from.

This morning we are one big apology to the staff at Da Luciano (except big grumpy drawers), to the old dears, to the *Football Phone In*, to anyone unfortunate enough to meet us.

We don't go out very often but when we do we really go for it. Ewen and Roughie once gatecrashed Willie D's overnight show and started giving out the phone number and talking about midfielders. They'd been out for hours and were clearly the worse for wear. The weird thing is, people absolutely love our tales of shame. They can sense our genuine regret this morning and we are bombarded with messages of support. Diane McArthur from Motherwell sent me this e-mail: 'Don't worry Cat you are not alone, after a few wines I've often tried to play pianos in pubs, the thing is I can't play when I am sober so I've no idea why I do it. I also think I can sing. I managed to persuade a pianist to let me sing one night and it was not appreciated. You are not alone!'

Mr W. calls Robin and me to a meeting and we are convinced we are going to get hammered for being hammered on the phone in; turns out he loved it, as did the phone-in crew and the audience.

It is Big in Falkirk tomorrow, I am staying through all weekend and my liver has quite frankly had enough. This has been one hell of a week, and the run is edging closer. I contemplate having a 'DRY' Big in Falkirk but there is as much chance of this as John Lambie has of netting an overhead winner at the weekend.

Saturday the 29th

I'm really nervous this morning and it is not the thought of presenting on stage in front of 30,000 people, it is the song. In a moment of madness we've decided to sing Bryan Adams and Mel C's 'Baby When You Are Gone' at Big in Falkirk today. Robin and I rehearsed it a couple of times yesterday afternoon in the studio and we went from horrendous to almost passable. It is a two-part harmony and to be honest the Mel C part that I have to sing is too high. I sometimes hit the notes, I sometimes open my mouth and nothing comes out at all apart from a pained croak.

I arrive at Callendar Park at lunch-time with Ewen and Roughie entertaining the crowds. Robin is already there and the first thing he says to me is, 'So shall we sing or not?' We go into the Real Radio bus and have a practice to the karaoke backing track and to be honest we sing it the best we have ever done. Confidence high, we take to the stage for the first of six presentation slots.

I let slip we might sing, but admit we are not the best and the crowd goes mental, chanting, 'SING, SING, SING'. I sing 'Heads, Shoulders, Knees and Toes' to get them going and it's fantastic to see so many people taking part. (I make another mental note – it is time this classic made a dance mix re-release. A sure-fire summer hit, don't tell anyone though.)

We tell them we shall sing in between the next two bands if we are allowed.

Bossman Jay comes on stage with us and tells the increasing numbers not to be so daft as to let us sing. I wish they had listened. Instead we decide to go for it, and for the first three seconds of the instrumental introduction we rock! Then it starts – the humiliation, the horror, our collective tumbleweed moment. Neither of us starts on the right note and it all gets progressively worse from there. Robin slips into the Mel C part and I don't know whether to sing the male part to salvage some harmony or to keep going. The chorus is worse than the verse and I can see in Robin's eyes he now comprehends the magnitude of our error. Thankfully the musical bridge helps us out and I plead: 'I know we are rotten so help us out by high clapping, Falkirk!' to which the whole field (by now about 30,000) are obliging. I love every one of them SO much. 'OK, now air guitar,' I yelp pleadingly, and again they oblige with enthusiastic glee. Thankfully the song ends shortly afterwards and we get a decent cheer, the kind the fat kid gets when he finally crosses the line at school races. Backstage we are met with overwhelming, well, silence. Nobody talks to us, not even to pass comment on how shit it really was.

'Do you want some cheese and biscuits?' asks Bossman Jay as he scuttles back to the buffet unable to make eye contact. Only Matt Bendoris, the cheery showbiz journalist from the *Scottish Sun*, calls it as it was.

'Bloody hell, you are the new Jemini!' Of course, he's referring to the worst UK Eurovision Song Contest performance of all time. Robin scoots away from the stage and heads home within minutes and I can tell he is actually quite upset at how bad we really were. He's been in panto with DANA, remember. I take the other therapeutic option on offer and hit the bar.

The Specials and The Beat are the headline acts for tonight and to be honest I'm not too fussed on either. I go for a wee wander and meet a lovely wee lassie called Marissa who wants an autograph and a photo (I blush again, I am so rubbish at being Z-list 'famous'). She gives me her pen and asks pertinently: 'How rich are you Cat?' Wow, a cracker. I'm not sure what the correct answer is but I tell her I have a horse and enough pocket money to buy chocolate every day and she seemed pleased. (I know, it is bad to lie to children about the horse . . .)

A huge posse from Real Radio end up in Behind the Wall in Falkirk for a night of high jinks and bad dancing and for a moment I forget those two and a half minutes of vocal assassination. With a pineapple pizza (it's a fruit portion) under my arm I head back to the Inchyra Grange hotel where the lovely staff have placed a bottle of chilled champagne in my room.

I open a large mineral water and scoff my pizza. Tomorrow is another day, and I want to be well . . .

Sunday the 30th

The best thing about staying in a hotel that advertises on the radio station is the little perks they treat you to, like the free champagne. However, to me, the fact that the head porter is a big fan of the show and agreed to let me check out as late as I fancied was like winning the pools.

I'd planned a twelve noon rise, a bath with all the lovely bubbles and stuff, and then a trip back to Callendar Park for day two of the festival. At 9.15 a.m., wearing a crushed pink tatty nightshirt with Patsy from *Ab Fab* hair and mascara stains right down my sleep-deprived face, the fire alarm went off – loudly, and right above my slightly throbbing head. I had to stoat down two flights of stairs hastily firing on my hooded top and trainers to meet lots of fresh-faced lovelies in the car park. Only the poor souls in swimsuits looked more ashamed.

With the all-clear signalling a return to bed, I found, as usual, I couldn't get back to sleep, so got up, showered and headed back to the park for the whole day.

The line-up today is cool. Sandi Thom, the Scottish singer–songwriter who podcast to 70,000 people and got a record deal, is fantastic. She has a great voice and seems genuinely stunned at the reception she gets. Chatting backstage she says she is amazed at how everything has turned out, although she admits she is knackered from her schedule. She has to fly back to London tonight, as she has promised her web viewers another concert from her flat tomorrow lunch time. I give Marcus from her band my two spare hospitality passes and he's made up, for it means his two mates from Linlithgow can come in to get a free beer.

Next on my backstage chat list are the River Detectives who do a great acoustic show. I'm quite embarrassed as I used to love these guys when I was about fifteen; I mention we chatted about them on air a few weeks ago and Sam beams: 'I know, my mum told me about it, she loves the show!' How cool is that. I tell him how 'Chains' and 'Train Song' are the only two tunes I can play on the guitar. He gives me an odd look. I didn't mean to imply they were basic or easy, just that I loved them so much I practised the relevant chords. Oh God, he thinks I am a nutcase. Anyway, they are polite enough to get a photo with me so I can e-mail it to my pal Lynn who used to sing 'Train Song' with me in bus stops when we were young.

Four Good Men are next on, a band made up with guys who used to be in Big Country and Simple Minds. They play a selection of their greatest hits and the crowd love it.

Backstage, band of the moment, Orson, arrive and cause quite a stir. These guys are from California and LOOK like rock stars. They've been at number one just weeks ago with 'No Tomorrow' and also had a massive hit with 'Bright Idea'. They wear quirky suits, theatrical glasses and dapper trilby hats. They are a cheery bunch who chat to everybody and instead of waiting in the confines of their private dressing room, prefer to mingle with us in the hospitality tent where they insist on drinking hot cups of coffee.

'It is SO cold here in Scotland we just need coffee,' lead singer Jason Pebworth tells me.

'Actually we were out in Amsterdam last night, and it was a bit of a heavy one so we need the caffeine,' confides the funky bassist in a giggling stage whisper. I can tell he relates to my bleary eyes and sees a kindred forty degrees proof spirit.

The guys heat up and play a sizzling set and the kids at the front go wild. Midge Ure is the headline act tonight and I meet him for a quick catch-up before he goes on. It's the biggest live set he's played with his band for years and he is really excited about it. It's great to see a guy who has done so much for music and charity, and is so used to big crowds like Live 8 and Live Aid, still having that pre-performance adrenalin burst. I was going to tell him I felt the same before murdering 'Baby When You're Gone', but I muted myself in time and wished him luck before he was swamped by autograph hunters.

It's been a cracking weekend and once again I find myself hitting my bed with four hours until getting up time. Still, on this particular occasion it actually is ROCK AND ROLL . . .

may

Monday the 1st

Mayday, Mayday. It appears Robin, Gordon from Burntisland, Raymond the trucker on the M8 and I are the only people in the world working today. The roads are empty, our building is empty and it is quiet on the texts and calls. That said, we are in super-laid-back mode and end up having a ball.

We decided to have a 'Bank Holiday Battle of the Bands' and suggest putting 'Bohemian Rhapsody' by Queen up against 'Stairway to Heaven' by Led Zeppelin. They are both classics, and both over six and a half minutes long. Generally, far too long for a breakfast show, but perfect for today where putting our feet up and taking it easy is order of the day. Queen wins the vote and I have time for replying to two e-mails, a cup of tea and a plate of somebody from the newsroom's Cheerios. They will never know.

We've been inundated with texts and e-mails over the weekend about our singing performance and thankfully the general consensus is that we were right to give it a bash, even though we did fail spectacularly. Next year we shall stick to throwing out T-shirts and lollipops.

I've had no luck with my last minute frantic search for Take That tickets, so I have resigned myself to an early night. The *Sun* reports that the boys were spotted in Mr Singh's restaurant last night before their big gig. I'm sure a nice spicy curry relit their fire.

Gareth, our hilarious stand-in news editor on loan from Wales, spotted Charlotte Church in Blockbusters in Cardiff handing back DVDs. She was in a rough area with her little designer dog tucked under her arm and a massive white limo sitting outside waiting for her. Not quite Jason Orange at the foot of my road, but a nice wee story nonetheless.

A lovely guy called Jim Rodden calls in to give me the phone number of Satay Singh's secretary on the off chance they left tickets as a tip. We both know it is a long shot but he adds, 'Ach – you deserve to go out and enjoy yourself, pet.' Our listeners are fantastic. And even if I don't get them I shall NEVER FORGET his kindly words.

Tuesday the 2nd

The first text I get this morning is from wee Victoria who has been to see Take That for the past two nights. 'Mark Owen is amazing and the gig was fantastic.' I never got tickets but I'm pleased she had fun. That said, if she mentions the concert one more time I may be forced to rip her pretty wee head off, in a friendly non-aggressive manner, naturally. Anyway, Take That are old news, for today – HE IS BACK.

The Real Radio Renegade is back on the streets and will be causing chaos for the next month. The sneak, previously known as the Real Radio Fugitive, is arguably the most exhilarating promotion we run. Basically you have to hunt down a man we set loose in the central belt. He can be anywhere in the transmission area and goes out during three bounty periods a day. He calls in with a disguised voice and gives a crossword style clue as to where he will be that particular period and tells us how much is up for grabs. To win, you must ask, 'Are you the Real Radio Renegade?'

There are numerous rules, you have to be over sixteen, he won't be in a car, he won't ask you to go anywhere with him and he won't be in a park, but overall it is a fun promotion that really captures the imagination of the listeners. Only two people in the whole station know who he is, where he is from and where he is based. This means all the presenters are as clueless as everybody else and can, and unfortunately do, inadvertently send people in the wrong direction at times.

Today's clue is 'I'll get you Butler' and he is worth £8,000. Instantly Robin reckons he is at a bus station, as it's a famous catch-phrase from the seventies TV show *On the Buses*. People call in from Edinburgh Bus Station, Dunfermline Bus Station and Buchanan Bus Station and you can hear chaos in the background with people screaming, 'Are you the Real Radio Renegade?' at each other. If nothing else, it is a fantastic awareness raiser for the station, but we take it a bit person-ally and really want winners on our show.

I've never actually been out in the middle of the madness but by all accounts it gets pretty frantic. People take weeks off their work for it, if it is a huge bounty lots of people phone in sick, and by the end of it lots of people who are regular hunters have made new friends.

This promotion can cause major disruptions – a Celtic European game was held up once, we brought Uddingston to a complete standstill and caused a commotion in Queen Street station, Paisley, Dunfermline, Falkirk, Stirling and Edinburgh too. That's what I like about this competition – we take in the big cities, the towns AND the wee villages.

I have to stay on air an extra hour a day until 10.00 a.m. but, hey, if we get somebody eight grand then I am more than happy to do so. Unfortunately he sneaks away this time (he was in Buchanan Bus Station) and he sounds a right cocky one. We shall enjoy tracking this character down.

E-mails are still flooding into the show about our Big in Falkirk 'singing' and to be honest we are still in shock as to the extent of the horror show. If I'm to become Sporty Spice to sing that part properly I'd better haul my fat butt down the gym and finally start this bloody training regime.

As you may have noticed, diet and fitness have been tell-ingly absent for the past few days and that's because I remain unable to stop eating and start running. However, I do have my gym bag and swimming stuff in the car and if nothing else I consider that a psychological start . . .

Wednesday the 3rd

I have a groin strain. In another moment of gross fitness negligence I decided that as I should be at 'week two day two' of the fitness guide, that's exactly where I would start. I went to Greens gym yesterday afternoon and ran for seven minutes then walked for three, not once, not twice, but THREE times. I actually felt OK, my knee wasn't too bad, but I had a totally wobbly moment when the running machine stopped and I stepped off like I was seasick. Quick stagger left, quick stagger right and then an embarrassing bump into the water cooler.

I would love to be an athletic type who strolls through these sessions with elegance but I can't. I go so red I look like I'm about to combust and end up sweaty just tying my trainer laces.

The Renegade was in Inverkeithing this morning and escaped capture again. It's quite funny to hear the chaos caused in the town, but all in good spirits.

Robin leaves straight after the show today as it is his dad's ninety-first birthday. He heads up to Aberdeen to take Dr Galloway, a highly respected paediatrician, out for lunch. What he makes of his eldest son making a living from pretending to be an eighty-nine-year-old lady, a gay man with a pet mouse and a Peterhead fish merchant is beyond me!

I fondly remember my Granny Harvey's surprise ninetieth birthday party. My dad assembled a nine-piece ceilidh band in a wee coffee shop in Milngavie, we gathered all her pals round (she talked for Scotland so had loads) and my mum, I seem to remember, rattled up a pretty good buffet. I had to bring my gran into the shop under the pretence of having to pick something up and everybody was told to be quiet as she approached, to heighten the element of surprise. When she walked into the room the lights went on, the band started and everybody shouted SURPRISE! Surveying the scene with 'Happy 90th' banners everywhere she remained the epitome of calm before saying, 'Surprise? Aye it's a bloody surprise all right – I'm only eighty-nine!'

And it turns out she was. Still, we had a great night and she lived through another seven birthday parties.

She was a great old dear who loved her budgie Joey to bits; the fact poor Joey changed from being bright green to pale blue during her summer break to Largs never registered, and my dad had to stifle a grin as she boasted proudly on a daily basis how fit Joey looked for his age. Even when she was on her last legs she remained wonderfully cheeky. When testing her lucidity and awareness in hospital after another bad turn, the doctor asked her, 'So, Mrs Harvey, who is the prime minister?' She replied, 'If you don't know that, how did you become a bloody doctor?'

Like Joey, she was a great old bird and I miss her lots.

Thursday the 4th

It is *Star Wars* Day – May the fourth be with you. Today we are celebrating 100 years of the first-ever holiday camp – a place in Norfolk. Robin won the talent contest in Butlins in Ayr aged eight, singing 'Fitba' Crazy', shame we never tried that one last Saturday at Big in Falkirk. This Butlins became Wonderwestworld, and is now Craig Tara, a Haven holiday centre.

Our listeners have fond memories of the glory days:

'I remember being told we were going to Butlins by Ayr, I told all my pals we were flying. I was only eight.' Allan in Stockbridge.

'We used to go in the 1970s when the pool had windows in the deep end so people could watch from outside. My brothers and I used to have competitions to see who could keep an underwater conversation going the longest with somebody outdoors. Ah the memories. Thank you.'

'My mum and dad took my brother and sister and I down to the beach and we would always compete to see who could dig the deepest. My dad was mortified when I kept shouting, 'Come and see the size of my hole everybody.' Angela, Airdrie.

'My mum won a trip on the QE2 at the bingo, it was only for one person so she sold it and took me and my brother and sister to Butlins. I want to say a huge thanks to her and happy seventy-fifth birthday.' Linda, Paisley.

'Following trends of calling babies after the place of conception, my dad told my sister recently she would have been called Butlins.' Amanda, Airdrie.

'I used to go to one in North Wales and it was always scorching. My mum would scrub me and my sister for hours trying to get the dirt off when it was a tan from the outdoor swimming pool!' Lori, Paisley.

We have a photo call this afternoon for the Race for Life. All of the Real Runners are kitted out in white T-shirts which feel too tight for me. I am the only person out of eight who has to wear a baggy Real Radio fleece. I have a dejected smile in the pictures and vow to never stop training until I can be the same shape as everybody else.

I feel quite teary and down with this latest 'fat' day issue. Twenty minutes later Bossman Billy walks past my desk and sees I look a bit gloomy. He returns five minutes later with a 'special present to cheer me up' and gives me a pack of three of the finest fresh jam doughnuts I've ever seen. I don't know whether to laugh or cry. Instead I do what any pre-menstrual dieting female would. I rip open the wrapper and munch one down without pausing for breath. Och, give me a break, I shall run it off later . . .

Friday the 5th

Three hours' sleep! The new guy in the flat above me with the penchant for loud heavy-metal music with the bass up full wasn't my only problem last night; the central belt endured one of the most amazing electrical storms I've ever experienced. The thunder shook my windows and remained immediately overhead for the best part of two hours. The lightning was a stunning mix of sheet and the most pronounced forks I've ever seen. Every two minutes my bedroom would light up before the claps rang out. I'm glad I was under my duvet and exceptionally pleased not to be in a plane.

The emergency services had a busier night than bonfire night as flash flooding stranded motorists and thousands of homes lost power.

We are inundated with calls from people who sat enthralled watching the show unfold. Everybody, it seems, turned the lights out, opened the curtains and just enjoyed the most astounding display of nature. It truly was an incredible spectacle. My favourite text said simply: 'Sheet, I forking missed it.' We also have hundreds of calls from folk in the east jealous because they missed out.

Today the Renegade clue is 'Not the London station' and I guess Charing Cross. Turns out for once I am right, he is worth £5,000 and instantly the area goes nuts. By twenty past nine, we have six calling cards but no sightings, the Renegade calls the show and says, 'Add a zero to my bounty.' He is now worth £50,000 and by all accounts people start pouring out of the offices in the area and start asking everybody. We even have lawyers and accountants downing tools and joining the chase.

Jim Gallagher phones in to tell us he has won. He has found the Renegade. We ask why he is not on the special line on the secret phone, and he stutters a bit. 'No, I've found him.' He insists indignantly. We ask him why he is not on the special phone again and he gets cross with his mate and with his hand clearly over the phone he shouts at his pal, 'Hand me a special phone, you never told me about a special phone,' before, clearly annoyed, huffing and puffing and hanging up. We piss ourselves laughing. Come on, for fifty grand you would give it a bash.

Tomorrow I am going cruising on the Clyde on Uncle Arnold Clark's boat *Drum*, the big fancy sailing boat Simon Le Bon nearly drowned on. I'm assured it is safe and I'm quite excited about it. Unfortunately the timing is not the best, because tonight I am off to the big STV leaving do as Shareen Nanjiani, Jane Lewis, Sarah Heaney and six reporters wave goodbye to *Scotland Today*.

I thin what the suits in charge have done to that company is an absolute disgrace. However, I shall go to the party and toast my old buddies and reassure them there is life after Cowcaddens.

I just hope that, erm, seasickness does not get the better of me in the morning . . .

Monday the 8th

Arrr, me hearties, Captain Cat at your service. I am still feeling all nautical but nice from our trip on Uncle Arnold Clark's boat *Drum* on Saturday. The conditions were absolutely perfect, calm water, sunny day but very windy.

I have to admit it was a lot harder work than I envisaged. I thought we would be sipping chilled cocktails on deckchairs watching the scenery pass with our feet up, but we actually had to roll up our sleeves and get stuck in. The engine was switched off at Gourock and we hauled the sails up. I took the helm for almost an hour and got her up to eleven and a half knots, which was bloody fast, as we cruised past Largs and Cumbrae. The boat was tilted at a thirty-five degree angle with the right side skimming the water and to be honest it was pretty scary. I had the others clinging on for dear life with the speed and slant, but the skipper reassured me that this was good and the way it should be.

We anchored in Millport Bay for lunch which was prawn cocktail, homemade chicken curry and chocolate mousse. How Ray the chef managed to cook for twelve people in a galley the size of a toilet cubicle is beyond me, but we wolfed down our scran in the great outdoors as the first bottle of wine was cracked open. Our sail back was a much more relaxed affair, more wine, the boat was level and the engine was on low.

It turns out multi-skilling is order of the day at Arnold Clark's as Ray the chef swapped his pots and pans for a guitar. He took a chair on deck and started strumming away happily as we all joined in.

The people on the Rothesay ferry that passed us must have thought we were multi-millionaire rock stars enjoying the high life. They'll never know we all ended the day in the quality old men's bar the Quarter Gill in Partick.

The yacht actually sleeps sixteen in very close quarters; Ray pointed out Simon Le Bon's bed and I sat on it and stroked it on my pal Alyson's behalf. It's what she would have wanted. She works in sports marketing and is always schmoozing with famous people, but this year I've sent her pictures of me cuddling into Lee Ryan, Orson and Shayne Ward; I think this latest experience will send her over the edge. She has only managed to send me pictures of her presenting an award to Andy Webster who plays for Hearts and is from her home town of Arbroath. The battle continues, but I am now definitely leading . . .

The *Football Phone In* is grabbing the headlines in the papers this morning, with Roughie missing his flight to London in a spectacularly stupid fashion. To be more exact, he was not allowed on the plane for carrying a deadly weapon in his hand luggage.

The boys were heading down for the Sony awards and planning to wear full highland gear. Roughie's skean dhu was in his hand luggage and he had to wait for the next plane as easyJet quite rightly refused to let him board with it. The fact that Ewen and Victoria left him in Glasgow Airport as they jetted off is hilarious.

Not since Alyson (who is slightly loopy) got stopped at customs for having two plastic water pistols in her bag have I chortled so much. Still, the guys are in with a great chance of winning something tonight and my fingers, knees and toes are firmly crossed for them. It is for this reason I have declared today another day of rest. Come on, you wouldn't want me toppling over on the treadmill now, would you?

Tuesday the 9th

Sometimes I even surprise myself. Despite chronic fatigue I struggled to the gym yesterday and ran for twenty-four minutes. My knee is fine today and believe it or not I am going to go back this afternoon. Oh yes, this is the start of the new me.

The *Football Phone In* guys didn't win last night in London, but they apparently had a ball anyway. We received an e-mail to the show from a random bloke who works in a radio station down south saying: 'Hi there, just thought you should know I was at the Sony awards last night and your station certainly knows how to party. They were the only ones singing on the dance floor and really going for it. What a great crowd.' As Sir Alex Ferguson would say, 'Pwoud, vewy, vewy pwoud.'

Good news for my dad today. Rothesay – his favourite place in the entire world – has been voted the best seaside resort in Scotland by *Which?* magazine. At the height of its popularity in 1906, the Victorian town used to attract 60,000 during the Glasgow Fair. It's been spruced up recently and the judges commended it on its fine scenery, deserted beaches, wildlife and walking. Are they mad? Rothesay is famous for Zavaroni's ice cream, Zavaroni's chippy, the putting green, the Winter Gardens, meringues the size of footballs at the wee coffee shop at Ettrick Bay, and the most lavish lavvies in the world.

Seriously, the artistically tiled bogs win awards every year. Apparently the gents' Victorian toilets have the original fittings from 1899. They have been described as the 'jewel in the sanitarian's crown' (honestly, folks, I checked) and when it is quiet they can arrange guided tours for ladies. Now you are talking!!

When I was wee my dad toured the Clyde coast in his VW campervan with his sellout Scottish stage show (*Scotland of the Seventies*) playing the summer seasons at Dunoon, Rothesay and Largs. The campervan always had water on tap (for the whisky) and a flaked-out member of the band catching up on sleep from the night before.

The famous Aberdonian comedy trio 'Scotland the What?' once wrote a fabulous ceilidh band song pastiche that contained the line, 'One more Scottische and I'll be off the leash for there's nothing drier than a dry musician.' How right they were. Still, my dad has been off the booze for twenty years now and is currently penning his showbiz memoirs. I'm sure the two pages' worth of material will be a hoot . . .

We have the quarterly night out with the Arnold Clark people this evening which should be fun. I promise not to wear pyjamas or sing karaoke, and in a moment of rare sense I am going to take my car; I have the *Offside Cup Final Special* in Gretna tomorrow night and a twenty-hour day from hell. With my new-found athleticism it should be a cinch. We have some cracking interview footage already in the can, and I think it will go down a treat. Just like the Japanese food at Yen tonight. Car or no car, car or no car . . . oh no, I am swithering . . .

Wednesday the 10th

I am an angel. In a moment of responsibility I drove to the restaurant, I drank two pints of soda and lime and now feel fantastic. We had a cracking evening at Yen, with the dexterity of our chef leaving us, for once, speechless. My particular favourite bit was when he started firing chunks of fried egg at everybody to catch in our mouths. Years of watching my dad, an expert at tossing chocolate raisins in the air, paid off and I'm proud to say my chunk was perfectly received without spillage.

Comedy moment of the evening, once again, came courtesy of young Baz who was reprimanded on the sly for showing more than a passing interest in Louise from Arnold Clark, a young and very pretty blonde. Ah, he tries; I think the wee soul was carried away by the large table-top grill which possibly reminded him of his last George Foreman moment!

Today I am off to Gretna for the *Offside Cup Final Special* which will be transmitted on Friday night. I was meant to be going to Hearts en route to interview the players. I was then to log the footage in the back of the cameraman's car and edit the package on site. However, at four yesterday afternoon Hearts cancelled the press day and made it on Thursday.

This means I have to chat in our makeshift studio with Tam about what I'd been up to for the show, we leave a space for the not-yet-shot package and then I shall film, edit and insert it tomorrow. So, done up in the pink outfit again, I smile: 'I've been to Tynecastle to catch up with the Hearts players.' There was then a space in the studio recording where Tam and I guessed what the players would say so we would have an audio track of laughter to cover the eventual package. He returned with: 'That was your best package ever, Cat.' The audience found this obvious piss-take hilarious.

Gretna owner Brooks Mileson was in splendid form. He truly is a one-off. He's bought over 7,000 tickets to give to local school kids but plans to go up in his car with his pals and sit in the crowd as usual. 'Why would I want to go to a boardroom?' he asked me, while he stood outside the hotel puffing on a fag with obvious pleasure. 'I like going to football with my mates so I'm not going to stop now. We're going to get a chippy at Hampden and then enjoy the game.'

Brooks spends thousands supporting his club, plus, rumour has it, up to seventy other youth teams in his area; he also has an animal sanctuary and spends his money for causes he believes in rather than because he is flash.

As the show is a BBC commission impartiality is important so we rip into both teams equally. We arranged for a coach load of Hearts fans to travel down to Gretna for the show to ensure a fifty–fifty audience. The only problem occurred when the bus was due to leave. Gus, our assistant producer, was running about trying to get the Jambos back on the bus but Brooks, in another moment of breathtaking hospitality, had taken everyone to the bar for a drink. Not only was this a funny gesture because they were Hearts fans who would be shouting against his team on Saturday, there were ONE HUNDRED AND NINETY people.

The bus left an hour and six minutes late, and I'm told bounced the whole way up to Edinburgh. This cup final lark is real good feel-good football . . .

Thursday the 11th

Four hours' sleep, and I'm up and ready to go again. I knew this week was going to be tough but I always forget quite how tiring working on *Offside* and the *Breakfast Show* can be. Still, just the Hearts feature to shoot, cut and insert and the *Cup Final Special* is in the bag.

The quarterly RAJAR (Radio Joint Audience Research Limited) figures came out this morning and the *Breakfast Show* is up to a peak of 158,000 listeners a day with 493,000 a week. I'm quite oblivious to the magnitude of these numbers but according to Robin, who's been in radio longer than Marconi,

'They are bloody good,' and that will do for me. We are still the biggest breakfast show outside London in the UK – which is quite terrifying when I think about having so many people know I fancy José Mourinho, am rubbish at fat class and cut out the labels of my increasingly expanding knickers.

Today we have a screening in Real Radio of the Torremolinos film. Everybody is herded into the lecture suite, the lights are dimmed, and yes, popcorn is actually served. Now, anyone who has ever watched back movie footage of a night out will know the cringe factor involved when those sultry dance moves are revealed to be awkward robot-like grindings. Well this video is murder!

Every misdemeanour, every bum karaoke note, every pole-dancing incident, all captured and replayed on the big screen for the ultimate squirm factor. I was quite relieved when my phone rang in the middle of it.

'Hi, Cat, Iain from the Pavilion Theatre here. Can you act?'

Sorry, what?!

'Can you act? We've just had a play about sex toys and a girls' night out and thought you would've been perfect for it. So I just wondered if you could act.'

I now can't talk for laughing. It is quite an eye-opener to hear what people think of you, and this examination is nothing short of terrifying. Does he think I am possible stage talent, or a psycho slapper? Anyway, as it happens, that play had already been cast, but as my name was bandied about for the part so much, he figured he would get in touch and ask what my acting background was.

'I studied Theatre for three years at Glasgow University and I love panto and that is about it,' I confessed.

'Funny you should mention that . . .'

Uh-oh . . .

'We would like you to be Tinkerbell in *Peter Pan* this year.'

I nearly wet myself. I have several emotions going through my mind:

   1. This is stupid – there are two shows a day and I get up in the middle of the night.
   2. It would be great fun.
   3. I may collapse with exhaustion.
   4. It will be great fun.
   5. It will be great fun and
   6. It will be great fun.
   7. I can fly, I can fly, I can fly . . .

I arrange to pop in for a meeting with him next week and promptly text all my pals this ultimate comical development in the emancipation of sensible Cat. I can throw sweeties at kids and fly. Fly . . . Oh shit. I wonder if there is a weight limit on Tinkerbell's magic wings. Back to fat class then.

I can hardly concentrate on my way through to Hearts for the press call. I'm about to enter a sensible cup final journalistic environment and all I can think about is how much cellulite row A will see through my fairy costume.

I manage to interview Paul Hartley, Robbie Neilson and Steven Pressley for *Offside*, and the three of them are good value. It is quite difficult to go to one of these press days and make the players answer *Offside*-type questions, but the guys are great. They even let me whack their bums to test their fitness with my golden stick. People would pay for this job sometimes.

I discover Czech star Rudi Skacel is the team nutcase and Hartley and Pressley both think they are the team heartthrob.

'There were only four Valentine cards sent to the club this year and you are looking at the man who got them,' beamed Pressley.

'Aye, but they were all from blokes,' grinned his Scotland and club team-mate.

Great stuff and easy to edit, I am back in Glasgow with the two-and-a-half-minute package cut, mixed and slotted into the show without too much hassle. I finish at quarter past seven, sixteen hours after I got up.

Sensible people would go and sleep for a week. However, tonight is the RAJAR night out with Real Radio in the curry karaoke (surely it should be curryoke) and I feel obliged to attend. I shall leave early though. Oh yes I shall . . .

Friday the 12th

The fact I am writing this entry a week after the date perhaps signifies my shame. I left a space in this diary as the magnitude of our Thursday night behaviour and the consequences of it kick in. It is only now (Friday, 19 May) that I can reflect and learn from what was the funniest (the listeners)/worst (the bosses) show we have ever done.

It would be fair to say Robin, Baz and I all stayed out far too long at the big do, and were still (I have thought long and hard about the level of truth I should write here and have gone for the honesty-is-best-policy approach) well, quite hammered on air. The show is carnage, I arrive ten minutes late, we have the giggles for four hours, Robin presses wrong buttons, and we have the following dialogue.

Robin: 'Are we on air at the moment?'

Cat: 'Yes, that is what the big red light means.' Laughter all round . . . We do the Hucklebuck, the cheesy dance, continuously and generally misbehave.

We have over 300 text messages and 150 e-mails telling us it is the funniest show they have ever heard, with most people saying we should go out every Thursday. The show, however, is not appreciated by those in charge, and to be honest, after taking vodka-flavoured stock and hearing the clips back they are totally a hundred per cent correct. Next week we shall be suitably chastised. Our wrists will be well and truly slapped, and we shall find out just how close we were to actually losing our jobs again.

MAY

However, as it is next Friday already, I can tell you we are now back in the good books, on our best behaviour and unable to spill any further details in the interest of our futures and to save me a right bollocking from my dad.

From now on we shall be as good as gold; I may have to be a magical fairy, remember . . .

Monday the 15th

What a weekend. Phew. I have been to every Scottish Cup final since 1994 and the one on Saturday was the best yet. The game finished 1–1 after extra time, before Hearts went on to win on penalties. Gretna took 12,000 supporters to the match which is amazing when you consider the population of the town is 3,000. There was a real carnival atmosphere and, as usual, the sun shone gloriously on Hampden.

I had a seat in the press box and laughed as Vladimir Romanov arrived with two Russian submarine captains both wearing full military attire. The man is clearly crazy; still it's the most impressive subs bench I've ever seen.

I felt for the Gretna players after such a brilliant performance but they were gracious in defeat and have won themselves a host of new fans after their fairytale adventure.

On Saturday night I attended the St Andrews Boxing Club charity summer ball. This time I did not have to speak which was great as I could sit back and enjoy myself. Tommy and Veronica Gilmour know how to throw a party and I found myself flamenco dancing wearing a feather mask by 11.00 p.m.

Sunday was a lazy day of complete rest, although it seems the streets of Edinburgh have been jumping since the final whistle two days ago. All the papers this morning have big spreads on the Hearts' street party yesterday. 125,000 turned out in Princes Street to cheer on the team. There is even a picture of Romanov sitting astride a life-size plastic cow (street art darlings) clutching the cup, all quite moo-ving really.

Our lines are buzzing with people reliving the moment and telling us their tales of euphoria. My favourite came in by e-mail from Megan and Robbie in Edinburgh. It read:

'We had a fantastic time, we met Jullian Brellier and he posed for photos with us, but can you please say a big thanks to Hearts captain Steven Pressley who waved up at my eighty-four-year-old grandma and smiled at her. She was in her nursing home in Dalry Road waving out the window and it made her day.'

Ah, bless Elvis. She may be getting on a bit but the old dear was all shook up uh huh huh.

Edinburgh wasn't the only place for a party at the weekend. Partick Thistle won promotion to the first division with a penalty shoot-out yesterday. I couldn't get up to Peterhead in time for the game but I phoned my mental football friend Janis for live commentary. After the winning penalty was scored I heard total mayhem, the sounds of feet running, cheering and finally the classic line: 'I'm on the pitch. I'm in the centre circle. We f***ing won!'

The line then went dead, but I got the message. Mr Cat, not for the first time, thought I'd had a turn as I was bounding up and down on his living room floor yelping like a banshee.

Oh yes, it is indeed a be-yooo-ti-ful game.

Tuesday the 16th

There is a cracking wee tale in the papers today about Max Arellano from Mexico, a six-year-old child prodigy who wants to become a doctor. He has devoured all the information from the medical journals he reads in his spare time and is now touring the country wowing academics as an expert in osteoporosis, diabetes and anaemia.

As a kid the only thing I really excelled at was fearless playing. If it could be jumped off I would, if it could be waded through I would and if there was a scab-free knee to skin – I would see to that pron to.

The wee boy who lives over from my mum and dad is three and speaks fluent cars. Uncle Arnold Clark would be so proud. Apparently when I drove into their drive in my Lexus he went mental, shouting the make, model and the size of engine inside.

As ever, our listeners have plenty to tell us:

'My wee boy can play the PSP at a year and a half.'

'My son is six and knows everything about construction. He draws up plans and knows the proper names for things.' Sam, Fife.

'My daughter has a great future in politics because she is very economical with the truth on a regular basis.' Gordon.

'My son Liam is ten now, but before he could talk he would commentate on the motor racing making the sounds of gear changes and everything. It was a total nightmare.' Fiona.

[And finally:]

'That wee boy wants to be a doctor at six? Well I played doctors and nurses for years so I must be a consultant by now.' Stevie, Wishaw.

The Renegade is still on the loose and causes chaos in Wishaw this morning. We have a great call from a woman who claims he is definitely standing outside the vets.

'He looks shifty, just hanging about and he's wearing jeans and a baseball cap.'

Minutes later we get a text in from Sandy in Wishaw: 'That woman was describing me. I was waiting for my pal to get rolls and sausage. I am not shifty and can you tell all the people now going mental that I am NOT the Renegade.'

Brilliant stuff, this campaign has been a riot this year. I love the local nature of it all. For one bounty period somebody's wee town becomes the focus of our whole transmission area. We learn about every coffee shop, bank, bus stop and public loo within the vicinity.

Thankfully he is captured this morning by Jackie Marshall from Bellshill who walked away with £1,500. She has been chasing the Fugitive/Renegade for three years now and seems more delighted with finally trapping the sneak than pocketing the cash. A huge crowd has gathered in the background waiting for verification that she has indeed won, and when Robin confirms that she has identified the Renegade, she squeals with delight and the crowd erupts.

There is a real sense of camaraderie within the regular hunters now and one of our talented kids' texts confirms just how successful the promotion has become: 'I asked my wee five-year-old what she wants to be when she leaves school and she paused for ages before saying, 'I want to be a real winner!'

Job done.

Wednesday the 17th

There's a sensational dilemma for us this morning. Baz has been going to his local gym a lot and has struck up a friendship with a lady in her late seventies who thinks she knows his mum. The only problem is she clearly thinks he is someone else, but the scenario has been going on for so long now, Baz plays along and tells her how his imaginary old dear is getting on.

The problem arose when he was on a cycle machine weeks ago and misheard her. He smiled and acknowledged her without hearing her actually ask, 'How is your mum?' The whole situation is comical because Baz is now starting to feel guilty and imagining the following scenarios:

- His 'mum' and Baz go to the gym at the same time as the old lady;
- His 'mum' actually passes away and he continues to tell old lady she is grand;
- Christmas presents are exchanged;
- He's actually kissed his 'mum' on a night out.

It always amazes me the incredible reaction we get to personal stories and dilemmas. Without our soliciting for calls the board is full and flashing with advice. The nation is split. Tell her the truth and laugh about the misunderstanding, or play along with it because it is not doing anyone any harm. Helpful texts include:

'Take her for a meal and break it to her gently, you never know your luck!' Davie, Alloa.

'Tell her she owes your mum money and she wants it back.'

'Baz has clearly been watching adult movies. Older woman meets young guy in the gym? Dodgy chat up line "How is your mum?" Aye right Baz, we've all had them.' Grant, Bo'ness.

'I think Baz sounds lovely, I'd be his imaginary mum.' Leeane.

[And it seems our boy from Pollok is appealing to everybody:]

'Baz sounds adorable, I'd willingly be his imaginary mum.' Fraser.

He's quickly becoming a *Breakfast Show* pin-up which is hilarious; the boy uses a George Foreman grill to seduce, remember.

After we come off air, Nicola, a fitness instructor from his gym, gets in touch willing to mediate; I look forward to an update on this intriguing situation and I hope, whatever the outcome, he remains pally with the old lady. Hey, she may be worth a fortune . . .

Thursday the 18th

I have been to the gym twice this week and appear to be developing quads like Fatima Whitbread.

The Race for Life charity run is only three weeks away and by my reckoning I could now run about eighty per cent of the way. The fact that I need a stretcher and taxi for the last twenty per cent is immaterial. I have faith. My gimp knee has been playing up a bit, though, so I popped into see Andrew the sports masseur at Greens gym.

'I have the perfect thing for you.' He beams. Great, it now feels like a sharp kitchen knife is being jabbed into my knee.

'It's a new machine, it cost us fifty grand but it works wonders.' Even better – advanced technology to save the day.

'We tried to phone you to test it out because we know you are perfect for it.' Shit, my knee is famous.

'It can shift eighty per cent of your cellulite within a few weeks.'

Ah. Like a story in The Broons where everybody is talking about one thing and the Bairn misinterprets it, I stood chatting about treatment which I thought was for my knee when he really thinks I have the best fat arse in Glasgow to see if the machine works or not.

On the show today things get quite heated when chatting about Sir Paul McCartney's marriage break-up. Heather Mills could get £400 million from the former Beatle who was too blinded by love to sign a pre-nuptial. It seems the majority of our listeners saw it coming. It is ironic really, he is sixty-three at the moment, and sang the infamous line, 'Will you still need me, when I'm sixty-four?' The answer is clearly not – your millions will do.

My pal Nichola is over in Cannes covering the film festival for the premiere of the *Da Vinci Code*. Apparently it was the biggest media scrum of all time. There were over 500 journalists with TV cameras surrounding the red carpet area trying to catch a glimpse of the stars and possibly a ten-second sound bite.

She sent me a fantastic text which had me laughing out loud. Her dad, Harry Kane, the most famous man in Dunoon, phoned her right in the middle of the mayhem and pleaded, 'Hi darling, I know you are in France. Can you get me an autograph from Tom Hanks for wee jessie behind the bar at the Commercial?' I hope she wrote one herself to keep the wee soul happy. She'll never know the difference.

On the Tinkerbell front, I approached Bossman Billy and Bossman Jay today individually. They both fell about laughing at the thought of me as a fairy. I really must start being more girlie.

Aside from the obvious worries (sleep deprivation, physical exhaustion and possible breakdown) they both think I should go for it. The problem of being Tinkerbell combined with my ever-increasing thigh width is that they'll need the bloody Finnieston crane to make me fly. I now know how Orville felt . . .

Friday the 19th

Tomorrow night is the Eurovision Song Contest with Daz Sampson (who?) representing the UK in their fiftieth year. The song is a sort of rap, although I am sure the 'c' fell off the description.

The competition has been ruined in recent years by awful songs and political voting but there have been some right crackers in the past:
- Sandie Shaw – 'Puppet on a String' – winner, 1967
- Cliff Richards – 'Congratulations' – 2nd, 1968
- Abba – 'Waterloo' – winner, 1974
- Brotherhood of Man – 'Save All Your Kisses' – winner, 1976
- Bardo – 'One Step Further' – 7th, 1982
- Gina G – 'Oh Aah, Just a Little Bit' – 8th, 1996.

Oh, and lest we forget, Robin's panto pal Dana who won in 1970, although she apparently wouldn't sing their duet live on stage in Aberdeen (post-Big in Falkirk, I can relate to her trepidation).

My favourite song was possibly Liverpool's singing chipmunk Sonia back in 1993 with 'Better the Devil You Know' (not the Kylie one) or the classic Buck's Fizz 1981 winner 'Making Your Mind Up'. However, Travel Gav, our Abba tribute-band singing travel guru IS Mr Eurovision. He hosts parties every year and could go on *Mastermind* with his immeasurable knowledge on the subject. He is hilarious on air, getting more and more carried away with trivia and conspiracy theories: 'Malta robbed poor Sonia. It was shocking.' and 'Ireland threw it one year because they couldn't afford to host it again, honestly. I know from an insider.'

Things really kick off when I mention I liked Michael Ball's song 'One Step Out of Time'. Robin refuses to believe he sang a Eurovision song and the phones go into meltdown. Michael Ball, the slightly portly but handsome-in-his-own-way singer, famous from West End musicals, is, it transpires, a bit of a favourite with the ladies of central Scotland.

Veronica calls in: 'Michael Ball is sensational. I go to every concert with my daughter and now my granddaughter. We all sit listening calmly to the beautiful classical songs then get up and dance down the front when he plays "One Step Out of Time", particularly if he is wearing his leather trousers.'

I have to confess I have been to FOUR Michael Ball concerts. It started off as a selfless gesture for my pal Lynn's birthday, for along with Bruce Willis, he was her ideal man. I only bought the tickets for a laugh and was mortified when I was spotted by one of the guys I knew from the pub working at the concert hall.

He was actually very good, Michael Ball not the steward, and on Lynn's behalf I returned again and again. However guys, unless you are Enrique Iglesias, please stay away from leather trousers, you hear?

We do get a great text in saying: 'What are you talking about, he played for Rangers and Everton.' There are TWO Michael Balls, but only one of them – and I checked with Travel Gav to make exactly sure – sang in Eurovision. He was placed second in 1992.

I love eccentric people to bits and enjoyed the e-mail sent in by Brian Murray from Airdrie at 7.57 a.m. It read:

> 'Hi Cat,
>   Did you know your online broadcast is about 30 seconds behind the radio broadcast? (I didn't.)
>   Did you also know I have too much time on my hands this morning? (Clearly!)
>   Great show, Brian.'

The Renegade is caught on our show for £5,000 this morning by Chris from Cumbernauld who is the most shattered winner of all time. He has been chasing him for three weeks and sounds genuinely fatigued with the mental and physical effort of it all.

Just think, with £5,000 Travel Gav could actually take his pals to the Eurovision Song Contest. On second thoughts, what a bad idea: I envisage a sequined cat-suited Abba looka-likey rammy if the UK were given their usual '*nul points*'. It is and will remain a small-screen, erm, experience . . .

Monday the 22nd

I am in agony this morning. I am nursing a full body's worth of strained muscles from over-exertion at the weekend. I'm afraid my going-better-than-expected running regime didn't even come into the equation; yes my friends, I have been wounded by Girls Aloud at a pyjama party. In my ever in-creasing catalogue of bizarre injuries this has to be one of the best yet.

My lifelong friend Denise sent her husband Russell and little baby Gregor packing for the night and invited all the Milngavie Posse up for an overnight adventure for her thirty-fourth birthday (at showbiz twenty-six I am obviously much younger than all my pals from school now). Jane, Debbie, Rhona, Lynn, Denise and I have been pals since school and we still meet up once a month; only Eilidh who moved to Wales, Julie who is pregnant and Tracey in London are missing. Collectively we have been through pretty much everything life can throw at you, both good and bad, and I love them all to bits.

Anyway, we all went out for a meal and a wee pub crawl in Drymen before heading back to Denise's at midnight (they are getting old, remember) where the madness really kicked in. As a wee extra present I bought her a CD and DVD called *Dance Party* which is a compilation of the cheesiest disco tracks which have set dances for them. The DVD breaks down each song and talks you through the routines move by move.

Well, with the pyjamas now on and the bubbly open, we stuck on track one which was 'Love Machine' by Girls Aloud. The dance teacher turned out to be a brash shouty Glaswegian who was actually very good at taking us through the moves wiggle by wiggle.

Needless to say, after half an hour, we thought we WERE Girls Aloud (bagsy me not the ginger one . . .) and if we had stopped here I would have been fine. But no, TWO AND A HALF HOURS later having completed the 'Macarena', 'Follow My Leader', and that song by Las Ketchup that goes 'a-hey a-ha a-hey a la la la la', there we were flapping our arms and perfecting the Fast Food Rockers. I had never realised there was actually a dance to this modern classic banned from Scottish Slimmers classes everywhere: 'A Pizza Hut, a Pizza Hut, Kentucky Fried Chicken and a Pizza Hut'.

I'm sure there is no gain without pain; I really hurt today so at this rate I shall be winning the 5km, not merely participating. I have an ice pack for every part of my strained body and still can't get 'Love Machine' out of my head. That said, it was a top weekend and I am giggling at the thought of our frenzied dancing through a pretty dull and uneventful Monday.

The Renegade is in Charlotte Square in Edinburgh this morning, but as it is a public holiday in the east it is pretty quiet and he escapes without capture. At lunchtime he heads to Dunoon, again he escapes, but I do hope he left a calling card for wee Jessie behind the bar at the Commercial.

For the record, Finland won the Eurovision Song Contest with a tongue-in-cheek heavy rock entry nobody will remember in two weeks' time, but the entire band were dressed like scary monsters and that at least earned them some novelty points. Having never even finished in the top twenty before, thousands of fans turned out on the streets of Helsinki to party the night away; I am quite worried on behalf of their nation.

The UK finished nineteenth out of twenty-four which was pretty fair for a song that was pretty foul. If only Girls Aloud had been our entry, ageing pyjama-clad girlies all over Scotland would be shouting 'TWELVE POINTS' at the telly.

Tuesday the 23rd

I am in total shock. I have just returned from my first experience of the Real Radio Renegade in action. Sitting in the studio while it's all going on can be mental at times, but the real chaos is always in the heart of the area people perceive him to be in.

This morning he came on at 8.15 a.m. with the clue 'What is the difference between snowmen and snowwomen?' The answer of course is snowballs, which could only mean one place, the Tunnock's factory in Uddingston. (I did have a chuckle at the guy who swore the answer was Whiteinch – naughty.)

In a complete spur-of-the-moment decision I announce I'm going to go and see what all the fuss is about. I can honestly say I expected it to be busy but not the total and utter mayhem which unfolded. I pinched the services of poor Ian, the commercial producer from upstairs, to be my driver because he lives in Uddingston and could navigate a quick approach. I called Robin from inside the Real Radio branded car heading towards the town and instantly we were peeped and waved at from pretty much every car, van and lorry on the road.

However, NOTHING prepared me for the frantic insanity of downtown Uddingston Main Street. Mothers with prams, men in vans, old ladies, joggers, workies, ambulance staff, Tunnock's workers, butchers, bakers and I'm sure there would've been a candlestick maker too if I'd asked, all running through the streets, over gardens, up back lanes, into shops and cafés, asking on the street, asking in cars (not allowed) and asking at bus stops, 'ARE YOU THE REAL RADIO RENEGADE?'

I met the regular hunters the Coatbridge Posse, the Parkhouse Duo, the Viewpark Virgins (aye, right), the Sisters of No Mercy and Camouflage Chris. Not to mention hundreds of others who were either out for the first time because it was local, or still on his trail after three years. I met a lady who had missed an appointment with her son's headmaster, a woman who was on the sick from Tunnock's asking everybody including her supervisor outside the factory, plus a bloke in full running gear who usually jogs round Strathclyde Park but ran to Uddingston from Burnside to see what all the fuss was about.

Then a lovely wee man called Jim Lowe came out of nowhere bearing the finest gift in the world. 'There you go Cat, I thought you may need sustenance, I got you a roll and sausage with potato scone.' I love our listeners.

I broadcast live from outside the factory, the main street, outside a pub and inside the Tunnock's shop in the main street, each time interviewing whichever particular hunter

was closest. Mrs Turner from the shop gave me a big bag
of goodies to take back to the studio and I quickly realised
Renegade hunting is bad for the health on many levels.

At one point, whilst I was talking on air on the main
street, Robin asked any cars listening to toot their horns. The
sound was deafening. Every vehicle in the gridlocked street,
which must have been about 700 cars and lorries, hit the horn
at the same time. I could not speak for laughing.

With only one calling card found at the bank, courtesy
of Margaret from Larkhall, the town went nuts and how he
escaped capture I shall never know. I have to admit I had a
blast and can see – prize money aside – why the competition
is such a success. People become friends with strangers and
have a laugh running through the streets.

I felt guilty when the bounty period ended with no winner. I was outside the factory with about 200 people and 100
cars all watching me and listening to me simultaneously on
their radios. The adrenalin really was flowing and it took
me almost half an hour to get back to the car after talking
to so many lovely folk. I was just about to get into the car
clutching my lovely bag of cakes courtesy of Tunnock's when
a big frozen-food lorry beeped, a huge guy wound down the
window and bellowed: 'Oi Cat – a roll and sausage and a bag
a cakes? Nice to see the diet's going well . . .' Ahhhhhhhhh-
hhhhhhhhhhhh!

Still, it was a scrumptious strawberry tart. What?! It is
another fruit portion surely . . .

Wednesday the 24th

Get your wallets out folks, the great airport rip-off is heading
your way. Glasgow Airport has announced plans to charge
ordinary people a pound for picking up their own passengers.
Not only this, it will cost a pound every fifteen minutes if
their flight is delayed. Given that airport taxis are extortionate anyway, I think this is ridiculous. Pick-up points will be

designated at the far end of the car park, which is fine if you are fit and it is dry, but imagine elderly people with cases or a stressed family with kids having to walk even five minutes in the rain, a total logistical nightmare.

Robin's wind-up gene kicks in, he thinks it is a great idea to encourage people to use public transport and he goes further by saying all planes should stop flying by 10.00 p.m. at night to give the people of Paisley a good night's kip.

To be honest, having lived under the flight path for twenty-seven of my showbiz twenty-six years, I can relate to the last one. That Air Canada jumbo makes the Harvey house shake! Naturally, Robin is the sitting target to everybody who doesn't have a chauffeur to take them there. I think he enjoys it, you know, and rises to his subject magnificently.

Ninety-nine per cent of the nation agrees with me, hurrah I am the goodie again. However, Jay (not of the Bossman variety) suggested this: 'Maybe they could put the cars in a holding pattern like they do with the planes. They could do big circles on the outskirts of the airport until their flight comes in.'

Mrs Turner in the Tunnock's shop has a lot to answer for this morning as my diet once again snowballs, quite literally, out of control. Porridge is abandoned for a snowball, a teacake and one of the treacle scones from the bakery microwaved for ten seconds and dripping in lovely melting full-fat gloriously calorific golden butter.

It's not all bad though, folks. I have my gym bag in the car and believe it or not I am actually looking forward to going. I reckon a large proportion of the fitness battle is mental and at the moment I am 'in the zone' as some fresh-faced skinny-assed gym assistant would probably say, sipping an iso-something drink and munching a carrot.

We are sounding like the healthiest breakfast show in the world at the moment with both Baz and Robin going almost every day. Robin did a forty-minute workout yesterday before nipping back into the changing rooms to change after one of the punters told him his shorts were on back to front. Baz met the elderly lady at his gym again, and – drum roll, folks – told her his mum was still fine but wouldn't be down this week.

I'm also getting quite nervous about Friday. In a moment of weakness and dimply-bummed depression, I have agreed to be Andrew from the gym's lardy-bottomed guinea pig for testing his new toy. I could probably save myself the effort and just hang about the airport; with all the lifting, carrying and walking we'll need to do, even Americans will be slim by the time they reach their lift . . .

Thursday the 25th

Our old pal Jack is making headline news this morning. Our esteemed First Minister (or that wee bastard McConnell as the smokers like to call him) has announced he will NOT be supporting England in the World Cup. Despite the fact most Scots, if they were perfectly honest, probably won't be supporting them either, this bold statement has caused a right old commotion throughout the not-very-United Kingdom.

English commentator and talking chin Jimmy Hill says he is 'a disgrace'; fellow Labour politician and PM-in-waiting Gordon Brown is shocked. He will be supporting England. Funny what the allure of the top job can do to one's loyalties. Jack, bless his wee Lycra Speedos, has even admitted he will support Trinidad and Tobago when they face the auld enemy because they have 'home-based Scottish players.' Nice one.

We are currently playing an alternative World Cup song on the show at the moment which pays tribute to St Johnstone star Jason Scotland. It is a cheesy ditty with a catchy chorus which goes: 'We can still support Scotland, Scotland, Jason Scotland,' and also boasts the marvellous lyrics, 'The Tartan Army are on the go with Trinidad and To-ba-go'. Jason Scotland has to be one of the best names in football. The only ones that come close are Danny Invincible at Kilmarnock and Emmanuel Panther who played for my beloved Thistle.

I have to confess to a shameful incident after a match at Firhill once where he had played one of his first games. I wanted to interview him and asked Michael Max, the Jags marketing manager, if Emmanuel, a strapping big exotic-looking black lad with model looks, spoke English. When I heard him shout to his team-mate in broad Glaswegian, 'Haw mate, gaunae wait fur me I'll no be long,' I learned never to judge a player by his moniker. Turns out he was brought up in Maryhill; one can only assume his parents hoped he'd be a porn star.

Anyway, in the biggest U-turn in history, Robin claims to be backing T & T too. I remind him of the day months ago when I decided to back Togo (T & T hadn't qualified yet) and he went mental at me on air saying we had to support our southern cousins. This worm hasn't just turned – he has done bloody somersaults rolling down a hill. It is his wind-up gene again; I'm convinced he can't help it. The Trinidad and Tobago Tartan Army campaign is gathering steam though. People phone in bemoaning the lack of available T & T strips for seven-year-olds in Alloa. I'm sure there will be plenty more to report as World Cup fever kicks off.

I am actually writing this entry on the train to Edinburgh where I'm heading to meet the lovely people from Black & White Publishing about this book. To say I don't have a clue what I am letting myself in for is an understatement. So far I have written 35,000 words and nobody has really passed comment. I am either in for the big thumbs up, or the biggest shock of my life if my ramblings don't match their expectations. At the moment this book has no title, no cover, no pictures and no direction. I hope that all, apart from the direction (my life has none so why should my book), will be settled by teatime.

I wonder if Jack will buy a copy. He might need something to pass the time if the southern Members of Parliament

banish him to the Tower of London.
all . . .

Friday the 2

All good on the book front: they didn
the mysterious world of publishing (ᵖᵒⁱⁿᵗᵉ
to let on) and I only made one glaring error. When admiring
their spacious open plan loft offices – the kind of trendy place
you see in adverts, all wooden floors and exotic foliage – I
commented on how it must be wonderful to let the creative
juices flow by working in such a wonderful open space. 'Er,
yes, but we only moved in last week and we don't have the
furniture yet,' Campbell the main man graciously explained.

Alison from Black & White has agreed to my idea of letting
the listeners choose the book title, which should be entertaining. More on this to come once the Renegade finishes.

Today my bottom becomes public property. Robin kindly
tells the nation I have agreed to be the sample bum for Andrew
at the gym's new cellulite-busting machine. In the interests of
pushing the fitness boundaries and editorial hilarity I have
waved goodbye to any last ounce/pound/stone of remaining
personal dignity. My orange-peel *derrière* is now water-cooler
chat. If only I'd stuck to that and not white wine, I might not
be here in the first place.

Anyway friends, let me explain. Endermologie, I am
informed from the scary-looking pamphlet, achieves cellulite
reduction perfectly. The Cellu 6 machine that will be used on
me 'restores metabolic exchanges by dramatically increasing
blood flow, lymphatic drainage and elasticity of the septa.
Independent motorised roller-like cylinders treat the skin
which treats cellulite from the inside, out. This is a gentle,
deep and soothing treatment making it possible to have the
defined figure you once only dreamed of!'

And THEY added the last cheeky exclamation mark,
almost knowing every psychologically damaged fat girl read-

the leaflet still harbours ambitions of resembling Wonder
Woman in her prime.

After much persuasion from Andrew along the lines of
'It doesn't hurt', 'It just feels like a really nice massage' and
'Your bum will look amazing', I finally agree when he adds,
'Go on, I'll let you have a go for nothing.' Ha, bingo (wings)!
OK, then.

Robin, who has never had a pound of excess fat in his
organic-soya-filled life, kindly tells our listeners: 'Today Cat
is off to get her cellulite-covered bum sanded.' He adds, 'The
machine is just like the Black and Decker ones you get at B &
Q – she lies on a DIY work table and a beauty therapist gives
her bum the once-over.'

This scenario captures the imagination and I'm touched,
although thankfully not literally, by the number of truckers
offering me the use of their 'equipment in their sheds'. After
promising to return on Monday wearing a name badge in
case nobody recognised me, I headed off for my 'sanding'.

What I was not prepared for was the horrific outfit that
you have to wear to get the treatment. Each patient/victim
is given their own see-through white body stocking, kind of
like a romper suit for adults made of nylon. Basically like a
big pair of tights with arms. Now I have a real phobia about
wearing clingy clothes; despite the fact I am now back down
to a comfortable size fourteen (come on, that's quite normal)
I still buy tops that are a sixteen or eighteen so they hang
really loose. I never tuck in anything, tops MUST have arms
and I never EVER buy white.

Amy, my inflictor, told me to put it on and stand next to
the couch to be measured. This is my other phobia. Despite
the fact she must have seen a thousand bodies worse than
mine, I was a gibbering wreck. My arms were clutched round
my blubbery bits and I breathed in everything I could, which
is stupid when it comes to being measured. The humiliation
partially over, it was time for the main event. The power but-

ton was switched on and 'Barbarella', as she has been named, kicked into life.

Well, I don't know what I expected but it was actually quite pleasant. It felt like a wee mini-steamroller going up and down my legs and over my bum. Amy, who was by now bemused at my extreme awkwardness in the white suit and at my stressed-out self-analysis ('I look like a big fat sperm!') performed wonders keeping me calm and explaining what was going on. When the rollers changed to a sucking action, like a big vacuum, it was the end of me. I thought my arse was going to disappear up a big tube and all I could think of was the tabloid headlines. I'm sure Tory MPs do this sort of thing at the weekends.

The sucking action actually tickled quite a lot and I ended up howling with laughter as the poor girl tried to do her job; it got so bad she had to join in and we were both helpless for about three minutes as my hysterical guffaws rendered me a hopeless case. The wee treatment room is next to the gym and God only knows what the muscle-bound hunks thought was going on. I can only assume that from the amount of laughter they should have a queue a mile long for feel-good sessions.

Once normal service had been resumed – that is, I stepped out of the white suit – I actually had a look at my bum and legs. Not too much difference but they did feel great. At this juncture Amy kindly informed me that you need at least SIX treatments to see any major difference.

'Andrew didn't tell me that!' I howled.

'Oh, did he not?' she smiled knowingly. 'When shall I book your next session?' They are good this lot, and as they say on *Mastermind*, I've started so I'll finish.

It is only a shame it is the weekend, and with a night out with my pals, a trip to the cinema and a christening to go to, I am sensing I may need more than six sessions to shift the orange peel that is becoming more of a grove. I wonder if little baby Ishbel needs a new outfit for the big day; I have just the thing . . .

Monday the 29th

Today is another May bank holiday – and another day that we're unfortunately NOT allowed off because of the pesky Real Radio Renegade.

We ease our way gently into the swing of things by putting 'Stairway to Heaven' up against Guns N' Roses' lengthy classic 'November Rain' in an early morning battle of the bands. Led Zeppelin wins this time. Result, seven minutes and twenty seconds of porridge-making excellence.

It is the last week of the Real Radio Renegade competition and already the regular hunters are phoning in saying they will have a massive void in their lives. To be honest, I have had enough now and can't wait to get shot of him. It is a fantastic promotion but also very draining on the presenters. We never get to leave the studio when it is on in case the magic line goes, the phones are constantly ringing and I can't go anywhere during the run without being asked what he looks like and where he will be next. As I have mentioned a million times on air, we do NOT know any more than you guys so it will be quite exciting to finally meet him come Friday.

Today is called manic Monday. He will have something to do with public transport and he says, 'I am Back And Angry.' He is worth two grand. Suggestions range from Buchanan Bus Station (he was there before), any place ending with a cross like St George's Cross, Glasgow Cross, Toll Cross, Edinburgh Airport (he was there yesterday and got caught) to Glasgow Airport.

Brian from Uddingston e-mailed in to say, 'Take first letters of the clue and it says BAA that is the British Airports Authority, try Glasgow Airport.' It is always a very difficult and frustrating show for us to do when we don't really have a clue where to send people. We can't create frenzy if there are potentially ten places for him to be, we can only hope a calling card is found early to help people out. I think people would be surprised at how much Robin and I really want him caught on our show. It does become quite addictive; I trawl the internet for clues and get quite shaky if the magic line goes.

By 9.27 a.m., we are still none the wiser with no calling cards to report. By 9.28 a.m. the secret line is flashing and a stunned Martin Banks from Bellshill is on the line to claim £2,000. The Renegade WAS in Glasgow Airport and Martin is an emotional wreck. 'This is my FORTY-FIRST bounty period. My wife and I have found eleven calling cards. I can't believe I have finally caught him.' The poor guy even explains how the Renegade was caught just two metres in front of him by three lassies in Wishaw. I reckon he has probably spent about two grand in petrol on his trail, but we have one very happy bank holiday winner.

The M8 is dead after the show and I get home and back to bed within twenty minutes. I sleep for three glorious hours and wake up not knowing if I still have to go to work or not.

The big run is less than a fortnight away so I am now off to shift my not quite so dimply ass on to a treadmill. I bolster my confidence, safe in the knowledge I can now run over FOUR times 'Stairway to Heaven' . . . surely that is enough to get round Glasgow Green . . .

Tuesday the 30th

It is official – I am a fairy. Confirmation from the Pavilion arrived today, they want me to be Tinkerbell and I shall fly, oh yes I shall. I text my dad straight away, who I know has never been more proud in his life. 'Ah, Toots – it is what you were made for. You were never meant to be sensible. I want a season ticket.' And he means it.

My mum, as ever, has much more sense. She knows that with EIGHTY-SEVEN performances, two shows a day for nine weeks, PLUS getting up at 3.30 a.m. for the *Breakfast Show*, I shall be a physical wreck. 'It's just not possible, you'll kill yourself,' she frets.

'Ach yir arse, she'll just sprinkle some of that fairy dust on her heid and get on with it,' Faither replies in a slightly less placatory fashion than I thought she deserved.

My dad, you see, is a seasoned professional in the theatre, having toured the world playing his fiddle and starring in sketches with the White Heather Club and the *Lex McLean Show*. He has also worked with Francie and Josie, Andy Cameron, Johnny Beattie, the Alexander Brothers, Fran and Anna, Billy Connolly, Tom Conti, Jimmy Logan, Calum Kennedy, Peter Morrison, Alasdair Gillies and pretty much every famous Scottish entertainer who ever embraced the rich variety tradition.

'You need to get the downstairs dressing room near the stage,' he adds. There is no point in even suggesting to him that the layout may have changed in the past thirty years; he is off on one and I let him enjoy the ride. 'The Pavilion can be the best audience in the world; the Glasgow public know how to enjoy themselves. If you get a good reaction at a full house you'll never get a better feeling in your life.' I'm starting to get goose-pimples. 'That said, Toots, if you're shit they'll let you know,' he concludes, not very helpfully.

He then goes into one of his many tales of yore where the entire *Lex McLean Show*, including backing dancers, and the Rangers first team ended up at a party back at the house I was brought up in. My brother Scott was just a toddler, and my mum was given no warning about the large impromptu party she had to host. Typically, she rose to the challenge and was soon cheerfully dishing out drinks and nibbles to everybody.

She is so unfazed by showbiz it is wonderful. Apart from Tom Jones and Peter Morrison, you could bring home any movie star or footballer in the world and she wouldn't have a clue who they were. And so it transpired. Passing over a beer to a polite man perched on the couch, she asked: 'So, are you one of the backing dancers at the show too?'

'Erm, not quite,' answered blushing Rangers and Scotland star of the moment Alex Willoughby, much to the amusement of his team-mate, Scotland centre forward Jim Forrest, who added, 'Aye, but he plays like one of them!'

I laugh heartily at this because my mum is still like that – I could show up with José Mourinho, Johnny Depp and Orlando Bloom (oh yes please . . .) and she would think they were Jags fans I knew from going to the games.

However, it turns out our Cathy, my mum, Knightswood girl and fine upstanding member of the community could be a bit of a dark horse too: 'Actually . . .' she teases ominously, 'did your dad ever tell you that I was offered a job at the Pavilion too?' Bloody hell, what have I started? 'The choreographer of the *Lex McLean Show*, at the same party, followed me about for two hours convincing me to become a dancer. He told me I had the legs for it and that with four weeks' training I would be on the stage and wowing the audiences.'

My dad clearly has no such recollection. However, prior to the great drying out of 1984 that is not particularly unusual.

To me this is the funniest thing, because my mum is quite shy and very unassuming. She complements Faither's eccentricities with a reassuring calm, although I bet she could have high-kicked with the best of them, given the chance. She did have a cracking set of pins, and I blame my squat globular physique firmly on the Harvey side.

There will be a photo call soon to announce the full pantomime line-up and I've been asked to give them my sizes for a fairy costume. I wonder if it is rude to ask for an extra large one, in black, with a hood, I'm sure Tinkerbell needs bringing up to date. Oh my God, I'm a fairy, I can fly, I can fly.

I send forty-eight hyper fairy-themed text messages and go for a lie down. Today my life has officially become a pantomime, and I love it . . .

Wednesday the 31st

Taxi for Harvey but not in Edinburgh – I think I shall walk thank you very much. A survey out today reveals a three-mile taxi ride in the capital is the fifth most expensive in the world. Only in Oslo, Geneva, Osaka and London will it cost you more.

At 7.00 p.m. on a Friday night, a three-mile journey in Edinburgh will cost you a whopping £7.00. When you consider the same journey will only cost you £4.82 in Paris, one of the most expensive cities in Europe, it is clear to see why home-grown Edinburgers are not chuffed with the latest findings. We are bombarded with calls from people who now get taxis from places like Dalkeith to come into Edinburgh for them because it works out cheaper. Texts include:

'I would rather get wet and sair feet than pay for an EMBRA taxi.' Tam, Embra.

'Edinburgh taxis? – don't get me started!' Dougie, the Edinburgh bus driver.

'They've got green taxi lanes now which should make them faster and cheaper but they are getting more and more expensive.' Ted, Livingston.

Taxi drivers fight back in their droves insisting it is Edinburgh council who set the fares and they have no choice. The Glasgow taxi drivers are absolutely loving this though, and also call in pointing out how they are a much friendlier bunch than 'those robbing b******s in the east'.

A guy phones in saying he reckons they have a 'weegie surcharge' adding on an extra few quid if you sound like you're from Glasgow. We have lots of lovely Edinburgh taxi-driving listeners who would never do such a terrible thing, would they?

Anyway, I can't concentrate today because I am having a real mid-life crisis. I've been house-hunting lately because my flat is the size of a cardboard box and I've come to the conclusion the houses I want and can afford are two entirely different entities. As a result I think I might now stay in my pokey wee flat and buy a VW campervan so I can have a new location to wake up in every weekend. Just think, open spaces, the great outdoors, a wee cooker and an accordion roof that goes up should I invite guests over for a party.

I could park next to Jinty McGinty's pub in Ashton Lane and flake out at closing time; hell, I could make a fortune from cooking hamburgers throughout the night and offering B & B. It's a sure fire money-making winner and now, with Mr W. playing devil's advocate on the internet, I have found my baby on eBay. She is called Bluebell, a type 2 Volkswagen, pale blue, 66,680 miles from 1975. With an oak veneer interior and fully working extendable roof, she is nothing short of magnificent.

My only previous encounter with eBay was the trampette I've only used once. Somehow clicking the 'place bid' button is a lot scarier when it is almost three grand. I shall do the sensible thing and sleep on, not in, it for the time being. Actually, I should just buy it and start doing taxi shuttle runs through in Edinburgh; I could retire by next Friday . . .

june

Thursday the 1st

I like to think I am quite an observant person, but today I am stitched up like Bagpuss. I failed to notice Baz and Robin scheming and chuckling behind my back as one of their evil master-plans came to fruition.

I had a cracking wee story lined up for my tale in the newspaper review section, when Robin goes off on an unexpected tangent. Cliff Richard's 'Summer Holiday' is the musical bed in the background and I think he has lost the plot. 'Cat, tell the nation what you nearly did yesterday.' I give him my finest vacant look, which I'm sure works a treat on radio. 'Tell our lovely listeners what you nearly bought on eBay yesterday Catster.' I have no choice but to own up.

'Yesterday, I thought about buying a thirty-one-year-old VW campervan I have never seen before.' Saying it out loud makes it seem even worse.

'Well Catster, here is the man selling it, speak to Nick . . .' Yes, somehow they had tracked down the seller's mobile number and lined him up for a bit of banter. The funny thing I learn later is that the man, from Dunbar, initially refused to go on air because he thought it was a wind-up!

I am mortified, but engage in some polite motor chat with Nick who reveals he is selling his van because he has just had a baby, and that the wardrobe is great for hanging wetsuits in. Everyone in the studio is in fits, I have only just got to grips with wearing the horrific white suit to get my bum sanded in a private locked room with Amy: to go out in public in a wetsuit is as likely as me knocking back the divine yet dirty Mr Mourinho on a night out.

'What do you think Bobby Harvey would say?' Robin asks, knowing fine well my dad would tell me not to be so bloody stupid.

'Erm, I spoke to him last night and he wasn't terribly keen on the idea,' I explain.

'Well Catster,' says increasingly evil Robin with a glint in his eye, 'Why don't we find out? It just so happens that we have your dad on the other line.' And true enough, Bobby is ready and waiting once again to steal the show.

'Ah Toots, the problem with a 1975 VW is the ageing chassis and let's face it, you know all about that.' Great, not only is my dad live on the radio, he is whacking out all the comedy lines.

I haven't been so embarrassed since he came on a year ago with Pink Pussy, my first ever toy that you wind up to get it to play tunes (again set up by my so-called chum the Robster). (I am sure you can guess the e-mails I received that week from people trying to procure wind-up pink pussies!) So despite being a mature and worldly-wise showbiz twenty-six years old, hired for my ability to ad-lib and react quickly, I am reduced to a squirming blushing teenager and all I can say in return is 'Da-aa-aad!'

Robin and Baz are in stitches and I vow revenge. The eBay deadline is nine o'clock tonight and I think I am now too embarrassed to make a bid. OK, the fact Nick is looking for six grand and not the £2,500 I may have been willing to pay has quite a lot to do with it too.

Mr Cat breathes a huge sigh of relief although he may live to regret it. I've found an authentic Romany gypsy caravan for sale that looks amazing, and I would need a horse with that too . . .

Friday the 2nd

The sun is shining, it's Friday and we are right in the mood for badness. This morning we get to meet the Renegade and we're expecting an influx of people to the station. Only people with calling cards have been invited because of the complete mayhem it caused the last time. We have been told, under no circumstances to make it an open invite, for health and safety reasons. We have also been told we must NOT use the George Foreman grill in the studio.

As Baz sticks on the third sausage and I spread ketchup in a roll, it transpires the sizzling noise can be heard right the way through the news bulletin.

'It's a lovely day to meet the Renegade' says Robin being good. 'Let's make it a gala occasion,' he adds, teetering on the brink. 'I think we should have a fast-food van for the hunters and an ice-cream van and rides.'

Brilliant – he has gone for it. We spoke previously about how much trouble we thought we might get into for this and agreed to throw caution to the wind. I wave my Real Radio career goodbye (for the third time incidentally) by adding enthusiastically: 'We have a great big bit of grass at the side, we could fit in waltzers and pony rides too.' We are told later that Bossman Billy nearly swerved off the road at this juncture.

Within minutes 'Gordon from the shows' is in touch offering us a 200ft crane to bungee from, a lovely old man with a coconut shy offers his services and Senga with a snack van says she is *en route*.

Maggi, Bossman Billy's enforcer, walks past the window looking stern; she looks in the studio window and runs her finger over her throat in that 'you pair of fannies, you are for it now' motion.

Tommy from Cranhill calls in: 'I was in ma bed but my brother's just called me and told me I had to go down to your studios. Do you really want me?'

Robin: 'Eh, what do you do, Tommy?'

Tommy: 'I'm the Cranhill Icey. I'm yir man if you want a double nougat or a ninety-nine.'

Me: 'Fantastic, get yourself down here Tommy, I'm starving.'

At this point, Maggi, who NEVER comes into the studio with the red light on, barges into the studio with the red light on. 'We specifically told you NOT to do this,' she says on air, not knowing she is on air. 'You will be in trouble if this gets out of hand, see you upstairs when Billy gets in,' and she storms out.

The Renegade, Jim Curtis, a thirty-four-year-old actor from London, comes into the madness – a studio wafting of burning sausage and phones going mental with people asking about the dimensions of the grass trying to work out if they could set up ghost trains and jumpy castles before half-eight in the morning.

Jim has been in *EastEnders* and *The Bill*; I recognise him, but don't watch either of these shows. I ask him what else he has been in. 'I used to model love dilemma photo stories in my pants for Deirdre's photo casebook in the *Sun*.' I've clearly never seen him before in my life.

We are inundated with calls from people thanking him for a fantastic month of fun, asking him questions and generally trying to cop off with the lad who IS pretty good-looking and pictured in today's *Scottish Sun*.

Suddenly we hear chimes. The phone goes and it's Tommy. 'Where shall I park, do you want to hear my chimes . . . ?' We roll about laughing with the bells ringing over the phone and through the so-called soundproof windows. Within minutes I am munching a splendid Crolla ice cream with flake and raspberry sauce. It is fair to say my diet is not going well this morning.

Tommy parks his ice-cream van right outside the studio window and caters for the Renegade hunters who come to meet their elusive man. The stories of near misses are hilarious; a nice old dear tells me she saw Jim in Airdrie. She recognises him straight away and kicks herself for not asking. Kenny from the Parkhouse Duo is there; he has about a million calling cards and still doesn't win the card draw. If he fell in the Clyde, he'd sink to the bottom, poor lad.

Once the madness dies down I return to my computer to find an e-mail from Bossman Billy. It reads: 'Come and see me before you leave.' Uh oh, here we go. Leave, does he mean leave, as in for the day, or for ever? I walk into his office and he has his best poker face on (what do they teach at Larkhall schools?)

'I've got this for you,' he says before handing over a new copy of *AutoTrader* open at the VW campervan page. 'If you are serious about buying one, my mate can keep an eye out. He's a brilliant mechanic and will sort you out. Oh, and by the way, great show today.'

I love that man. Our MD is a maniac and it's fantastic, and the good news is we were also forgiven by Maggi when she realised Tommy's van sold fags 30p cheaper than the shops. Fridays are great.

Monday the 5th

Weekends go so quickly, and once again circumstances plotted against my attempts at having a restorative one. With the Renegade over, I decided that on Friday I would like to relax and recover from what has been an exceptionally tiring five weeks.

I booked a very cheap room in Dunblane Hydro for me and Mr Cat for one night through a late deal site on the internet. There was a button saying, 'Click here for a three-course dinner for £10.' Now the Hydro is a four-star hotel so this was obviously a bargain.

I assumed, given the cheap nature of the deal, the hotel was empty and desperate for custom. Big mistake. On arrival, we couldn't get parked in the car park, the overflow car park

OR the staff only car park. When I finally abandoned (lovingly, Uncle Arnold) the car and walked into reception I was greeted by a male nun and a female in a Mexican outfit with a painted moustache.

'Oh, you must be our internet booking,' said the very sheepish receptionist. Not a good sign. Well it turns out the hotel had been booked for a conference for the Scottish Wholesale Association for three days. The hotel was told NOT to sell any vacant rooms as they were preparing for a right old shindig. However, as fate would have it, internet bookings through a third party could not be cancelled. I only booked on Thursday, so they couldn't warn me.

'It may be noisy in your room I'm afraid.' Great, my hopes of a quiet night evaporated, and when a giant Dalmatian introduced himself as one of the organisers chuckling, 'Oh, you must be the internet couple, how funny is that,' I knew what was going to happen next. 'You might as well come and join us because you probably won't get much sleep. Oh, and it is a free bar.'

Twist my rubber arm! At 4.00 a.m. we said goodbye to our new best pals Sandra, an English teacher from Stranraer and her grocery store husband at the beer bar.

I vow to have a quiet one next weekend, Sunday is the big run, I must NOT be led astray, I am an athlete.

On the show this morning it seems that I was not the only one having a wild time at the weekend. Fiona, our new newsreader, spotted Bossman Billy at the Bon Jovi concert. Actually that does not do the situation justice, Bossman Billy was ON STAGE with Bon Jovi, playing air guitar like a nutcase and high-fiving the main man. Keiron Elliot, the weekend breakfast DJ, who plays 'Duncan' in *River City*, was also at the gig and apparently captured the entire performance (Bossman Billy's not the band's) on video.

We get both on the phone and the interaction is hilarious. Billy admits he may have got a little carried away, Keiron threatens to put the footage on the internet, Billy is forced to concede he got SO excited he danced on stage for an hour and 'nearly took Jon Bon Jovi off his feet with my high-five'.

There is a fantastic picture of the concert in the *Sunday Herald*. The shot is taken during a ballad; it shows 45,000 people snapped from behind, facing Bon Jovi. There is one pair of hands in the air clutching a pint of lager and pointing at the sky. These hands are the same hands that nearly took the star of the show off his feet. Ah, what is it they say, you can take the boy out of Larkhall . . .

Tuesday the 6th

Julia Roberts is the new face of Avon. For two million dollars she is now the glamorous image of the company most famous for their army of wee wummin ringing doorbells and shifting talcum powder sets by the dozen.

My pal Denise's mum, Betty Morrison, was our local Avon lady and had a four-street patch to deal with. I have a vague memory of sneaking through to their posh room (the sitting room, only used by visiting guests and the church elder) and being amazed by the Aladdin's cave of boxes of interesting potions and lotions for her customers. I also recall going out in the pouring rain with Denise who was her designated dispatcher in downpours.

We are inundated by Avon ladies who are still doing a roaring trade. It appears the products are quite trendy now, and their 'Skin So Soft' is still our favourite midgie repellent!

Angie from Fife phones in: 'There are over 400 Avon ladies in my area and we have representation in over 156 countries. Our products are excellent and we go to conferences to keep up with the latest goods and marketing strategies.' That's us told then. I wonder what wee Betty Morrison would make of that.

It seems we are very fond of our Avon ladies:

'My mum is an Avon lady. It is great because I never run out of cosmetics and toiletries. Woo hoo we love Avon!' Kirsty, Fauldhouse.

'I still do Avon and I'm up early this morning because I get my order. We are very much alive and kicking.' Debbie, Kilsyth.

'Shouldn't they be called Avon people nowadays?' Mr PC.

'My mum used to spend a fortune on their lavender Christmas gift packs from a wee woman called Mrs Gallagher. She was about a hundred and used to sit in our kitchen slurping tea really loudly and getting really excited describing new lipsticks.' Chrissie, Edinburgh.

[This final text was a bit naughty but it made us chuckle so I've included it. Profuse apologies to you if you are said Avon lady still in therapy from the incident:]

'I grew up in Partick in the early 1970s. Our Avon lady was robbed one day and all her make-up was stolen. The next day all the local lads were hanging about the cross made up like Ziggy Stardust. It was hilarious.' Gary.

Today Uncle Arnold has outdone himself. We have been given two cars to test drive for a few days, a bright blue Mazda ZX5 convertible for me, and a Mazda RX8 for Robin. Both are sporty wee numbers and go like the clappers. Robin says he feels like a footballer driving his, which is ironic because I feel like a footballer's wife driving mine.

I must get my Visa card out and give Betty Morrison a call; I have the car, now I just need the look. Some nice Avon lip-gloss and a bit of mascara and I'll give Victoria Beckham a run for her money . . . oh no, did I mention the 'run' word? Training is still on and going, well, let's just say it is still on.

Wednesday the 7th

Today is a momentous one – I reveal on the show that I am cataloguing our mischief and misadventures in the form of this book. Robin's face is ashen. As a responsible father of three fantastic kids and husband to Aberdeen's only supermodel, he doesn't want his crazy breakfast antics to be stored for posterity in the annals of Real Radio history. I take on board his concerns and pacify him with the fact that his lovely wife and kids know he is a nutcase anyway.

The working title (it's a publishing term my darlings) for this book so far has been *Cat's Breakfast Diaries*. However, everybody concerned knows we can improve on this. And who better to ask for some much-needed inspiration than our listeners who don't disappoint with their inventive and inspired ideas?

Every now and then we hit on a subject that strikes a chord and today everybody wants to play. The phone board is full and flashing for two hours and we receive pages of texts. The prize, given that we are making this up as we go along, is to have your idea made into the book title. Cracking text titles include:

Through the Catflap, Life Through Cat's Eyes, Cat-stir, The Cat Chronicles, The Cat that Dished the Cream, Cat: The Secret Nine Lives, Really Catty, The Cat amongst the Robins, The Cat's Tails, Careless WhisPURR, Cat's Tails of the Unexpected, The Cat Files, Confessions of a Kitten, Feline Fine, It's a Cat's Life, Lady Catersly, Purrfect Moments, The Cat's Pyjamas, Letting the Cat out of the Bag, Paws for Thought, Memoirs of the Catster, Cat's Claws-it, Cat-astrophe, Cat-alogue of Secrets, When the Cat's Away . . ., The Real Exposé, The Cat Vinci Code, It's a Real Good Life, The Cat's Breakfast, and Get REAL.

I love the really random ones like:

- 10 to Porridge – Des, Airdrie
- Antlers and Champagne – Campbell
- Miaow! – Lorraine
- Radio Gaga – Jimmy the bus driver
- How to Work with Idiots – Sammy
- A Fash called Robster
- Harvey Head Banger – Caroline, Cambuslang
- Working 5 to 9 Ain't No Way to Make a Living – Paula, Falkirk
- The Real Pussy Cat Doll – (with the bit on the back reading 'Don't you wish your hardback was hot like mine?' – Alan, Coatbridge.
- Cat O' Nine Tales – (because it has a sting in it for Robin), Wullie.
- Catster: the REAL Pink Panther – Mo (that bloody car!!)
- Robin – CAT by the Short and Curlies.
- Cat's All Folks – when it comes out you'll both be finished! Stu, Uddingston.

Others picked up on Robin's anguish: Robin's Divorce, Robin Galloway the Obituary and A Tropical Holiday for Mrs G, were some of the classics, while it is safe to say Pussy Galore and Cat Loves Boaby did not make the cut. John phones in to say: 'Why don't you call it "The morning memoirs"? I like the sound of that.' Not bad at all.

'That sounds like a fancy coffee table book, read by ladies who lunch.' I add, liking the upmarket feel.

'Aye, in a Partick café!' quips John, with perfect comic timing.

However, the two that really catch my eye are 'The Cat's Whispers' which Carole Rintoul from Bo'ness, Chris from Bruce's taxis in Falkirk and Kaz suggested, and 'It's a Cat's Life' from John in Govan. I shall e-mail both to the publishing gurus and see if we can hijack Cat's Breakfast Diaries. I also hope to add a subtitle like 'Mischief and mayhem from the Real Breakfast diaries' or 'Breakfast diaries uncut', just to make sure elderly ladies don't expect nice fluffy tales of feline fun with Tammy the Tabby and Terry the Tomcat.

Cecil's Boaby would run a mile . . .

Thursday the 8th

I come in this morning to a nice friendly e-mail from the publishers. They loved The Cat's Whispers, It's a Cat's Life and Careless WhisPURRs. Once again, it is time to ask the audience. We opt for an early morning text vote and at 6.30 a.m. the name of this award-winning ('fastest to discount bargain bucket 2006', surely!) book was decided. It's a Cat's Life came a close second, but the winner by a whisker was *The Cat's Whispers*.

We call up Carole who was first to text it in and she is absolutely delighted. I shall invite her to the launch night, assuming I'm allowed to have one. We are on our best behaviour, remember!

The impact of THAT Friday has been far-reaching; this morning Robin and I are awake and alert and a hundred per cent sober. This is despite the fact we attended the launch of the 'Scotland, Scotland, Jason Scotland' song last night and it was a free bar. I confess we teetered on the brink for a while as we stared lovingly at paws full of free booze tokens, but we still have our warnings ringing in our ears and we stuck to soft drinks. Kind of ironic when we were charged a fiver for a can of Diet Irn-Bru and a sparkling mineral water.

The night was a hoot – what other country in the world would release a World Cup song without qualifying? At the door of the packed pub, I met a really nice bloke called David who I knew from working on the *Fred MacAulay Show*.

'Are you here to see the big song launch?' I asked.

'I'm singing it,' he replied with a wry grin. Oops. David and his pal Richard, who also used to book me as a guest on the *Fred Show*, are 'The Trinidad and Tobago Tartan Army' who wrote and recorded the song. They are in shock at its success and love the celebratory atmosphere of a pub packed with Scotland fans wearing T & T tops and taking pictures of the life-size cardboard cut-outs of St Johnstone's most famous export Jason Scotland, who is wearing a kilt.

The shops have sold out of the record, and new copies are being pressed to try and force it into the national playlists. Apparently if a song is in the top forty it has to be included in national stations' playlists; last night, the latest tracking showed it was sitting at number forty-three in the UK charts, top five in Scotland.

Richard assures us that Robin and I will be on stage on *Top of the Pops* if they are invited. That would be hilarious and we take them up on their offer. Not since the blootered Scotland team of 1982 singing 'We Have a Dream' and swaying all over the stage, will our English neighbours have had such a shock.

Today is my final training run before the big race on Sunday. I head to the gym with a mixture of determination and acute fatigue. This shift really is a killer. Somehow I manage to run without a break for thirty-eight minutes, this is my best yet and I feel confident even the tropical weather predicted for the weekend will not hamper me struggling over that line.

In a double dose of healthy activities I have another session with Amy and her big fancy bum Hoover. This is now my fourth session and I am still a fat pie. That said, it does feel tremendous after the treatment and she did say it will take at least six to see a visible difference.

'The camera arrived so we can take your pictures,' she says with glee. I almost sprint out the door faster than Linford Christie with a firework up his jacksey. Think of the worst photos of you ever taken, and then multiply that feeling of mortification by a million. Close-ups of each bum cheek, a wide (oh the irony) shot of the whole bum area, the tummy from the side, the tummy and thighs from the front – the misery goes on and on.

'Turn your back to me and clench your bum cheeks as hard as you possibly can,' she adds. Now any woman – even the slimmest of wifies – knows that clenching botty cheeks as hard as possible will result in a skin surface like a big dimply Jaffa orange. Anyone carrying a pound or twenty-eight more than they should will have craters like the moon after a mining excavation.

The Polaroids, which incidentally are now destroyed, any budding blackmailers, are jaw-dropping-clutch-on-to-a-table shocking. Let's face it, when have you ever really seen your arse so close? I vow to run every day for the rest of my life and never eat chocolate again. I ask if she has used a magnifying lens, but alas, every inch of the image is my own hand-reared organic free-range *derrière*.

It is a roasting hot sunny Thursday, so I try to keep the power of positive thinking – I feel faintly better acknowledging my bum would be significantly larger if we'd scudded the free Tennent's last night . . .

Friday the 9th

The marketing gurus at Mars are no doubt regretting their latest campaign. They've changed the wrappers on the bars to 'Believe' for the duration of the World Cup. The aim is to instil confidence in England, but it has massively backfired north of the border.

Even the salvage attempts of putting up billboards with 'Believe' and 'Scotland Commonwealth Games Bid 2014' can't pull the wool over our eyes. In just two weeks since the Believe bars were launched Mars sales have dropped eighty-two per cent. Supermarkets are selling boxes of our favourite snack as two for one because nobody is touching them.

We send Baz out to Easterhouse to see if he can shift them. He phones in live from the traffic lights and it is hilarious. 'I can't give them away, I have free chocolate, everybody, it's free, help me please!' he yells. The boy is fast becoming as daft as the two of us. In an hour he only gets rid of four bars out of a box of forty-eight.

Texts this morning include:

'Tell Baz to stick them up his MARS.'

'Buy a Twix instead and give them the two chocolate fingers!' George the trucker.

'I work for a vending machine company and nobody is taking the Believe bars, we are selling loads of Bounty bars though. I think this is because they are Bounty crash out soon.'

[A lovely wee woman phones in with this tale:]

'I work for a newsagents and we knew months ago about this promotion so we bulk-bought normal Mars bars in case our customers didn't want the Believe ones. I'm glad we did because we are doing really well. So if anyone still needs their fix, come to Gordon's in Camelon for a proper Mars bar.'

Loads of listeners call in about our latest tabloid splash. There's a massive picture of Robin and me with the cardboard cut-out of Jason Scotland at the song launch in the *Scottish Sun* today. Robin opened the paper and said, 'Oh look Cat, we're in the paper.' Quickly followed by, 'F*** me Cat, you look like a right munter!' It is just as well I'm not sensitive. For those of you not fluent in colloquial insults, a munter is like minger without the affection. A right munter is about as bad as it gets.

To be fair, it is a cracking snap of Robin and cardboard Jason, and quite possibly the worst shot of me ever taken (apart from the dimply arsed ones from yesterday – this has not been a good week for my self-esteem). I have to admit I am actually shocked at quite how rough I look, my eyes are half shut and I look drunk and angry when I was on soft drinks all night. Naturally, Brad Pitts everywhere have their say:

'If that is you sober, you'd better start drinking quick.' Ronnie.

'I don't think you look that bad.' 'David Blunkett'.

'I'd say you were an eight pinter, I'd nip you after eight pints I suppose.' Big Jock, in Glasgow.

'You're pretty rough but her to the right might get it.' Johnny, Falkirk.

I pick up the paper again to see what he was on about, only to see a stunning picture of video star Paris Hilton, in what can only be described by nice normal girls everywhere as a total 'slut-frock', the boot!

I know the run is on Sunday and I am meant to be on a diet, but only one thing can cure the munter blues and that is lots of chocolate. So did I betray my lifelong Tartan Army roots and tan Baz's box of unwanted Mars bars – better BELIEVE it!

Monday the 12th

I AM an athlete! Yesterday was the big 5km Race for Life in Glasgow Green and I survived. I have to confess I was actually extremely nervous on Saturday night and couldn't sleep ahead of the run. I'm not sure why because it turned out fine, but I was worried I wouldn't be able to finish with my dodgy knee and I didn't want to let people down.

I had to do a wee bit on stage in the centre of Glasgow Green in front of 12,000 ladies before the race began. I warmed them up nicely with a rendition of 'Heads and Shoulders, Knees and Toes' which thankfully everybody joined in with. In fact they were so good I only had to sing the first line, which after the Big in Falkirk vocal disaster, is probably a blessing.

I actually surpassed all my hopes and expectations and ran the race in thirty minutes and thirteen seconds which I am told is not bad at all. I ran the whole way (even up the wee hill) and met loads of fantastic people.

The race raises money for cancer research and it was one I very much wanted to do. To say it was emotional is an understatement. Official statistics suggest that one in three people will be diagnosed with cancer, which is quite terrifying. Lots of ladies that came over to chat to me had lost loved ones or were undergoing chemotherapy; several had lost breasts or were going through with reconstructive surgery. These brave souls were raising awareness and money despite their situations and I was exceptionally moved by their determination and positive outlooks.

Everybody taking part had a race number pinned to the front of their T-shirts and could have handwritten personal messages pinned to their backs to remember loved ones or to dedicate the race to somebody close who is battling cancer. These are incredibly touching and on two occasions I wiped a wee tear from my eye as I was running behind somebody with a moving message and photo on their backs.

I dedicated the race to my mum who has had almost thirty lumps of skin cancer removed. She is the most selfless person in the world and is always more bothered about how everybody else is doing rather that focusing on herself. I've not told her about my wearing her name on my back as she would think I have gone soft in my old age, and she doesn't want to cause a fuss.

We are a very close family but rubbish at sharing emotions. I love you and admire you to bits, Mum, and hope my thirty minutes and thirteen seconds' worth of sweaty pain will help show this a little bit.

Six girls from Real Radio ran the race with me and it felt great at the end meeting up and sharing our tales. Aggie from Sales said she was just about to start walking when a wee old wifie came out of a shop with her Sunday papers. She hadn't put her teeth in, but gave her a massive big smile and yelled,

'Go on yerthelf darling.' It made her laugh and put a spring in her step to keep on going.

On the show this morning lots of the ladies call in and share their experiences. The general consensus is that it was a fantastic day and we all feel like we have achieved personal goals along with the fund-raising. When I started going to the gym about five weeks ago I wouldn't have believed I could run the whole way in just half an hour. It really is an eye-opener to see how just a little bit of regular exercise can make such a difference. I intend to keep going, and might even contemplate doing another run for charity as well. I can't believe I have just written that. It must be all those crazy endorphins playing with my sanity.

Phone call of the day came from Isobel McRorie who called in from Scottish Slimmers. She organised a collection at all of the classes in central Scotland and her dieting darlings have donated £1,838.05 which is absolutely fantastic. I think we shall have raised about £4,000 by the close of play today. Brilliant.

I've been really moved by the cancer-related stories, the courage and conviction of the ladies who are battling the disease, and the generosity of others. With all the misery we witness on the news every night we can easily lose sight of the good out there. Today I happen to think the world is a very special caring place. I'm off on one again, normal service will resume tomorrow . . .

Tuesday the 13th

Eat vegetables – they make your willy grow bigger. This gem of information is a direct quote from Scottish culinary legend Gordon Ramsay. Now on further inspection (and it is my duty as a properly trained journalist – yes really – to review this statement carefully) it turns out oor Gordon doesn't know this for sure, but reckons it is a good way to make his son eat his veg. However, the poor wee lad, and I shall let Gordon take up the story, 'looks down at his shorts to see if anything is happening every time he eats a carrot.'

Our phones buzz instantly and first on is 'Big Boaby the Vegetarian'. Honestly, you guys have all the best lines. He tells us, 'I've just come down the stairs and the wife is force-feeding me turnip soup.'

I used to be told to eat fish to make me brainy while Robin was fed the old classic, 'If you don't eat your crusts you won't get curly hair.' We've touched on this subject before, but once again we are bombarded with funny comments made by mums and grannies:

'My mum used to say, "Go on, cry more – it will make you wee less."

'I was always told I'd get knocked into the middle of next week if I misbehaved.' Paul, Edinburgh.

'My mum taught me to walk and talk, then spent her life telling me to sit down and shut up – you cannae win!' Big Piper, Dumfries.

'My grandfather used to say, "I'll marmelise you." We never knew what it meant but we used to take cover because we knew it wasn't good.' Nick, Falkirk.

'When my dad burnt toast he told me to eat it as it would put hairs on my chest. I'm his eldest daughter!' Shell.

'My mum used to tell me if I drank lemon juice the midges wouldn't bite because I would be too sour.' Fiona, Glasgow.

[Helen has a fair point:] 'I can only imagine what Gordon Ramsay would tell his daughter to make her eat her veg!'

[Gary from Kirkcaldy calls in with this tale:] 'When my wife and I started going out it was tradition in my family to take a new girlfriend up to my grannie's for the once-over. She said to my wife, "If you keep both your legs in the one stocking you'll do all right." She obviously failed – we've got three kids now and have been married fourteen years.'

A Tesco delivery driver phones in telling us he has a cargo of fresh produce and wonders if he should head to Ann Summers instead of the supermarket he's been dispatched to. Personally, I think it is all nonsense and I'm going to put it all behind me as I head home to cook Mr Cat a nice healthy tea of carrot soup and vegetable casserole . . .

Wednesday the 14th

Batten down the hatches and grab on to the remote control – telly wars are erupting across the country. With three World Cup games a day on terrestrial TV, blanket coverage of *Big Brother* on E4 and soaps getting shuffled about the schedules, it seems keeping control of the control is paramount to keep sane. The anguish is heightened in homes with just one telly, but it seems loads of you are seeking retreat (or being sent) to watch the wee portable in the spare room/hut/garage/kid's room to avoid a stooshie.

Robin's pal Kevin has an iPod holder that goes round his arm in the gym, but he uses it for keeping his TV zapper in when he gets home. His wife is not best pleased.

Texts today include:

'My wife is going nuts because the soaps are all over the place. She sends me to my room with the tiny portable and mopes in her chair. She's got control of the remote and always will have.' Davie, Cumbernauld.

'My wife watched the Brazil game and I had to go upstairs to watch *Big Brother*.' Tony, Falkirk.

'This month is murder. My fiancée is Scottish and I'm with the other side! She's a real "rest of the world" supporter.' Andy, Helensburgh.

Tomorrow, remote control wars will intensify as the growing number of Trinidad and Tobago fans in Scotland clamour to watch our adopted side play England. The Soca Warriors are eighteen-to-one which means the bookies reckon they'll get totally thrashed.

We manage to track down Kenny Phillips from the radio station WACK FM in Trinidad and get the low-down on the build-up. The good people of T & T have no idea Scotland and oor Speedo pin-up Jack are backing their side. With six Scottish-based players, a striker called Scotland and the tournament's official under-dog status, we have no choice!

Kenny thinks it is hilarious that T & T strips have sold out in Scotland and that we have a song in our charts about their player who is not even considered to be that good. Kenny has a fabulous laid-back attitude with a deep Caribbean lilt to his voice, and you can imagine him sipping cocktails under a palm tree without a care in the world. He sounds like the happiest man in the entire world.

He tells us the locals are so excited about the big game that nobody will be working. It also transpires you can no longer buy TVs on the islands because there has been such a rush they've totally sold out. 'My pal lives near the beach in a tiny house, man, and he had to buy a seventy-two-inch screen thing because that was all that was left. It takes up half his wall, man.' He chuckles. He is so chuffed that Scotland are supporting his side he calls his programme director and sets up live interviews with us for his station. So this afternoon Robin and I make our broadcasting debut in the Caribbean.

The link is brilliant fun and finishes with him trying to teach us a traditional T & T dance, which basically involves a lot of hip-wiggling, bottom-shaking and groin-thrusting. It is becoming quite clear why Caribbean Kenny is so cheerful all the time . . .

Thursday the 15th

It is officially Trinidad and Tobago day on the *Breakfast Show* this morning. Kenny our new best Caribbean friend has voiced all of our radio station imaging including all the weather jingles, breakfast songs, traffic and travel and sports intros. All our backing beds are steel drum hits and the whole show has a crazy Caribbean feel. We get him on air and instantly he is a hit with our audience with his enthusiasm and humour.

At 6.30 a.m. Robin announces we have a box of T & T goodies to give away and shall be doing so in a competition. He is winging it as usual as we haven't actually made up a competition, which we have a good laugh about. I come up with the idea of making the competition, 'What should the competition be?' A daft idea with top response:

'It should be the first person to pronounce five of the Saudi team correctly wins.' Tony, Edinburgh.

'The best Trinidad limerick should win.' Graham, Easterhouse.

'Have a "How many England flags can you fit in a wheelie bin?" competition.' Jackie.

[But my favourite came in from James in Cumbernauld:]
'What about dookin' for pineapples?'

Our backing of Trinidad and Tobago is meant to be a good-natured venture so we link up live with James Gibson, the IRN England correspondent, at the team hotel. His update has me in stitches. The England team's hotel for this game is in the centre of Nuremburg which is, ironically, twinned with Glasgow. Last night there were steel drums and BAGPIPES playing outside their base until the wee small hours.

'Your mob is definitely up to something,' he laughs, 'there are loads of people in kilts with Trinidad and Tobago tops on over here. They never shut up all night; to be honest I'd be surprised if the team got any sleep at all.' While this news is clearly devastating for Mr Beckham and Co., we know for certain ninety-nine per cent of people driving to work are now absolutely pissing themselves.

James also informs us Rooney may play and the atmosphere is amazing but, more importantly, he walked past Ashley Cole's girlfriend Cheryl from Girls Aloud and she was 'amazing'.

We play out a clip from WACK FM's breakfast show, *Morning Wake Up Call* with Kent and Tamara. It is kind of funny talking to their version of us. However, it is reassuring to find they are also slightly barking. Tamara tells us her producer wants a kilt. I ask if he has the legs for it and she replies in a fantastically teasing slow drawl, 'Oh yeess, man, yes.' I ask if they know what he has to wear under the kilt and they have no idea.

'ABSOLUTELY NOTHING!' I explain, relishing the moment. But as quick as you like Kent bursts in, 'Well in that case you better make it a long one then.'

We are on the floor laughing and I smile all day at that killer line as I buy one-way plane tickets for me and all the girls to Trinidad . . .

Friday the 16th

Glorious failure – the Trinidad and Tobago team are the new Scotland. For eighty-three wonderful minutes we held on to a goalless draw and dreams of the unimaginable, but late strikes from Peter Crouch and Steven Gerrard spoiled all the fun.

Robin, Baz and I watched it in Tennent's Bar in Byres Road which had an interesting mix of supporters. We were decked out in the red and black of our adopted side, and standing next to a bunch of Scousers cheering on their lads. A *Sun* photographer was in the pub and instantly I feared the worst. However, this morning I enjoyed a silent snigger to see this week Robin is the 'right munter'. Revenge is indeed rather sweet.

After the game Robin and Baz headed off, and I stayed for the first half of the next game with my pals. A bloke came over to chat and introduced himself as Dave the Edinburgh Airport fireman. Funny surname I thought. Anyway, Dave's fire-fighting colleague David Montgomery has been slagged for years for being 'Robin Galloway's illegitimate son'. David is from Montrose where they get Grampian telly, and in the black and white days when Robin was reading out birthday cards the poor wee soul got pelters at school because he was the double of him.

Nowadays his mates on the watch open the *Sun* on a Friday and say, 'I wonder what your dad's been writing about today.' David is mortified, but gutted he missed his 'daddy'. Reuniting families is a lovely pastime so I call 'Daddy' on his mobile. Daddy, however, is sitting on the cludgie. Not quite the reconciliation David had no doubt dreamed of but hey, contact was made.

They chat for ages and establish that Robin would have been thirteen when David was born. The possibility of Robin having a secret wee brother is then examined. He returns my phone to me and I say cheerio to my partner in crime who returns to waving a wee friend off to the sea.

This morning we almost get sacked again. Not for being steaming (we went home before nine last night with the fateful Friday finger-wagging still etched on our minds), oh no, this time it was for opening the Real Radio car wash.

Robin has been thinking about buying a power washer all week so we hired one to give him a wee trial. In another moment of unstructured madness, we decide to plonk Baz out in the Real Radio car park with the washer to take care of any passing listeners who could do with a wee shine. Within ninety seconds of opening our impromptu service, Baz has two clients, a black Volvo and a white van. He does a grand job, and soon we are queued out. Lovely Maggi from upstairs texts in, 'Please tell me you are kidding!' The poor soul says she now dreads Fridays because she never knows what to expect next.

The arrival of a blue tanker and a forty-three-foot articulated lorry in the car park causes a bit of commotion, but hats off to Baz, he washed them both with a smile on his sweaty wee face and soapy water all over his trainers.

Mr W., in his new role as station power-meister, looks stern. 'This had better not have been planned,' he growls, forgetting that not too far in his distant *Breakfast Show* producing past HE sanctioned the REAL SKIP episode. However, when Bossman Jay arrives and Baz is getting down and dirty with another grubby lorry in the front car park, he is almost crying with laughter and we live to fight another day.

My career hanging in the balance seems to be happening on a weekly basis, and I have to admit I am looking forward to my wee break now. I'm off to Spain for five days with the girls for some much needed relaxation and plenty of early nights.

As I click to save this document I receive a text from Alyson. It reads: 'Wey-hey, it's party time – bring it on.' I'm only slightly scared . . .

Monday the 26th

Phew. I've just returned from a five-day girlie trip to Spain and I need a holiday more now than before I left. Relaxing can be so tiring. Comedy moment of the break was a night out with *Coronation Street* star Beverley Callard who plays Liz McDonald. After her cabaret set, I asked her to leave a message on Robin's phone for a laugh and she rose to the occasion.

I was obviously still in 'what would make funny radio' mode and wrote all the important details for her to say on the back of a vodka-soaked napkin with a red scratchy felt pen. It read: 'Hi, I'm Beverley Callard, Liz from *Corrie*, and

I'm in Puerto Banus with Cat and the girls. Say those words .
. .' At which point my squad would all shout the Real Radio
catch-phrase 'I'm a real winner' with assorted Spanish addi-
tions like 'yaribaa yaribaa' and 'under-ray under-ray' (correct,
I have no idea how to spell these).

However, she's a professional actress and obviously felt
the need for some late night creativity. In fairness she was
polite enough to ask if it was OK to improvise. I was still
cracking up with laughter that she was about to do it in the
first place and readily agreed. 'Aye, say what you want.' I
giggled.

Well, she was class, absolute class which is ironically the
opposite from her trashy character in the soap: 'Hi Robin,'
she gushed provocatively. 'I hear you are very hot. Well, let
me tell you, gorgeous, I'm Liz MacDonald from *Corrie* and
I've locked Jim in the cellar of the Rovers Return. Steve is still
mucking up his love life so I've come away with Cat and the
girls and we are all at the bar in bikinis – make that thonged
bikinis – and let me tell you, my naughty boy, we are having
a ball.' Etc. etc. you get the drift.

Robin played out the message on Friday morning to major
laughs in the studio. It is only this morning when I hear the
clip back that I realise quite how funny it sounded: we were
obviously in exceptionally high spirits. Still, she was one of
the nicest celebrities I've ever met and even Janis, who had
previously commented, 'Good God, she's a slapper!', admitted
she was actually rather lovely.

It's all very A-list with my peculiar celebrity encounters
at the moment; this afternoon we interview socialite heiress
and video star Paris Hilton about her new musical career. As
a self-confessed addict to gossipy magazines, I feel I know
her before we've even spoken and my gut instinct is that I
shall also dislike her immensely. Well she turned out to be
OK actually. Not brilliant, but OK. She just sounded so jaded
with the whole interview process.

In fairness, we were probably her fiftieth show in a row. So she was expecting more of the same: why have you fallen out with Nicole Ritchie? What do you actually do? And THAT video – discuss.

Well, we had a few ideas to perk things up and she rose to the occasion. Pardon the pun. First of all we made her phone the Hilton in Glasgow to blag a room for the night. The bloke in reservations was so dour it was unbelievable.

Paris: 'I'd like a room tonight – I'm Paris Hilton.'

Bloke: 'Do you have a corporate deal?'

Paris: 'My grandad told me to call – he owns the hotel.'

Bloke: 'I could give you a queen room for £170 a night.'

Paris: 'I'm Paris Hilton – my grandad owns your hotel.'

Bloke: 'I appreciate that, but I can only offer you a room for £170 a night.'

Paris: 'You need to lighten up. Oh, and I'm only joking.'

It was very amusing I have to say. Not quite as funny as her introduction to Cecil and his wee mouse Boaby. With Paris in a studio in London and us in Glasgow, she never clicked that Robin and Cecil are one and the same. It was interesting to hear her say she loved Boaby, she could make Boaby a choker, and that Cecil must look after his Boaby because he obviously loves it very much.

She was blissfully oblivious to any double entendres that I am told may exist, ahem, and we had our fun. She spends £500,000 on her dogs a year but as far as I'm aware she's not yet splashed out on wee Boaby. All in all, a very wacky day . . .

Tuesday the 27th

I'm not paranoid, but they clearly want rid of me. There is no other possible reason for my latest task.

'Would you like to go to Thailand?' said Bossman Jay sweetly.

'Yes of course I would, why?' I added the why because he had that 'not quite telling you the full story' look.

'It will be great for the station and the charity.' He has clearly not got to the bad bit.

'What is the catch?'

'It's not really a catch, just a challenge.' Oh shit.

'What kind of challenge?'

'A jungle trek, we think you should be called Jungle Cat.'

I used to like Bossman Jay. He knows more about music than anyone I know, he's a fun boss and possesses a sensational ability to kick-start a party. Now he wants to kill me. It's all after THAT Friday. I am sure of it.

I sit statue-still, not quite sure how to react. Thailand, fantastic, a wee fund-raising walk, no bother, but a jungle trek with spiders, snakes, beasties bigger than coconuts and, get this, the natural habitat of the tiger – jings, my mum will freak! Not since jumping off a mountain in Arran with only a small parachute on my back or wearing my white bum-sanding suit have I felt so vulnerable.

My sensible head tells me not to be so daft – this will be gruelling and my dodgy knee has only just managed to run 5km. My not-so-sensible head, which generally wins, says, 'Aye, why not? Bring it on. I AM Jane . . . ah ye ah ye ah ye ah ye ah.' Well, I know two Janes so that is at least a start.

The plan is to trek for nine days (9–12km a day, rugged terrain, often through rivers), kayak for one (rapids) and to complete the journey on elephant back (sudden urge to place arm in front of nose and wave it about like, well, like an elephant) in order to raise thousands of pounds for NCH Scotland. The guys there do a fantastic job, and I feel special they've chosen me, or at least that's Bossman Jay's second wave of attack-flattery in the face of a tiger-mauling.

The details are borderline horrific. There will be open-air camping, nights spent under canvas with village people (thankfully not doing YMCA), a night on a floating boat thing with a tarpaulin roof, and three days where there will be no toilet or washing facilities whatsoever. Broadcasting has never been this glamorous. I shall also be spending the trip with sixteen fund-raising listeners, who will share every grubby, smelly, wonderful experience on our adventure.

I make a mental note to self to get Alyson very drunk and persuade her she would love it too. She's my only pal fit and daft enough to even consider it. I need an ally if I'm to poo outdoors with no paper. In the world of camera-phones, it is the least she could do. After all, she owes me, she made me dress up as a big stupid squirrel, remember. Payback time . . .

Wednesday the 28th

It's an exciting morning for us. It's the final of one of our major competitions, 'Work your way to the USA', where we send an entire work force off to the States courtesy of Real Radio and BMI. Any workplace can enter any amount of people, and four have been drawn out for the final day. We dispatch presenters to all four locations.

The most nerve-wracking thing about this competition for those in the running is that they may be heading straight to Vegas after the big draw. This means that everybody, in all four teams, has had to pack their cases, look out passports and make arrangements for four days away. The disappoint-ment from the losers is palpable, the elation of the winners infectious.

Last year we sent the Yorkhill Fire Service to the bright lights of the Strip and by all accounts they set the place alight. This time we have Dougie Jackson whipping up frenzy at the East Dunbartonshire Taxi Owners' Association, Shareen Tulloch is with the Army in South Queensferry and Steve McKenna is on the buses with First Scotstoun, while Ewen and Roughie are chatting up the ladies at Falkirk Housing Association.

We chat to all of the presenters and the atmosphere in each venue is nothing short of acute hysteria. Dougie appears to have landed the biggest bunch of head cases. The ten taxi ladies are all in cowboy gear, they have a Chevy outside the office and an Elvis impersonator singing away in the background.

We call the Lucky 24-hour Café in Las Vegas live and explain the competition to Suzette the charming receptionist. She has no idea who the teams are but opts for company one, Dougie's nutters. Well, there have been screamers and there have been shouters on the show before, but this lot take the chocolate chip cookie. For over a minute we can't speak to Dougie for the noise. They go absolutely mental.

Eventually Dougie manages to grab a word with the girls. Wee Jeanie sounds like a right character. She is sixty-seven and full of energy.

'What are you going to do in Vegas?' asks our Dougie over the racket.

'Pull George Clooney!' she screams to a rousing cheer before adding, 'Ya beauty!'

Maggi and Stephanie from the station are joining the girls as their chaperones, and I suspect poor Maggi, who has possibly taken on the trip to get away from our naughty antics, is in for the biggest shock of her life. Robin and Cat with ice-cream vans, a skip and a car wash in the car park will seem like a day off compared to the Bishopbriggs girls on tour. A great competition, great winners and Viva Las Vegas . . .

Thursday the 29th

Today is the big pantomime photo call at the Pavilion and I am ridiculously nervous. I'm not sure if it's meeting the cast, the whole adventure of embarking on something totally new or the fact that I am completely paranoid about not fitting into the fairy outfit, which is making me queasy.

When I actually think about it I'm convinced it is the latter. At the moment I'm not worried about standing on the stage and singing in front of 1,500 people although I'm sure that will come, but all I can think of is 'the costume better have arms, it better have arms'.

Tinkerbell (which has been changed to Tinkercat for this Peter Pan production) in my mind is a cheeky impish elfin creature. She will wear a wee green tunic (baggy) with a hood maybe and comfy flat pixie boots. She will have a fabulous glitter wand and beautiful sparkly wings. She is cute, her cellulite bum and bingo wings are totally covered by said tunic, she looks young and she can fly.

It seems almost inevitable, given the way my life pans out, that when the moment came to dish out the costumes and the lad said, 'Oh, I think they have sent a wrong one by mistake,' that it would be mine. The whole cast of Peter Pan and one wrong costume – Tinkerbell's.

Instead of a fairy, I had a fairy godmother costume and an uber-glamorous ice queen one at that. I am handed the biggest meringue dress this side of Princess Di's wedding attire, which is covered from head to toe in blue and silver feathery glitter panels of chiffon. The colour is nice actually, but I know I shall feel like Elton John in drag, in drag! I am also handed a three-foot-high blue wig like Marge Simpson.

'Erm, is Tinkerbell not a wee impish fairy?' I plead, hoping not to have to wear the dynasty on acid creation.

'Yes,' smiles Iain from the Pavilion with an evil glint, 'she will be for the panto, but today, that is all we have.'

The good news is it is so big I could fit two of me in it, and you would need a microscope to see any arm flesh at all. The bad news is I look like Elaine C. Smith's great-granny, whom I'm sure was lovely but not showbiz twenty-six like Tinkercat. Thankfully, Peter Pan, Cameron from *Big Brother*, can't fit into his tunic and a bit of reworking is required there too. He really is a lovely lad. So smiley!

Shellsuit Bob and Zoë from *River City* (Stephen Purdon and Laura McMonagle) look sweet in their wee nighties and baffies, while Dean Park looks so comfortable in make-up and the dame's dress it is scary.

The photos are painless until the snappers decide it would be better to take some outside – in public, in Sauchiehall Street.

Well, what a sight to behold – the full cast out on the streets in glorious technicolor. The snappers keep giggling at me which I suppose is fair enough – only two years ago I was at sensible press conferences with them, operating as a proper journalist.

Today, in Glasgow city centre in my sensationally sparkly camp get-up, surrounded by teenagers snapping away on their camera phones, I have another antler-like moment. If only the First Minister could have seen me, I would have thrown sweeties at him and I'm sure he would have been so proud . . .

Friday the 30th

All my hours spent watching *Diagnosis Murder* have reaped dividends. We went to a Murder Mystery night at Pollok House last night and I worked out who did it and with what! I'm shamed to admit I took the whole thing far too seriously and knew I would be in for major stick if I failed. My team won and Robin has been slagging me for watching too many *Miss Marples*, which is incidentally one of Mrs G's favourites too. She's one of the most effortlessly glamorous and genuine people I've met, with great taste in telly too, it now transpires.

Marie from the Pavilion has e-mailed Robin the shots from the photo call yesterday and he is in bits. They are shocking, truly munteresque once again.

'You look like Mrs Slocombe from *Are You Being Served?*,' he laughs. I can't reply because he is right.

We are flooded with suggestions for what Tinkercat the wee Glesca fairy should wear, and these include Irn Bru tunics, tartan wings, a Partick Thistle frock, a magic shell suit tucked into sports socks, a Burberry fairy dress, and loads far to rude to mention.

Today is a unique day for the show – all of the bosses are away. Every single one of them. This spells danger. They're not only off, they are all out of our transmission area, so anything really does go. Robin asks what I like best about panto and I list things off as he hits the cheer or boo sound effect.

I begin: 'The atmosphere, the baddies, the goodies, the songs, the mischief and the ponies if they have them.' I know exactly where this is going.

'The ponies?' he smiles, acknowledging that we are about to go for it. I can smell our next official warning but we can't help ourselves. 'We've always wanted a pony in the studio, so to help get Cat in the mood, if anyone has a Shetland pony, then please get in touch and come and see us.' There, he has said it, and there is no one official here to tell us not to be so daft, that horse pee could frazzle forty-grand worth of equipment in seconds and that it is a major health and safety issue.

Brian from Livingston calls in. He can pop Princess the Shetland into a horsebox and be with us in half an hour. She has never been inside before, but she is generally well behaved.

'Bring her in!' we yelp like ten-year-olds. Fridays are becoming increasingly daft and, when the horse box arrives in the car park during the news, I have to leave the studio for fear of laughing through a murder story.

Princess and her helpers come into the studio and she behaves impeccably. She is cartoon cute, and munches cheerfully on carrots, until her helper says with more than a hint of fear in the voice: 'She's just farted. That could be a sign.' Oh shit. It is one thing getting into trouble for being irresponsible; it is another to spend two hours cleaning a mound of poo from the floor with a brush and shovel. In a Derby-style dash we get Princess back out into the car park before those carrots show us just how much roughage they really contain.

After the show I e-mail Maggi in Las Vegas with a picture of us in studio with the pony. She would only be wondering what we were up to anyway. I don't mention that Gregor Bell has just called in with the news that East Links Family Park has six lovely wee piglets that would love to be on the radio. She needs a nice surprise to return to . . .

july

Monday the 3rd

What a weekend of sporting happiness. Scottish tennis ace Andy Murray knocked number three seed Andy Roddick out of Wimbledon to reach the quarter-finals, and England are out of the World Cup. I shall say that again just to make sure I've taken it in – England are out of the World Cup.

I know I should be kinder to our southerly neighbours' feelings but I can't help it. I've been indoctrinated by my Tartan Army travels and have a pathological dislike for John Motson and Gary Lineker.

They were knocked out by Portugal on penalties, Wayne Rooney was sent off for stamping on a player's bits, David Beckham has retired as captain, and Sven has disappeared into the sunset with over twenty million pounds for winning them hee haw. Even the Wags (wives and girlfriends, for those of you not up on your girlie banter) were booed and taunted by el Portuguese Wagios when they left the stadium greeting into their Gucci hankies.

After Cristiano Ronaldo scored the winning kick, I immediately sent a cheeky text to Mr W. who has been waving his St George's flag in my face for weeks. The reply did make me laugh: 'Mr W. is unavailable to take your message so please f*** off.' It has since transpired that he was bombarded with twenty-one texts within two minutes of the final whistle.

I feel a tiny bit sorry for the genuine fans, but the hype has been ridiculous and we can now breathe a sigh of relief and enjoy the rest of the tournament.

There's some interesting news on our Paris Hilton interview – it's been picked up by *E*, the TV entertainment show presented by Ryan Seacrest in LA. It was voted number one in their top ten celebrity moments of the week. It is also mentioned in the *New York Post*, and the clip is running across the Australian radio network. Grumpy Kevin in the Glasgow Hilton is now an international star.

Big news on the diet front as well. Isobel from Scottish Slimmers has organised a woman to come into the station to weigh all of the Real Radio dieters every Wednesday. There is no getting out of it, my diet resumes properly in two days' time. For that reason, I had pizza on Friday, a Chinese on Saturday and Indian last night. Tonight it will be chips and cheese with a kebab shop visit planned for tomorrow. Unlike England, I am going out in style . . .

Tuesday the 4th

It's always a worry when the internal studio line flashes – we know we've done something bad or forgotten to mention something important. This morning we decide to take the rap live on air, and expect Bossman Billy or Jay to be in rant mode. However, it's Robin's seventeen-year-old daughter Hayden who is on the line and subsequently on the radio! The conversation is a hilarious typical father–daughter chat.

Hayden: 'Dad, do you know what day it is?'

Robin: 'Eh, Tuesday.'

Hayden: 'Yes, but what day?'

Robin: 'Tuesday the fourth of July.' (I'm watching expectantly, but his expression is still vacant.)

Hayden: 'But what day?'

Robin: 'American Independence Day?'

Hayden: 'It's YOUR twentieth wedding anniversary and Mum is going nuts.'

Yes, in 1986, on American Independence Day, Robin ironically lost his. And he has forgotten his big day.

Our phone lines are red hot with lots of irate ladies giving him a piece of their mind. Most are of the opinion he should be sent to the spare room without supper, however, most also agree a nice new diamond, a trip to the Caribbean, champagne and flowers may soften the blow. Another interesting suggestion came from David from Glasgow by text: 'Give Mrs G a new pet mouse called Mickey, let's face it Boaby wont be welcome in the house for the foreseeable future.'

Elsewhere, Andy Murray has been knocked out of Wimbledon, Germany take on Italy in the World Cup semi-final tonight, and the eagerly anticipated film *Pirates of the Caribbean: Dead Man's Chest* is released today. Forget the trip to the Caribbean, exotic blooms and expensive gifts – an evening with Johnny Depp and Orlando Bloom is just what Mrs G deserves.

Just before I head off, I open an e-mail from Iain at the Pavilion to see the all-singing, all-dancing flyer and poster for this year's pantomime. Everybody looks great in their costumes from the big photocall, except me. I AM Mrs Slocombe. They have used the shot of the fairy godmother costume and I look about a hundred. This shot will be in every newspaper, bus stop and train station in Glasgow.

I may cry, or simply accept the fact that even in the fantastical world of panto-land I am destined to be a munter unhappily ever after . . .

Wednesday the 5th

I've always lived my life in a state of organised chaos. I never prepare for anything properly and have an overly laid-back 'ach – whatever' attitude to my appearance. Today is a perfect example. I open my diary and it tells me that tomorrow is the big Duke of Edinburgh's Awards presentation at Holyrood. I've to meet Prince Phillip and present awards to gold achievers on the fiftieth anniversary of the scheme. I have nothing to wear (believe me this is not the typical female line, I actually have NOTHING to wear) and I've forgotten to ask a guest.

I dig out the official paperwork and see that a biography of the presenters (me) is required, plus the date and place of birth of both attendees must be registered for security purposes.

Robin is utterly disgusted with me for living such a muddled existence. I am too polite to mention at least I remembered in time. (Mrs G has forgiven him yesterday's *faux pas*.)

We are inundated with suggestions for people to be my guest for the glamorous affair. They include:

- Robin – no chance, he would show HRH wee Boaby.
- Bobby Harvey – he thinks HRH killed Diana.
- John Lambie – his language would take the heat away from the Prince.

Others include: Old Mrs Galloway, Hector Brocklebank and Cecil and his wee pal.

As I've mentioned before, Mrs Goodlet, my old Girls' Brigade leader, is the person I should've asked, although I suspect I've left it too late. However, Robin has been up to his super-sleuth tricks again and at half-eight, Mrs G – my ex-leader not his wife – is on the phone live on air and very excited. She would love to come to the big do, and reveals in acute detail how ridiculous we looked coming down from a hill aged fourteen and dressed as soldiers.

I'm not sure what it is about talking to people about my past, but I am all giggly and embarrassed again. I don't have anything to hide (apart from a few beer-goggled pulls who no doubt feel the same, the taxi driver catching me pee in Great Western Road dressed as a Viking, and the night I tried to steal a digger) but it is that feeling of vulnerability which is disorientating.

Thankfully, Mrs Goodlet is reasonably discreet (hey – she's not going to jeopardise a nice free lunch) and I arrange to meet her at Easterhouse station tomorrow morning.

She has a nice floaty summer dress and a pretty hat to wear, so it's with complete despondency I acknowledge my only dresses are bridesmaid's ones (six to choose from, all floor length) and that a trip to the shops is actually a necessity.

The rest of my diary for today reads as follows:

11.00 a.m. – Scottish Slimmers, 12.00 noon – shops, 3.00 p.m. – gym assessment, 4.00 p.m. – bum sanding.

I may as well have root canal treatment with no anaesthetic and make it the miserable full bhuna. With rice, naan and full fat mango chutney . . .

Thursday the 6th

Today I am officially by Royal Appointment – and I've got the gear to match my lofty status.

Yesterday, I endured the worst afternoon of shopping in history which resulted in my sitting in a dressing room in Monsoon, Buchanan Street, with a pile of clothes that wouldn't zip, having a partial breakdown. I was totally distraught, the feeling of isolation and despair overwhelming. I sat for at least four minutes, tears streaming down my face, before snapping out of it, remembering I am back on the slimming trail, and taking Robin's fashion advice – buy a fancy hat and nobody will notice the dress.

This morning, I do the show wearing a spectacular black hat with black and white fake wispy feathery things. It goes nicely with my jeans and black hoodie, which will be replaced with a plain black and white frock thing later.

I'm quite excited about today, probably more for catching up with Mrs Goodlet than meeting the Prince. I pick her up at the station and she hasn't changed a bit. She is as chirpy as I remember. We arrive at Holyrood and are escorted through to the palace grounds. They are spectacular and the sun is beating down; at 10.45 a.m., the temperature dial on my car says it is twenty-seven degrees. One shall pure melt, so one shall.

There are fifteen groups of about thirty recipients and their guests, and each group has a presenter. What happens is the Prince meets each group, talks to a few people, is presented to the presenter (I was going to say introduced but got told off, not royal protocol apparently), his aide hands the presenter the certificates and we dish them out.

The atmosphere is very colonial with a brass band in full military uniform, sitting in a white bandstand playing 'jolly tunes'. I like to think the Queen is curled up on her couch in the palace watching *Diagnosis Murder* with toast and cheese and a can of Diet Bru. She surely can't deal with this all the time.

I am astounded by the number of people who come up to me and say: 'Nice hat, Cat,' or 'It's the Cat in the hat.' What is funnier, though, is celebrity of the moment, Mrs Goodlet, who is flabbergasted with the attention she is receiving. Until yesterday, she didn't even know I was on the 'wireless'. Everybody who listens to the show knows that she is my guest and they all come over for a wee chat. She's been to the ceremony several times before with some of her Brigaders to receive awards, but she has never been close to the Prince before.

Today she is next to me and we are formally presented to the man his aides simply call 'HRH'. He is wearing a pale linen suit and a panama hat and looks like the man from Del Monte's Grandad. He is also very short.

It's always funny when preconceived ideas about people are blown away. He always looks so tall in photos; maybe the Queen is actually a midget. Anyway, he asks me if I have my gold award. I explain I did bronze, silver and three-quarters of my gold. I only forgot to hand in the log-book. He turned to his aide and said: 'She should have the gold. If she's done the work and is here today she should have her gold.' I reply inappropriately: 'Brilliant, the main man says I've to get it. It's come right from the top so there's no going back now.' The aide looks disgusted.

Pip smiles and decides I may be worth chatting to for longer, for no other reason than most folk appear to be too terrified to respond. He finds out I work on radio and asks about the show.

HRH: 'What time do you start?'

Me: 'I get up at half-three, we are on air five until nine.'

HRH: 'Five?! Who listens then? Only truckers I would imagine.' He then gives me a cheeky grin before adding: 'Yes, I imagine you are very popular with truckers.'

I let out a raucous dirty laugh, implying I know exactly what he's implying. My mum would be mortified! One must not engage in flirty chat with ageing royalty. My dad will be mad I never nutted him. With this killer line he disappears to the next group and my tiny glimpse at royal life is over. We have loads of truckers who listen to the show and I'm glad they now have the recognition they deserve.

We are then bussed to Edinburgh City Chambers with the other VIP presenters including curling legend Rhona Martin (who I can't catch eyes with after saying she looked like Colin Hendry on air) and Colin McCreadie from *Taggart* (a pal of Tam's and a lovely lad). We are ushered into a grand drawing room when I hear: 'Oh NO, they let anyone in these days!'

Sitting in the corner and looking all tanned and mischievous is my old buddy, Aberdeen manager Jimmy Calderwood, and his lovely wife Sue. We join them for lunch (a Scottish Slimmers' check counting nightmare – a fancy buffet) and have a lot of fun.

If you told me last year I would be sitting at a table lunching with the Aberdeen manager and my Girls' Brigade leader after sharing a joke about truckers with the Duke of Edinburgh, I'd have thought you were quite mad.

We left Edinburgh delighted with our wee day out. Mrs Goodlet said it was one of the best days of her life, and that alone made mine . . .

Friday the 7th

I'm getting worried. T in the Park is tomorrow and I am currently without a ticket. We have been giving two pairs of weekend passes away every day all week and I can't get one for love nor money. Bossman Jay is trying for me, and with his contacts I am still hopeful. It shows how successful the festival has become that Scotland's number one station can't blag the breakfast presenter a bloody ticket. I've only missed two in ten years and even camped when the event was much smaller and at Hamilton.

My friend Fiona and I pitched our wee brown tent next to the fence in Strathclyde Park early doors when it was fairly empty, and returned a bit squiffy in the dark to 5,000 wee brown tents next to the fence. Pulling down a stranger's zip is one of the joys of festival life. We looked in about fifteen tents before discovering our own!

Anyway, back to my predicament. 'Stevie the Fish' from Clydebank calls in and offers me passes. He is a fish merchant and has been delivering to the site: 'You just have to pretend you're a caterer and go in that gate.' If he hadn't said it on air, alerting stewards and officials everywhere, I was heading straight to town to buy chef's whites and a rolling pin.

We chat about survival tips for the festival and are swamped with the same response – remember bog roll. Pack your own, put it in a waterproof bag, and enjoy your week-end – a 'Pee in the Dark' is much better with soft paper.

When the show finishes I send a text to Dave Corbett my mate at DF Concerts and e-mail George Kyle the chief cheese at Tennent's. I have a feeling they will both be on site and not responding to their inevitable stack of last-minute pleas. As I go to log off my computer, I am still ticket-less and on the cusp of either my best or worst weekend. I shall be absolutely gutted if I don't get in, do they not know I hang about with royalty . . .

Monday the 10th

I love George Kyle. He is my favourite person in the entire world at the moment and Tennent's is the finest lager in the universe. Yum, I love Tennent's.

At 6.45 p.m. on Friday, after a day of unbridled misery, I started making alternative plans for my weekend. Nobody had replied to my horrendously beseeching texts, and my cagoule and wellies were back in the cupboard. As old ladies are alleged to say in the east, my 'T' was well and truly oot!

At 6.46 p.m. Elaine, George's glamorous assistant, called from Tennent's. He'd checked his e-mails, loves the show and pulled out all the stops. I think I actually got the last two hospitality tickets to T in the Park. Yet again my ice cool façade disappeared as I yelped like a banshee down her ear.

'Er, right Cat, I'll see you tomorrow then,' she concluded, hanging up as quickly as possible to get me off the phone.

Well, I had a blast. Alyson and I got the jakey bus up at half-ten with a bottle of 'special water' to keep us going. I made a point of seeing plenty of bands and took in sets from The Zutons, The Feeling, the Kaiser Chiefs, Franz Ferdinand, Orson, Goldfrapp and headliners the Red Hot Chili Peppers.

For the last half hour with rain teeming down I squeezed into the King Tut's tent for a blistering set from my old pals The Charlatans. They went down a storm and seemed to be lapping up the atmosphere. Tony the keyboard player sent me a text later that night saying he'd had an absolute ball, and that the rest of the band were on their tour bus raving about the Scottish crowd. Despite the wet weather and the wellies, we rock!

Today the papers are full of pictures and tales of misadventure and mayhem from the weekend. It really is one of my favourite trips of the year, but not good for the waistline. I retrospectively counted my Slimmers' checks for Saturday (we are allowed forty-five a day) and stopped at 119. Fruit and veg for the next two days before the big, potentially expensive weigh-in.

Zinedine Zidane is also on the front pages of every paper this morning. Italy won the World Cup last night on penalties, with Zizou seeing red with minutes to go for head-butting Marco Materazzi. The Italian defender obviously offended him enormously and we ponder on the nature and content of his killer line. Suggestions include:

'I bet you cannae crack my ribs with your heid, baldy?' Martyn.

'I've got yir wife's drawers on.' Andy, Falkirk.

'Haw he haw, haw he haw, you've got a heid like a snooker ba'!' Gus the gadgy.

I'm off for another bum-sanding session later on to shift the cellulite; I'm not sure how many more I have to endure as their dimpled guinea pig before they declare me a lost cause. I'm sure my lovely lager-laden weekend will give Amy lots of new bumps to work on.

Did I mention that I love George Kyle who works for Tennent's and I'd dearly love to go next year too . . .

Tuesday the 11th

He's back. Our Speedo-loving First Minister Jack McConnell is our guest again today for an open question session and a general catch-up. Today we declare the show an official 'politics-free zone' and have a klaxon sound effect on standby if he starts to slip into any form of sensible discourse.

We open the phones before he arrives for questions the great Scottish public want to know about our main man. Our first caller sounds very solemn indeed: 'I have a question for the First Minister that I think we need to know a truthful an-swer to . . .' Robin and I just look at each other despondently; this is going to be deep and dreary. 'Does Jack ever fart under the duvet and hold Bridget's head under it?' We are in bits; we later learn that Jack, his aide and his driver are all killing themselves laughing in their car too.

Robin has put a tie on for the occasion, I am wearing a hoodie and Jack comes in all casual, which makes Robin's tie even funnier. During the opening link, Jack's mobile goes off. It is his wife Bridget. He's mortified he's forgotten the number one rule of broadcasting. No mobiles!

I suspect he is even more mortified that it's his wife who has lost her car keys and is running late for her work. Today she just happens to be opening the Kelvingrove Art Gallery after a three-year refurbishment programme. Mark from Glasgow sends in this helpful text: 'Tell Jack, his missus's keys are still roon at ma bit!' He laughs heartily.

In a very amusing hour he answers all of the questions from our listeners superbly, including:

- Do you have your own teeth? – 'Yes, although a few have fallen out now.'
- Do you watch reality TV? – 'I quite like *Big Brother* and want the Welsh guy Glyn to win.'
- Have you ever tried Buckfast? – 'No!'
- Did you ever wear the Speedos? – 'I wanted to but they were too small!!!!'
- Do you own a hoodie? – 'Yes, I was given one at a youth project with 'McConnell' on the back.'

The Conservative leader David Cameron has recently launched a plea for people to be nice to youths in hooded tops, which the media have tagged 'hug a hoodie'. Robin asks if Jack would ever hug a hoodie, at which he leans over and gives me a massive bear hug on air. I bet Gordon Brown would never be this much fun.

To be honest, most of the questioners ask if he has ever been to a party with Tommy Sheridan, and if not, can he get invites. (The former SSP leader is currently in court with a defamation case against the *News of the World* which claims he's had extramarital affairs, five-in-a-bed sessions and goes to swingers' clubs.)

Jack tells us we were a welcome addition at his Christmas party and assures us we shall be there this year – and our antlers are expected. I suggest karaoke to liven it up and he says he'll think about it. I can see his aide through the studio glass shaking his head.

At the end of the interview Jack says: 'I'm so glad I never had to answer the question I heard in the car.' It just so happens we have re-edited it and hit the hilarious clip inquiring about any nocturnal wind games with Glasgow Council's executive director of culture and leisure services, better known as his wife. He can hardly speak for laughing but eventually concludes: 'No, I have never done that – Bridget would probably kill me.'

I can only imagine what Tony Blair would have said if faced with the same question on *Newsnight*.

A text comes in from Jim the Trucker: 'Who would have thought, the First Minister is actually quite cool!' Robin and I happen to agree . . .

Wednesday the 12th

Rangers star Fernando Ricksen is on all the front pages this morning after checking into a rehabilitation centre for booze addiction and anger management. He's been sent home from the club's pre-season training trip to South Africa after getting steaming on the flight and throwing water over a stewardess. In the past few years he's been in trouble for setting off fireworks in his garden, bouncing on a trampoline with a model, and cavorting in a nightclub with Jordan. It seems like he's always been a bit of a loose cannon but I hope he gets the help he needs.

I sat next to him and his wife Graciela at a charity ball the week he joined the club and to be honest he was great fun. She ate nothing at all, not a bite, and reapplied lip-gloss in a wee mirror – at the table – most of the evening. He enjoyed the wine before getting a bit too animated during the auction. He was determined to buy the signed Celtic strip, but was politely warned by another guest that supporters of his new side might not take this charitable gesture the way it was intended.

As it happened, he was mid-story about something entirely different and waving his hands about in a dramatic fashion when the MC said: 'Sold to table forty-eight for £700.' The bold Fernando without realising had just paid the best part of a grand for a hand-embroidered quilt! Fair play to him, when the girls came over for his details he agreed to pay straight away then turned to ask me the classic line:

'What IS a quilt?'

'It is a very expensive duvet for your bed,' I smiled.

'Oh, I would have preferred the Celtic top,' he added nonchalantly before scudding more wine.

I've interviewed him several times since then and he has always been pleasant enough. I hope he can tackle his demons and makes the most of his considerable talent. Anyone who has pulled Jordan and entertained another stunner on a trampoline must be able to bounce back . . .

It's the Real Scottish Slimmers' first weigh-in today. I am petrified after my T in the Park binge. However, against the odds (and all reason) I've lost five pounds which is my biggest drop ever. I'm not sure if it is the running, the bum-Hoovering or wonky scales, but I'm elated. Clearly lager is indeed good for you. Made by Tennent's, home to my friend George Kyle, who doesn't know it yet, but is desperate to send me tickets for next year . . .

Thursday the 13th

My cheeks are sore. Yesterday afternoon I endured two hours' worth of posing into the lens for the picture on the front cover of this book. I have to confess I am rubbish at getting my photo taken, and get nervous giggles when asked to give 'smiley eyes, friendly eyes, demure eyes, medium smile, full smile, semi-head tilt', etc.

Alistair Devine, the photographer, is quite a laugh with his exotic tales of snapping Elizabeth Taylor, Lauren Bacall and Elton John. I can't help feeling that a day in an industrial estate in Ballieston with me is probably not his finest hour. Neither was it mine, as I got stuck between the arms and back of a chair attempting to recreate the Christine Keeler pose. My face went purple as I tried to free my chunky thighs (thankfully this snap is not available for perusal).

It's by complete chance that I open the paper this morning and staring out at me is Alistair, friend of the stars and clearly quite a bit of a character. His latest project shows naked ambition. He is looking for willing participants, over eighteen, to be photographed nude in a Glasgow West End bar in the name of Art. Similar to the famous 'art projects' organised and photographed by Spencer Tunick in Barcelona and Newcastle, oor Alistair is trying to cram a pub full of scuddies for a promotion. His pictures will then be used to decorate the bar.

It sounds hilarious, it sounds liberating, it sounds Bohemian; to be honest, it sounds perfect for oor Baz. His face is a picture (no pun intended) but I can tell his mad mental Pollok side is thinking, 'Magic – naked burds.' Texts of support flood in:

'Go on, Baz, take one for the family!'
'Get your kit off, you will make a bored housewife very happy.'

'I am offering my services to hold his hand if he is nervous.' Avril in Broxburn.

'OFF, OFF, OFF, get yir kit off, in the name of art, obviously.' Kim.

He is now really looking forward to his latest task, and it's clear our boy is creating quite a big stir with the ladies of a certain age. I only hope the same doesn't happen to him as he mingles with his fellow artistes . . .

Friday the 14th

I'm a bit tetchy this morning and it's all down to animal instinct. With *Diagnosis Murder* off our screens, I have become obsessed with *Big Cat Week* on the BBC. This follows various families of cheetahs and lions in Kenya. I am in love with wee Toto the featured kamikaze cheetah cub who in the past two days has narrowly avoided a horrible death from hungry baboons and lions.

Last night I was out on a power walk (two cracking blisters to prove it) and missed the episode. I endeavour to find out if the cute feline one is still with us at the back of 6.00 a.m. Our phones go mental, which is unusual for so early in the morning, with updates, mostly from laughing workies, with elaborate tales of the wee soul's imaginary demise. Texts included:

'Toto was lovely, could've done with a bit more salt though.' A. Lion.

'The man in the jeep squashed him.' Bonhill Pat.

'He's now a rug in my mammy's house.' Davie, Bellshill.

[However, loads of people confirmed he is alive and well, although he needs a feed. I was particularly grateful to Derek who informed me:]

'Toto still cool as cheese, hyena scoffed by lions and wildebeest migration has started.'

There are not many shows on radio that let you know the news, sport, weather, travel and migration of wildebeest progress. I love our listeners.

Today we decided to offer Baz as a prize in a blind date competition we devised ten minutes before the paper review because all of today's news stories are miserable and depressing. We open the phones and ask any lady, or guy for that matter as we are a cosmopolitan show, who fancies a date with oor Baz to get in touch. Loads of people phone in to nominate their relatives or pals, but we need to hear from the contestants themselves. Only one sounded like the scary lady from *Misery*, the rest were lovely.

However, as we hadn't really thought of any formal rules, we whittled down the entrants to the two liveliest ones – Eilidh, a trainee solicitor from Edinburgh, and Stacey, a car sales assistant from Cumbernauld. Both sound great fun and both have no idea what they are letting themselves in for. To settle the tie-break Baz asked the following questions:

1. I like wondering through the streets of Pollok on a nice night. Where would your dream date be?

Stacey: 'Any park would do me, I love going for walks in parks.'

Eilidh: 'It would have to be the Taj Mahal – very romantic.'

2. I love keeping fit. What do you do to get hot and sweaty?

Stacey: 'I love speed, so driving fast cars would get me hot and sweaty.'

Eilidh: 'I love riding. [Baz's eyes pop out.] I ride to get sweaty [he may combust], on horses, I should add,' [and I'm glad she did].

3. I love the Real wind-ups. How much do you like Boaby?

Stacey: (laughing) 'It's great.'

Eilidh: (very excited) 'I love Boaby. Boaby is fantastic!'

We let the listeners choose his date and Eilidh scrapes victory with fifty-four per cent of the texts. I'm sure her love of small mice helped her victory. Texts pour in offering to take Stacey out, and I'm sure it won't be long before she is snapped up.

Baz now has to organise a date with Eilidh for next week and give us the low-down. I hope for her sake that he doesn't ask her if she likes 'ART'. That could be a VERY interesting first date . . .

Monday the 17th

It's Fair Monday in Glasgow, there's a public holiday in Fife, the sun is shining and the schools are off.

This morning we've been granted free play of the music, which only happens about twice a year. There will be no dreary Dido, Kelly Clarkson or slushy ballads; instead we opt for a comical mix of sing-along classics, extreme cheese, TV themes and one-hit wonders. We ask for suggestions for our 'making it up as we go along' play list, and end up with a hilarious selection.

Status Quo's 'Rockin' All Over the World' is followed by the theme from *The Muppets*, Frank Sinatra's 'New York New York', 'Save Your Love' by Renée and Renato and then the *Benny Hill Show* music. We have a little bit of Dolly Parton, some Guns N' Roses, Jim Reeves, the *Rainbow* theme and Billy Connolly singing 'Supergran'. I can only imagine what people tuning in for the first time would be thinking. It's eclectic to say the least but the feedback is fantastic.

On a more serious note, Davie the trucker calls in to inform me Toto, my lovely little Cheetah cub, did not survive the weekend. The *Big Cat* team caught up with his mum but there was no sign of the wee fellow: they suspect he may have been washed away in a river. I am very saddened by the news, but allow myself a small chuckle as sympathetic requests flood in for 'Africa' by Toto.

Robin sends me over the edge by ending the show with the tear-jerking theme from *The Littlest Hobo*. It is like *Finding Nemo* all over again . . . hankies please . . . Talking of which, reports over the weekend have revealed that Rangers star Fernando Ricksen was actually told off for watching porn films on his pre-season flight of shame. Rumours that it was a True Blue movie are unconfirmed . . .

Tuesday the 18th

Heatwave! Today is officially the hottest day of the year and close to the hottest day in Scotland ever. At thirty degrees across the central belt we're all sweltering and unable to function in the working environment. Glasgow and Edinburgh are actually hotter than Hawaii, and the *Scottish Sun* has pictures of girls frolicking in the sea in Aberdeen. They had red sun-skelped faces, white pasty midriffs and blue North Sea legs.

For me, the best thing about nice weather is getting my toes out and eating Twister ice lollies (only four Scottish Slimmers' checks so almost healthy). The blokes in particular appear to love the Scottish scenery, as Gerry from Airdrie pointed out: 'The best thing about summer is all the lovely ladies taking the twins out for a walk!'

On the show this morning we decide to test the old saying: 'You could fry an egg on the roof.' Robin suggests Baz tackles this latest challenge on the roof of his brand spanking new bright blue Clio sport, delivered by Uncle Arnold only yesterday. Within seconds the phones kick into life, all from irate taxi drivers urging us not to be 'so bloody stupid'. Apparently the albumen damages the paint work on impact. Again we are torn between being good or bad eggs (sorry, it had to be cracked).

A solution is agreed upon, whereby Baz folded a sheet of tinfoil into a wee tray shape, placed it on the roof and finally added the egg. After about eight minutes the egg white did indeed start to sort of change colour a little bit although he refused to eat it, which for our Baz says it all.

After the show I open more e-mails, all telling me where we went wrong. Boffins from all walks of life (clearly adults who loved exploding things as kids) explain it has to be at least thirty-one degrees and the metalwork must have been in direct sunlight for over four consecutive hours. I prefer Graeme from Edinburgh's simplified approach: 'You should have used a black car. They go hotter.'

I decide to go for a run round the Milngavie reservoir this afternoon, working on the theory that I shall be able to burn off all the calories I consumed at Mini-Me's BBQ on Saturday night in one go. When I return bedraggled to MY Clio, it is like a furnace. If only I'd had a square sausage in my joggers . . .

Wednesday the 19th

It's another belting battle of the sexes this morning. Scotland is set to swelter again and Robin claims he'd prefer to be a girl in this weather. We, apparently, have it easy.

According to Mr PC, we can wear not very much to work and get away with it; we can put our feet up and enjoy the rays and we can send the kids out to play in the garden. I know he's at the wind-up here, and argue back that guys can wander about with their tops totally off thus enjoying more freedom and coping with the heat better. Girls have to deal with melting make-up issues, bad humidity hair, and sandal sores.

Every pregnant woman in the country gets on the phone. The poor souls are melting, knackered and according to most 'just want it out'!! However, the lads do fight back valiantly: 'Try fitting a three-foot hot water tank in lofts in this heat.'

The show always zooms by when we polarise opinions, and there's nothing the Scottish public likes better than a good natured burds v. blokes rammy.

'All I'm saying,' says Robin with an evil grin, 'is that it's much easier to be a girl in this weather. They can wear nice light dresses, guys have to cover up and it is not fair.' I have an equally evil brainwave: 'OK then, if life is so much better in a dress, why don't you wear one tomorrow?' He shoots me 'a look' but I continue: 'In fact, I shall buy one for you, nice and summery and cool for this hot weather.' He knows he has no option.

'OK then. I'll wear one.'

I know in his head it is a long plain sundress of a certain quality, while in my head it is a short luminous Lycra abomination with 'seventeen-year-old tart in Ibiza' written all over it. I may even treat him to underwear and accessories. For the first time ever I pack up quickly to go shopping at the Fort and I'm actually looking forward to it. He should be afraid, VERY afraid.

My run yesterday in extreme conditions clearly wasn't far enough. I only lost half a pound at weigh-in this week which is actually quite depressing after munching on rabbit food all week (apart from my two-day weekend binge). Today I shall try the same route in a padded ski-suit. Like Franz Klammer, I can see my dieting dedication going downhill fast . . .

Thursday the 20th

This is momentous day in Real Radio history – it's the Robina and Cat show in a morning of absolute mayhem. In fairness, he did ask for it, and I must admit I'm exceptionally proud of my haul.

After an intense two-hour shopping spree yesterday (nothing was quite, well, sluttish enough really) I spotted the perfect frock. It came from deep within the sale rail at Quiz clothing, the kind of place teenagers go for their under-age disco gear. At £9.99 it was possibly the most expensive item in the shop, but it was worth every single penny, believe me.

Robin told me he was a size twelve, and how he knows this is a worry, but my chosen delight claimed to be a size twelve, fate really. To be honest, if the label had said age twelve it would've been more believable. Drum roll, please . . . Robin's creation for this morning's show is a buttock-skimming black and red floral Lycra number with spaghetti straps and a built-in padded cleavage. It is so wrong on so many levels, which made it just perfect for the task in hand. Now every girl knows the correct underwear is a must with summer dresses, so at great expense I also snapped up a red lace thong for 99p in New Look.

I was concerned the dress wouldn't actually go on, but Lycra proved more stretchy than I could ever have imagined. He put his outfit on during a live link, including dropping his briefs and stepping into his new pants. Baz and I were crying with laughter as Robin left us and Robina blossomed into life. The cleavage looked too real and I hate to admit it, he has a better rear and set of pins in a dress than I shall ever have, no matter how many times my bum is vacuumed.

Poor Baz really should have seen it coming though, because I couldn't leave him out on his own when it is sale season in the shops. The wee orange sun dress with gold chain straps in a size fourteen from Top Shop was just his colour, and the pink gingham thong at 50p was also too good a bargain to resist. And so it came to pass that everybody on the show sat in pretty dresses for the entire broadcast.

Not surprisingly the calls come thick and fast, everybody wanting a piece of Robina. My favourite came from the gruff-voiced lorry driver called John who asked breathlessly: 'Ah just want to ask Robina a question, which side does she dress tae?'

The doorbell goes at 8.30 a.m. and on the security screen we can see a tall man delivering us an unsolicited breakfast – wearing a black and white strappy ladies' dress. The world has gone quite mad. His name is Sammy from the Radisson Hotel, and we can't work out if this is his usual look, or a quickly executed PR stunt (my *Diagnosis Murder* training spots shaved legs – I suspect he may dabble in dresses more than he admits).

Not since the visit of Princess the pony have so many Real Radio staff popped in to see us. Most are in hysterics at Robin squeezed into his figure-hugging garb; however Bossman Billy genuinely looks very disturbed. He usually pops into the studio for a wee chat every morning, but today he looks at the boys sternly (without catching Robin's eyes), mutters, 'It's not right, you know.' and leaves. He is from Larkhall, remember – men in frocks don't last long there apparently.

It was therefore inevitable that, when the programme finished, Robina and Bazia sprawled like pouting page-three, erm, lovelies over the bonnet of his brand-new car and e-mailed the picture round the office. I'd like to say there was a sensible conclusion to this episode but there really isn't. Robin stands by his theory ladies have it easier in the heat because his legs shoulders and back were cool. He has however conceded that thongs are evil, unhygienic and possibly the most uncomfortable invention since the chastity belt.

That, if nothing else, has made his 'tranny on the tranny' episode, like his silhouette, an interesting learning curve . . .

Friday the 21st

At 4.45 a.m. this morning all my karaoke dreams come true. I open an e-mail from Maisie at the SECC who informs me she's managed to find me a late ticket for Guns N' Roses tonight. OK, so Axl Rose is the only remaining member of the American rock legends, but it should be mental. As a bit of an Indie kid I have to admit I've never been to a proper ROCK concert before and I'm looking forward to the full lager-drenched crowd-surfing experience.

'Sweet Child of Mine' has been my only karaoke song since a very odd night in a bikers' hostel in New Zealand about eight years ago. Nichola and I were over there working for STV, covering the Edinburgh Tattoo's visit to Wellington, and took a trip to the outlying town of Nelson on the South Island.

The only bar open was the bikers' bar attached to the cheapest hostel in town. We were the only people not clad head-to-steel-capped-toe in leather, and without beards (including the one tattooed woman). Walking in the door was like the music-stopping moment in *Police Academy*, when the officers stumble into the Blue Oyster Bar.

Believe it or not, it was karaoke night, which meant that after a few swallies to get in the mood (or to stop feeling so scared) I reached for the song book. Previous performances from the locals included AC/DC's 'Highway to Hell', 'School's Out' by Alice Cooper and 'Paranoid' by Black Sabbath, so I knew what sort of song to go for. 'Sweet Child of Mine' was the obvious choice and I took to the stage with NZ chardonnay-fuelled bravado.

Well, it was my finest performance ever, the crowd went mental and I've loved the song ever since. The fact they went wild because I was one of only three girls in the bar, we were Scottish and clearly not rock chicks but a pair of mentalists up for a laugh, has not sunk in yet. I probably didn't hit a correct note the entire performance but I air-guitared with energy and sometimes enthusiasm can mask a lack of talent. My street cred disintegrated rapidly though.

Nic, inspired by the reaction to my song, bounced over to me beaming: 'I've put us up together, you were great but this one will be better.' Even all these years on I can still remember exactly what happened next. It is my tumbleweed moment. Time quite literally stood still.

There I was standing on the wee stage, next to my bubbly sidekick, looking down at all of those expectant eyes in a room packed full of big burly bikers, waiting for the opening chords of a rock classic. The anticipation, the pheromones, the testosterone, the opening notes of recognition . . .

'De de dee – de de de deedee de de'. Eyes opened in shock and every muscle in my body tensed as I turned in horror to Nic who – oblivious to our disgusted audience – threw her hands dramatically above her head in a massive big Y shape and screeched, 'YOUNG MAN'.

Yes, she'd chosen 'YMCA', by the Village People, the band with the stereotypical gay biker with the vest top and the chained leather cap. How we escaped without a kicking I shall never know, but we finished the song looking at the floor, nipped to the loo after a solitary hand clap from the drunk at the front and headed out a side door. Fast. Anyway, 'Sweet Child of Mine' holds great memories and I'm looking forward to the gig.

This morning, the Tommy Sheridan defamation case reaches new dramatic heights. The *News of the World*'s legal team is planning to call him as a witness, in his own case against them. After sacking HIS legal team, Sheridan is representing himself. How he will cross examine himself is anyone's guess. It really is better than the telly.

Back on our show, Baz is getting a bit nervous ahead of his 'artistic' debut on Sunday. To help him with a few useful tips we get Richard Collins, 'The Naked Cyclist' on the phone. He is a prominent naturist (oh such boasts) and keen to advocate getting one's kit off and hanging loose in public. 'Just be yourself, relax and enjoy your surroundings,' is his learned advice.

We are sending Baz, a twenty-four-year-old single male from Pollok, into a room crammed full of naked ladies. I'm sure he will LOVE the surroundings; and I hope dearly for all concerned he is relaxed . . .

Monday the 24th

What a weekend! I've got a big Monday morning smile.

I dragged Alyson to Guns N' Roses on Friday, she made me drink snakebite and blackcurrant like we were students again, and we rocked, or at least we did in our minds. I've put the chips and cheese covered in salad cream munched on the way home out of my thoughts, though. It was salad cream light right enough . . .

On Saturday, my party-planning skills were tested to the max as I coordinated my pal Starsky's sixtieth birthday day out. As we pulled up to the Science Centre in Glasgow in a taxi I could see his bemusement. His face broke into the biggest grin when we turned the corner and he spotted the *Waverley*, the last sea-going paddle steamer in the world. He always goes 'doon the water' for the Fair, so I'd booked eleven of his close friends a return trip to Rothesay, his favourite place, and I quote, 'in the whole world'. 'You can bury me there and I'd be happy,' he added. I pointed out I had a mental day in store for him, but that I did expect him to make it back in one piece.

As we walked up the gangplank, Bobby Harvey, resplendent in tartan jacket and bow tie jumped out of a door and started playing Scottish tunes. He led us down to the Caledonian tea room which we'd decorated, and Starsky nearly wept when he saw all his buddies dressed in pirate hats and eye patches. I must admit I nearly cried when I saw how surprised and delighted he was at the gathering.

Well, the sun shone, the Clyde was as flat as a mill pond and sparkled spectacularly all day. We disembarked at Rothesay for a four-hour stopover which zoomed by courtesy of a promenade stroll, a Co-op carry-out, fish and chips wrapped in the *Sun* with Robin wearing a dress, and a big Zavaroni's cone. The boat continued to Tighnabruaich before returning to collect us. Well, I've no idea what goes on up the Kyles of Bute but when we got back on, it was raucous.

There was a stag party, a hen night, a fiftieth wedding anniversary, a sixtieth birthday and a twenty-first all celebrating in the lounge. We walked into a floating slosh. The old dears were in the mood, on the gin and out of control. It was without doubt one of the funniest few hours of my life.

We docked at Glasgow where my mate Peter decided to treat the boat to his famous Drifters medley, and we had the mother of all sing songs tied up at the quay. I fully intend to repeat the trip for his seventieth, by which time he may have the insanity required to keep up with the pole-dancing high-kicking octogenarians.

Our Baz had quite a weekend too. He actually went through with it and got his bits out for Art. The Bobar in Glasgow was apparently full with people enjoying their freedom and the free lager on offer to participants. He's actually got the phone number of a cute blonde and fully intends to take her out. His reasoning, 'Well she knows what's on offer so what do I have to lose,' is Pollok logic at its finest.

I politely remind him he has a blind date with Eilidh in Edinburgh this evening and that she'd probably prefer him to be wearing clothes. At least on the first one . . .

Tuesday the 25th

'Is this love that he's feeling, is this the love that he's been searching dodgy websites for?' as the song sort of goes. Oor Baz has a certain glow about him this morning, and it's down to a very successful blind date.

He sent me this text at 7.21 p.m. last night: 'This is worrying. She is HOT. I was expecting a right dog but she is lovely.' He is such a romantic.

Stevie the limousine driver, whisking Baz to his destiny, created a boy code on route: 'I'll ask you what the weather is like, if you like her say it is a nice night, if she is minging say it looks like rain.' Sure enough, when they picked Eilidh up Baz was asked the big question, to which he replied: 'It looks like being a lovely evening.' And they say girls play games! Huh.

Well, they got on splendidly, he behaved impeccably (for Baz) and he hopes to see her again. However, he admits he is aware her father (who is apparently loaded and drives a

Porsche) will probably be standing with a shotgun if he even tries.

I've never been on a blind date before for two reasons: (1) I am too chicken; (2) nobody would ever set their friends up with me. I am shocked at the number of listeners who get in touch with tales of successful first encounters:

'I went on a blind date with a school teacher – she taught me quite a lot!' Gerry, Wishaw.

'I met my husband on a blind date twenty years ago and we are still happily married today.' Mags.

'I was set up on a blind date by two women who run my local burger van. Neil and I have now been together three years and married for two.' Gill, Kirkcaldy.

[True love obviously doesn't always run smoothly, however:]

'I had a nightmare blind date. The guy was so dull I did a runner when he went to the bar. Do I feel bad about it now? No, he was a munter!' Nikky.

'I only went on one blind date; she had a voice like an angel, face like a gorilla, never again.' Ross, East Kilbride.

Eilidh actually calls in the show to give us her take on events. She thought he was great fun, looked a bit too 'studenty' but would love to see him again 'probably just as friends.' Awww. To be fair, Baz is fairly upbeat about the whole experience. He would definitely like a wee kiss but accepts she's 'not up for the Cup' (another 'Pollokism', my friends). The fact he is now texting his nudie buddy from the Bobar photo shoot makes me think he will survive this latest chapter of his emotional development . . .

Wednesday the 26th

Another two days of eating only fruit and vegetables in a vain bid to balance out my crazy weekend has blatantly failed. I'm the only person in the Real Radio fat class to put on weight. Half a pound to be precise and I'm sure I can pinpoint it to the blackcurrant cordial in the snakebite. The whole regime is beginning to get me down again. I can't seem to be able to enjoy a weekend and lose pounds. The fact that everybody else seems to be able to manage makes me feel even worse.

Still, I'm not the only one who has to give up the good stuff – Rangers manager Paul Le Guen is on the front pages this morning after he's banned his players from eating curry. The Frenchman is a fitness fanatic, having completed the six-day desert *Marathon des Sables* in the Sahara. He's now insisted his players must follow his strict regime, so out go chips, fast food, take-away, and top of the list, curry.

Jim from Netherlee makes me laugh with this text: 'No curry? Does he want Fernando Ricksen to drink on an empty stomach?'

I can only imagine how upset famous Glasgow restaurateur Satty Singh is going to be. The Rangers squad use his restaurant, Mr Singh's, like a second home. He even called his sons after two of his favourite players; spare a thought for Oleg Kuznetsov Singh and his brother Mark Walters Singh. Previous Gers bosses Graeme Souness, Walter Smith and Alex McLeish often treated their squad to curry nights out for team bonding.

So far the rumours filtering out of Murray Park suggest Le Guen has already started severely kicking curry-filled ass. He has apparently insisted on bunk beds at the training facility so the lads can rest between their twice-a-day fitness sessions. He has also seriously reprimanded one player for leaving a newspaper on the floor, and another for putting his feet on the canteen table.

I wonder if he fancies becoming a slimming class teacher. With a reputation like that I'm quite sure I'd stay away from *les frites et le fromage et le snakebite* for ever . . .

Thursday the 27th

Some days the papers are worth poring over. Today the entire centre spread in the *Sun* is the final shot from the naked bar photo shoot. Oor Baz is there, but you need a magnifying glass to see him (hee-hee, cheap but childishly enjoyable gag!). He is literally the furthest away figure. We can see the side of his head and a glimpse of his right shoulder, and that is it. He is relieved, but secretly quite gutted. If you are going to get your kit off for Art it might as well be worth your while. Over 500 people applied, only thirty-five were accepted, and it strikes me they are all fairly fit looking.

Fun-time Steve McKenna is standing in for Robin at the moment which always makes for an interesting show. He is so wacky and off the wall I have to be constantly alert to keep up. The thing is, he is like this off air too, a kind of whirlwind of mayhem and insanity, with a heart of gold.

Talking of fit naked people, his tongue pops through his cheek when asking me how I got on at fat class yesterday. I have to admit my shameful news. 'You need to go spin-ning,' he grins. We have mentioned this off air once, and my thoughts are as follows: spin cycle classes at the gym are the closest thing to self-inflicted torture one can get. They're intense, high-energy sessions for the super-fit; in short, pure murder. Steve knows my thoughts but continues with glee: 'I think we should get you fit with a spin class tomorrow. I'm sure we could get bikes in and an instructor.'

True to form, the phones go nuts. Within five minutes we have equipment, a scary instructor, and kind offers from a paramedic, a physiotherapist and a man that fits stair lifts just in case. Tomorrow, it seems, I shall spin my way through the show. They plan to dangle a roll and square sausage in front of me on a stick, and 'Zander'?!! is coming in to shout at me to go faster. Every now and then I wonder why I don't have a 'proper' job. This is one of those occasions.

As I go to leave I catch sight of another disturbing photo in the *Sun*. Poor old *Knight Rider* has been pictured steaming drunk again – we shall have to start calling him David Hasselhoff and a hauf . . .

Friday the 28th

It is now 9.25 a.m. and I feel as if I've been speared up the bum. Anyone who says THAT is good for you can go and spin! From 7.15 a.m. , for an entire hour – including my 7.30 a.m. sports bulletin – we cycled on our stationary spin bikes. Not gentle 'round Millport look at the pretty scenery' cycling, but *Tour de France* 'trying for the yellow jumper hill race' cycling.

Zander, as expected, was a fitness fanatic with a penchant for inflicting pain with a big smile on his distinctly non-purple and non-sweaty face. After a short warm-up (by which point I was already quite knackered) he went into the full routine. Up for eight, down for eight, up for four, down for four, up for two, down for two, up, down, up down up down – fall over in a heap. Dance music is blaring in the background as we go through our paces.

I've kept up my running since the 5km which I am fairly proud of, but my quads, the muscles at the front of my thighs, feel like I've never been on a bike before. Within twenty minutes I am more purple than a bruised blackcurrant drinking Ribena. Through adverts we cycle, through tunes we cycle and I somehow manage to read a sports report like I'm making a dodgy heavy-breathing phone call.

Zander screeches, 'Up on your feet, Cat. Come on, put some effort into it. Turn up the resistance, kiss that saddle with your bum cheeks.' WHIT! My bum cheeks will never be able to move again, let alone kiss anything.

I am geed on by texts of encouragement including: 'Faster, FASTER, FAAAAAAAAASTER.' The Paisley Painters; and 'My radio alarm has just woken me up with your panting and groaning. What on earth is going on? It sounds like fun anyway!' Michelle.

Bossman Billy pops his head into the studio and has tears in his eyes. I'm not sure if it is the surreal vision of the studio with all chairs replaced by bikes, Steve dressed in eighties fitness gear complete with pink sweat band, or my face, which I've mentioned on numerous occasions goes the most horrific colour of red.

The studio now reeks of man sweat (I obviously smell like a fresh daisy) and I am so soaking wet with perspiration I look like I've showered with my clothes on. At the end of our workout Zander informs me I've just burnt off the calorific equivalent of two rolls and square sausage. For the first time in the history of the show I actually have to leave the studio to have a shower during the wind-up section. I return refreshed, with adrenalin pumping and craving that roll and square sausage he mentioned more than I could ever have imagined.

When Baz dropped a little hot brown bag in my lap twenty minutes later and placed a can of chilled Irn Bru at my desk I could've kissed him. But I've seen him naked and in a dress, so I just said thanks and set about enjoying the fruits of my labour.

Fridays are great again after all. Only a big fluffy cushion for my tender tush could make me any happier . . .

Monday the 31st

There's a cracking wee yarn in the *Daily Express* today about a terrier called Ratty who gets the bus three times a week to the local pub. It started by accident one day when he followed a crowd of people getting on to a bus near his home in York. He popped off when everybody disembarked and walked into the pub where the landlady, who recognised him from the neighbouring village, fed him sausages, then drove him home. Wee Ratty had such a top day that he does the same unaccompanied trip on a regular basis and has become quite a celebrity. First Bus even commented: 'We never charge for dogs so there is no reason why he can't continue his adventures.'

Bert from Glasgow is on the phone straight away. 'My mum used to send our dog out to the icey with a pound for marshmallows.' My cheeks hurt laughing at this wonderfully eccentric opening line. 'He would go with a pound note in his mouth and come back with a perfectly intact bag of marshmallows.'

Steve has a valid point: 'How did your mum discover this?' Bert has no idea but who cares, it's a belting story. Texts included:

'My collie Bruno skateboards; the local kids come round and ask if he is coming out to play.' Kath, Galashiels.

'My gran had a border collie that got his dinner on a plate at the same time as my grandparents. One time my dad was round and saw a plate of spaghetti bolognese on the table. He was about to tuck in when my gran shouted, "Don't touch that it's for the dog!"' Paddy in Falkirk.

We have a right laugh on air this morning about my Saturday evening attempts to get young Baz a girlfriend. I sent him a text from the party I was at in Glasgow, Nichola's twin sisters Michelle and Angela Kane's thirtieth birthday bash.

I told him there was loads of talent and free booze and he arrived within eight minutes of my invite.

Michelle caught his eye straight away, although my opening introduction of, 'This is my friend Baz, he gets naked in public,' needs a bit of work. Her dad, the famous Harry Kane, has listened to all of Baz's blind date exploits and his artistic endeavours. Giving him the stern fatherly once-over, he finally caught his eye and said: 'You seem like a decent lad, on you go – fire in!' I'm not sure who was more shocked, Baz or Michelle, but the heated flames of passion were definitely cooled, and they both scuttled off to different ends of the party all youthfully coy.

The thing is, Baz gets a glowing beamer whilst I'm recounting this tale which makes me think he may actually quite like her. I shall e-mail him her e-mail address and see what happens. Whether he takes her daddy's advice remains to be seen but I shall keep you posted. Cilla Black had better watch out . . . there's a new Cat on the block.

august

Tuesday the 1st

My new-found talent for matchmaking is tested to the max this morning. I've received an e-mail from Sharlene, Susan and Jill in Edinburgh with the following tale of woe:

'Hi Cat,

   My friend Lisa met a bloke called Brian on Saturday and she's not stopped going on about him ever since. He was on a stag do but his pal Monty was too drunk to get into Espionage so we took them to a club called Massa. Anyway, they forgot to swap numbers and now she is devastated. He loves the wind-ups and always listens to Real Radio. Can you help?'

Instantly we are bombarded with texts saying: 'He is clearly married.' This is not the happy ending I was looking for. Another text says: 'I think Brian will be OK. If he is like me and my married mates, he will have used a false name and the ring will be in the pocket, from BRIAN in GLAS-GOW.' This is NOT going according to plan. However, one wee text grabs my eyes.

'This is Bryan. It was not a stag do it was Monty's birthday and we were very drunk.' I reckon this could be our man and we call him live on air. He eventually answers and sounds very sheepish. It turns out he is sitting on the bus to work and mortified about the call. However, he did like Lisa and wants to meet again. He reluctantly admits he hasn't a clue what she looks like but knows that she was 'OK'. Ah, men they say the sweetest things. I duly forward Sharlene the mobile number and insist on getting the full juicy details as they unfold. Hey, if it doesn't work our there is always young Baz!

I'm intrigued by yet another survey in the *Record* today – the 100 most annoying things in the world. I'm sure we had one of these a few months ago. However, some of the answers do make me chuckle. At eighty-nine – chihuahuas, at sixty-three – estate agents, at forty-six – Americans, and at thirty-eight – Jehovah's Witnesses.

The new top ten is:

10. Noisy neighbours.
 9. Ex-smokers
 8. Chantelle and Preston
 7. Brown-nosers
 6. Tailgaters
 5. Traffic wardens
 4. James Blunt (I laughed out loud; still, he has a semi by the sea so he shouldn't be too despondent)
 3. Queue-jumpers
 2. Caravans
 1. Cold callers.

These surveys are all about opinions so spare a thought for those chihuahua-owning American Jehovah's Witnesses listening to James Blunt in their caravans. They must feel very picked upon indeed . . .

Wednesday the 2nd

It's 5.00 a.m. BST, 6.00 a.m. European time. Wey-hey, I am in Spain. Steve is in the Glasgow studio and in total shock. In a sensational last-minute Direct Holidays secret operation, Mr W., Jacob Chan and I are now in Salou, in the PortAventura theme park. We have outside broadcast equipment, passports and about three T-shirts between us, and we're here for three days to 'enhance the vacation station promotion'. We are not on a jolly having fun in the sun, we are here to work. I choose to ignore the fact all three of us have had two hours' sleep after a late night visit to Idols Karaoke Bar. We arrived late last night and decided to get into the spirit of the resort for research purposes.

I can tell Steve is totally stunned and thinks I am actually in the studio next door. The wonders of technology soon change his mind. Mr W. takes a photo of me outside our hotel in the morning sunshine inappropriately dressed in my winter hoodie, and puts it straight on to the website. Thankfully, the general opinion from the listeners is 'good on you, nutcase!' To be honest I blame Sophie and Alan from Direct Holidays who came up with the plan and managed to get us flights at the very last minute.

I haven't written any sport but who cares, it is eighty-seven degrees and the forecast is for clear blue skies all day. I ask the listeners to text or call any friends and relatives in the Salou area to tell them to look out for us. I have a microphone and a bin bag full of Real Radio goodies to give away. I've not got enough underwear, but I've enough branded lollypops and caps to keep all the kids in Spain happy.

After the show, we head for the Caribe water park where we splash around in rubber rings and throw ourselves down flume rides with bravado. However, we also did a little bit of 'work' and handed out merchandise and interviewed every Scot in sight. The best thing was – they all knew we were coming.

Helen and her two kids from Airdrie were first to say hello: 'My brother-in-law told me you were here so I came to track you down.' Billy from Port Seton was next: 'I love Real Radio. I can't believe you guys are here. Where is Bossman Jay, he's great.' I explain that Bossman Jay is probably lying in a darkened room wondering why three of his employees are currently in a water park!

Next up it's the magnificent PortAventura theme park where I stupidly keep up with the boys and go on every ride that looks terrifying in the brochure, and absolutely horrendous in real life. The Hurakan Condor is a 330ft free-fall ride which the park's PR girl described as 'horrific'. I should have listened.

Still, as the three amigos watch the closing fireworks and spectacular floating finale, we conclude that it's been a pretty good day at the office . . .

Thursday the 3rd

It's tough on these shifts let me tell you. Four hours of sleep this time, and up like the lark and on air for another award winner. Ahem.

We all popped out into Salou late last night to sample the nightlife and to meet as many listeners as possible. We actually managed to find the only authentic tapas bar in the predominantly English-speaking resort and it was brilliant. I hadn't a clue what half of the dishes were but the drinks Fredo (for that was his name) served were quite special, very special in fact, no room for mixers or ice but tasty nonetheless.

The most memorable Real Radio listener we bumped into was Big Ali from Whitburn, ironically a wee blonde bombshell about five foot nothing. She runs the Whitburn Judo Club and within seconds had me upside down with sandals at the ceiling, head two inches from the ground.

This morning's show flies by playing loads of audio clips that we recorded yesterday. This is brilliant on several levels. It sounds great having Scottish people in holiday mode, on air and sounding all excited. We are quite tired and it means I can have a relatively easy show and pop out for ten to enjoy the hotel breakfast – bacon baps with hash browns (euro-checks, remember).

Trip of the day was a jeep safari ride up through the Montsant National Park. It's sometimes called Spain's Grand Canyon, and the views are magnificent. We get to swim in a freshwater lake in the mountains, and conclude once again that this can be the best job in the whole of the world. I somehow manage to record audio on the 4x4 off-road section of our trip and it is hilarious. I am clinging on for dear life; there are massive engine revs, squeals of fear and a very shaky interview with Paul the Jeep driver.

Back at the hotel we conclude that as it is our final night, we had better go out and play. It is what our audience would want. Comedy moment of the night came courtesy of Jacob, our commercial writer, who is a very proud Scottish-Chinese guy. After a few 'special waters' Jacob tells me it's about time he kissed a nice girl. 'Let's face it,' he grinned with a cheeky glint in his eye, 'everyone fancies a Chinky at half-two in the morning!'

His words, my friends, not mine . . .

Friday the 4th

And now, the end is near . . . it's been an amazing trip but thank goodness we are heading home after the show. For no other reason than that I am SO tired. This morning, we've had fifty-five minutes' sleep!

Mr W., Jacob and I hit the town and made loads of new pals. We air-guitared with mops in a bar, murdered karaoke, Irish-danced in sombreros, and basically broke poor Alan from Direct Holidays who I suspect would've preferred to have a quiet night in, wee soul.

Mr W. informed the owners of Idols Bar that pictures of us in action on previous nights were on the Real Radio website. He gave the owner his business card and we never had to fork out for another drink all night. Not surprisingly, my Chi-Chi the Panda look has returned, but amazingly I am wide awake and raring to go. Steve is in great form and says that text messages have been flooding in from listeners in Scotland who love our adventures.

It really is an odd situation to be in; professionally I feel I should have been in bed earlier, however, I feel from the listeners' point of view I would be letting them down. I'm in Spain for three days – they expect me to enjoy it. And we really have. We have been broadcasting from Hotel PortAventura within the resort and I keep giggling through links as Betty Boo or Woody Woodpecker strolls past. This must be the dream holiday location for children.

The weather in the Costa Dorada is perfect, the Spanish people have been lovely to deal with, and we've met so many folk who love Real Radio that from our perspective it's been a worthwhile trip. Direct Holidays have thoroughly enjoyed the broadcasts too, and word is they will be delighted to take us away again. It really is a magical place to be working from and I'd love the opportunity to return. I'd like at least two years to recover first, but I shall be back.

I get a text today which muddles my head a little bit. The lovely wife of Gav, my ex-boyfriend, has just given birth to a wee boy. Gav and I were together for five and a half years until about four years ago and never, ever fell out. I just kind of went through a mad phase, got a bit scared and sort of drifted away. He was seven years older than me and at a different stage of his life in that he was sensible and mature and I wasn't. I still miss his friendship, but genuinely wish him all the best in the world. He will be a fantastic dad.

My phone goes text mental moments later; I assume it is my pals texting me the big news in case he's not been in touch but no – Tommy Sheridan has won his case against the *News of the World*. It is unbelievable. He took on the lawyers and was awarded £200,000 in damages. The paper called eighteen witnesses which the jury have chosen not to believe.

Many of these witnesses are MSPs and there is talk of retribution, perjury charges, a new SSP leadership battle, polygraph tests and book deals. The *Record* whisks Tommy and his Jackie O wife Gail, whose testimony won him the trial, away for exclusive interviews.

It really has been quite a day!

Monday the 7th

Two hours' sleep thanks to my reccuring insomnia, and I'm possibly the most run-down person ever. I have a spot on the side of my nose that has its own heart-beat. I am sure you can see it from space. It throbs and glows, and no amount of make-up will be able to cover it up. Steve welcomes me back from Spain on air with the loving line: 'Will you look at your plook it is massive. I think it should have its own show.'

Without asking, I am overwhelmed with advice. Toothpaste, aftershave, rose oil, aloe vera and arguably the most helpful one of all: 'Stop eating so much shit.'

Some out-of-this-world news this morning: UFOs have been spotted in Aberdeen. Over 120 phone calls were made to the police and coastguard after red lights, not of the Northern variety, were spotted floating in the air. After investigation it transpired that they came from little romantic Chinese lanterns lit at a wedding that floated lovingly into the air.

My friend Angela married a lovely German bloke called Markus. One of their traditions is for the guests to tie forfeits on to helium balloons and let them loose. If found, the finder would send the good luck message back to the married couple and the pledge has to be upheld by the guest who signed the card. Most people wrote things along the lines of, 'We shall look after the dog for a week,' or 'We shall paint your fence.' I wrote, 'I shall treat the couple to a night out in Clatty Pats nite-spot.' I'm not sure whether they got my tag or not, maybe it is quite telling they have so far not tried to cash it in.

Today's show flies by with a mix of e-mails and calls about our trip to Spain. Like the Hong Kong adventure, it is really nice to see that people enjoy our travels as much as we do. To be honest, that makes it worth while. This one from Joanne Coull made me laugh out loud:

'Hi Cat, My mum is Big Ali. I was wetting myself when I heard your tales about her. I hope she didn't throw you too hard. She is quite a character.
Love Joanne – I'm also from the Whitburn Judo Club!'

I leave the show with one closing thought – can you imagine playing Twister with this family at Christmas?

Tuesday the 8th

Teenagers across Scotland are sitting by their front doors this morning. It's exam results day and I can feel their pain. I remember the anxious feeling waiting for the big brown envelope to pop through the letterbox. Somehow I did OK, but all the reassurances in the world won't help the wee souls' nerves today.

I'm also a bit nervous. This afternoon I have to talk to all the staff at Black & White Publishers and explain what this book is all about (nonsense), where the idea came from (Jack's party), and what I hope to achieve (a right good launch party and some free Christmas prezzies for my family). It's weird I can murder songs in front of 35,000 people but get a bit wobbly having to speak to ten people in suits. I think I have 'proper job syndrome'. I'm scared of grown-ups that have them.

Well, it goes OK I think, the people were lovely although I just started yapping and wasn't sure when to shut up. Ali, one of the heid yins, asked: 'Describe your book in one word.' My reply, 'Eh, mince?' was not my finest.

The funniest part of the day was meeting Reg McKay, Robert Jeffrey, Alexander McGregor and Les Brown. The first three have written books about true crime, the latter is a former policeman who has also written a book. It was like being stuck in an episode of *Taggart*, but with real people. They swapped stories and concluded that people really are buried in the concrete pillars of the Kingston Bridge. My lovely uncle Vic will be so pleased; he was part of the original design team. I can now assure him it is gangster bones in the structure, not bad planning, that is making it fall apart.

Anyway, I sat enthralled and drank far too much of the wine that Oliver, the sprightly work placement guy, kept pouring. He spent the day asking what he had to do to be included in this book and at one stage he agreed to have CAT painted on his bum to perform naked street theatre in the Royal Mile. The fact he kept refilling my glass was enough to merit a mention, but hey ho, I had fun seeing just how far he was prepared to go.

Despite arriving at 11.00 a.m. for the meeting, I catch the 7.30 p.m. train home, vowing to attend more publishers' meetings. During the journey, I spoke to a fifteen-year-old boy and his pals from Falkirk about their exam results and told them the only way to get rich and pull girls is to chuck it and form a rock band. I am sensing I am NOT a careers guidance officer for a reason . . .

Wednesday the 9th

This morning I have a mission. Most books have launch parties and the publishers have stupidly let me chose a theme and venue. To market the book, they are hoping to attract *No. 1* magazine, Scotland's version of *OK!* or *Hello*. However, it is quite a glossy publication and apparently they say they only cover glamorous functions and black tie balls.

I find this quite amusing given the lack of real A-list events in Scotland. In the *Hello* social diary they have Princess Caroline of Monaco wearing Versace in St Tropez. In the last *No. 1* they had Debbie from Dundee at a bank opening wearing TopShop, I kid you not. Debbie looked great, though, and to be honest that is why I like the magazine. I want to be 'Cat from Real Radio wears her maw's frock'.

I'd quite like to have a karaoke night at Firhill, but I suspect they are looking for something a little more highbrow. The natural thing to do is open the forum to our audience, who once again come up with some cracking suggestions, most of which involve recruiting Tommy Sheridan as party planner. My favourites include:

'What about a Pirate Party at your local baths?' Paul McKenna.

'A pyjama party on the Waverley.' Una, Dunfermline.

'Have a prehistoric themed do at Edinburgh Zoo.' Elaine.

'You could have a black and white party, men in black, women in white.' Karen, E.K.

'Have it in my house.' Dave, Coatbridge.

'Have a wind-up themed night with Old Mrs Galloway, Hector, Cecil and as many boabies as the room can hold.' Keith, Hamilton.

'Have it in the Thistle trophy room – plenty of space in there.' Gordon.

I love them all but am particularly drawn to the pirates and pyjama party themes. A big Cat's pyjamas party, how much fun is that? I can imagine the headline writer in *No. 1* now: 'Here is Bossman Jay from Real Radio wearing a fetching Paisley pattern ensemble.' I would go for the full length stripy Wee Willie Winkie look complete with droopy nightcap; Robin, with his cute bum and toned legs could pick up a nice silk negligée in a summer pastel shade.

I shall send all the ideas to those in charge to see what they say, but my Jimmy Choo sheepskin baffies are ready to party . . .

Thursday the 10th

I've become a researcher in my own right. I've commissioned, embarked upon, created and concluded my own official high-brow survey. A Nobel Prize for informative data collection is surely forthcoming. Here goes: ninety per cent of Scottish people have an aunt or elderly relative called Jean. The boffins at the universities will be gobsmacked.

This stunning statistic, albeit only based on evidence from twenty Real Radio staff, was quite a revelation. I thought many of us had Auntie Jeans, but eighteen out of twenty is a proportion, in my learned opinion, that is, erm, quite a lot.

I have an Auntie Jean who lives in Helensburgh and is very nice, Robin had one, Bossman Jay's mum is Jean and Dougie Jackson has two Auntie Jeans while Mr W. claims he has an Uncle Jean, who is French. The problem is there are very few young Jeans, and I start a campaign to introduce more.

The phones almost crash with people sharing Auntie Jean stories. Ann is first on the phone: 'My Auntie Jean was a legend. She made crispy egg pieces and special Angel Delight.' When we asked what they were, she laughed: 'She made boiled egg pieces with bits of shell through them and the Angel Delight always had a powdery bottom.'

Along with the hundreds of 'I have an Auntie Jean' texts were these crackers:

'My granny was Jean, she had four daughters who all gave birth to daughters and called them Jean!' Jean in the Crook.

'You know how everyone has aunts or uncles that aren't actually relatives, well I have a brilliant Auntie

Jean, and I think everyone should have one.' Lorraine, Hamilton.

'My wife has an Auntie Jean, she is a drunken nutter.' Steve, Edinburgh.

'My dog is called Jean.' John.

'I have an Aunty Jean Parker, nosey Parker by name and nature. We hate her.' Lynn.

Paul Smith from Airdrie tells us his wee girl Jean was born last Wednesday, while Fab in Falkirk's husband's Auntie Jean lives in Ayr and is 102. I'm delighted to hear the Jean gene pool is going from strength to strength . . .

On a more sombre note, the UK has just been placed in a state of 'critical alert' after a plot to bring at least nine jets down in mid-air has been uncovered. All flights in and out of Heathrow have been suspended and for the first time ever, hand luggage is banned in all UK airports. Twenty suspects have been arrested and Scotland Yard say they have 'disrupted an attempt at mass murder'.

In another bit of unfortunate timing, I have a flight booked for 6.00 a.m. tomorrow morning for a *Sunday Mail* travel feature in Prague. Getting on flights at the best of times terrifies the living daylights out of me, and with extra tension I am not actually sure what to do. I shall Czech out the situation in the morning . . .

Monday the 14th

Big smiles all round. I'm just back from Prague where I spent the weekend. Despite all the chaos, Mr Cat and I decided to go for it and had a ball. Travel writing really can be the best fun in the world, and it helps that lovely Liz the magazine editor at the *Sunday Mail* is my friend and keeps commissioning trips.

I managed to wangle Friday off for winning the Real Radio employee of the month award, much to the surprise of, well, everybody to be honest. Along with a £50 cheque and a wee trophy, I was granted a 'duvet day' – this is basically a cheeky wee day off that's a reward for being such a diligent and valuable asset to the company. Hee-hee.

Robin was in tears when he found out I'd won. I am many things but a compliant cog in the corporate machine I am most definitely not. If something is wrong I moan about it, if something could be improved I make myself unpopular by saying exactly how I see it.

My dad used to quote Robert Burns to me from an early age: 'A man o' independent mind – is king o' men for a' that.' Turns out he took these two lines from two different verses, but I like the sentiment, and he was on the Glenmorangie at the time. I've taken this on board and remain very much in charge of my own destiny. (I'm chuckling as I write this, remembering the feng shui man's 'destructive, but only to yourself' warning.) I've had many ups and many downs but they've all been of my own doing.

The Real Radio employee of the month award is generally given to an outstanding member of staff who has gone over and above the call of duty to help the company. The only thing I can think of which gave me the edge was cultivating a spot bigger than the one Bossman Billy has been sporting on his forehead recently, thus alleviating the pressure on our esteemed MD.

Anyway, I took Friday as a 'duvet day' and wrapped myself up in a nice Prague hotel blanket.

Security at Glasgow Airport was extreme. Only people travelling were allowed into the airport. Hand luggage was banned. We had to take travel documents and passports in a clear poly bag, and at security everybody was thoroughly searched with shoes and belts being removed and scanned.

Robin flew to Manchester for a stag do on Friday and was stopped by the police going into the airport. He'd booked an e-ticket and didn't have proof. The police asked for ID and he showed his Visa card.

'Robin Galloway?' questioned Glasgow's finest. 'Robin Galloway, so you're Robin Galloway?' He continued to stare; Robin by this point is getting a bit twitchy. 'Can you do Hector Brocklebank and we'll let you in?' Robin naturally obliged, they were in stitches and he was cleared for take-off. It's nice to know in a state of critical alert a decent rendition of a fish-delivering Peterhead lorry driver can get you straight through . . .

Tuesday the 15th

'Dirty Harry' is the headline grabbing attention this morning, complete with a full page picture of the royal prince in action. He's not in a trench with his regiment; he's in a nightclub with a pretty blonde that is not his girlfriend. He is kissing her cheek, and quite frankly copping a right royal feel! It's a nickname I'm sure will stick, as he's been a bit of a lad for his tender years.

Baz had a pal called 'Gary Cartwright cannae fart right', although only the first two parts of this name are official. With school starting back for the kids on Monday we get some cracking nicknames from our playground pasts:

'We'd a classmate called "Janice Kelly broke her belly slipping on a piece 'n' jelly".' Big Kev.

'My brother was called Wire-nut because of his hair.' Kevin, Milton.

'Kevin Dyet was called "Dyet Dyet pick your nose and fry it".' Kate, Motherwell.

'Lydia McAuley was called "Lydia tea-pot" or "Lydia dustbin".'

'We had an "Ian Cooper, paratrooper, super duper pooper scooper"!'

'At school my mum was called "Gladys padys nikyradys red heed carrot nose" – thank God I'm not named after her.' Ann.

'I was at school with a Chinese boy called Foo Kin Chan. We used to have great fun in the playground in front of the teachers shouting "Foo Kin come here."'

And Derek Spence in Edinburgh made me smile with this e-mail:

'I went to Craiglockhart Primary in the mid seventies; we had one lad called "The Dirty Apple Man" because he picked up an apple from the playground once. I think he actually put it in the bin but kids can be cruel. His name is Scott but I won't mention his second name in case he is a hit man now or something.'

It's always entertaining to learn what old school friends are up to. The most amusing example I can think of is my friend Gail Easdale who I sat next to in O-grade and higher music. She became a dancer, married Paul Robinson from *Neighbours*, aka 1980s' pop star Stefan Dennis, and now lives in Australia with their son. Ah, school tales, 'Don't It Make You Feel Good Baby . . .'

Wednesday the 16th

Elvis is alive and living, well, everywhere in central Scotland it would seem. Today is the twenty-ninth anniversary of his death. Robin was, ironically, a teenager sitting on the toilet when his dad broke the news that the King of Rock and Roll had been found passed away on *his* throne.

I comment that I saw a guy on the Largs to Millport ferry once who was the absolute double of the great man and we inadvertently kick-start bedlam. There are plenty of conspiracy theories about his death with fans hoping he'd merely gone into hiding. As the song says, 'There's a guy works down the chip shop swears he's Elvis' – well, let me tell you, he fair gets about. Texted sightings include:

'Elvis works for the Co-op in Harthill and goes by the name Ian Mathews.'

'I've just had him in my cab. We went to McDonald's for a happy meal.' Ian the Bellshill cabbie.

'Elvis is working at the Blochairn fruit market and calls himself wee Tam.'

'Elvis is the safety officer at Longannet Power Station and is called Martin Hall.' Jack.

'My sister Moira Dobbie is marrying Elvis, or Jon Scott as he is now called. He is Elvis mad, he sings like him, he styles his hair like him and their four-year-old son Brendan says 'thank you very much' in Elvis's voice.' Jackie, Cambuslang.

'He is working in Asda in Robroyston, although he is now black.' Andy.

'He is currently emulsioning a kitchen in Anstruther, I have just seen him.' Dougan.

'The rest are fibbing, Elvis is the head chef at Carluke golf course.' Wee Dunny.

And we have two cracking calls. The first, a bloke from Airdrie says: 'I go with the theory he is in Glasgow. I nipped into the Ladbrokes in town for a pee and it said on the wall "Elvis lives in Duke Street". I for one believe that. If it is written on a lavvy wall it must be true.'

Next up it is Louise from Clackmannanshire: 'Elvis comes to Clackmannanshire every year. He appears as a shape on the hillside in the bracken, sort of like an Elvis crop circle. He loves the place that is why he comes back every year.'

Robin and I have sore cheeks from laughing but sure enough we get at least ten separate texts from Clackmannanshire residents assuring us this is one-hundred-per-cent true and a well-known fact about the area. I'm not sure about Elvis, but I'm certainly all shook up with this tale uh huh huh . . .

Somehow, after my two-pound gain last week, I lose half a pound at fat class this morning which just doesn't make sense. I've lived on fattening beer, yummy grub and Czech ice cream and lost weight. Maybe Czech checks are like my euro-calories. My only other big loss was after T in the Park which was a bit of a drink-fest too. Maybe if I give up solids and just stay steaming I shall be Kate Moss by next month. On second thoughts, if that mean's I'd have to kiss that grubber Pete Doherty, I'd rather stay a wee porker . . .

Thursday the 17th

Folk can be right daft. There is a story in the *Record* this morning about a bloke from Ayrshire who is lucky to be alive after sustaining six bites from two poisonous adders. He picked up the snakes for a photo whilst out walking in Arran. However, because he was a big fifteen-stone lad, the venom didn't kill him. His brother is now complaining, 'They should have signs up warning of the danger.'

Is it just me, or is picking up two snakes for a photo quite an obvious thing NOT to do – kind of like NOT throwing petrol on a fire and NOT jumping in front of a train? Still, at least he'll not be doing that again anytime soon.

There is something grating Robin this morning that he won't be doing anytime soon as well, playing golf. Today is the annual Real Radio golf day, an executive day out where the great and good of the station plus top clients and contacts pretend to play golf and spend far too much time in the nineteenth. The thing is, in the five years since its inauguration, Robin has not been invited. As the station's obvious number one asset, he is a bit miffed. The fact that he bought new clubs on eBay a few weeks ago, in anticipation of the big day, is only adding to his angst. He claims it is obviously because the chief cheeses assume he will be too busy, but says it would be nice to be asked.

When I subtly ask Phil the engineer why Robin has been overlooked he replies instantly: 'Because he is rubbish.' Still, Jim the taxi driver from Livingston phones in and offers to take him fishing next week. He's a Reel winner!

Scott, the marketing guru from Arnold Clark is one of the important guests going. Seeing Bossman Billy, Gav from sales and Scott heading off together makes me smile. The last time I saw the trio together they were on a 'corporate break' to Norway. I had just checked into Prestwick Airport with Alyson and Janis *en route* to the Scotland game in Oslo when Aly said, 'Is that not your boss?', which is not the best line to hear when wearing a Scotland top, draped in a saltire and heading for a three-day party. In fairness they looked equally shocked to see me – their client goodwill trip partially exposed as a freebie to the football!

However, it turned out that rather than hindering each other's fun, we enhanced it. We hooked up for the full three days, Scotland won, we all ended up in Viking hats and they went from being colleagues to firm friends. I've learned lots about the transitional path from boy to man in Larkhall, why Scott from Arnold Clark likes big holes (a bizarre digger fascination) and how good it must be to be the MD and own a company credit card.

For the record, if our lovely big chiefs down south, John Myers and John Simons, are still reading this, Billy bought six diet cokes and a baguette and worked tirelessly to secure another year's sponsorship for the *Breakfast Show* . . .

Friday the 18th

This morning we cause possibly the biggest commotion in Real Radio history. The phone system crashed three times and we've literally thousands of angry/congratulatory texts and e-mails. This morning, I beat a nine-year-old child in a competition. (Pantomime booooooooooooooo!)

All week we have been running a quiz with MacB flavoured water. Basically, a kid comes on and takes me on with two questions each about general knowledge. All week I have deliberately lost, with my questions being nigh on impossible to answer. This means the kid gets £500 to spend on whatever they choose. Today I got both of my questions right and the little girl, Becky Galloway, cried. Her mum came on and shouted that she was taking matters further and hung up. I sound mortified.

Hundreds phone in to complain: 'That is a disgrace, you can't do that to a child,' while a proportionate amount also phone in to placate: 'You won fair and square, she was a wee brat anyway.' We run about six calls on air from the favourable to the absolutely furious.

I read the 8.00 a.m. sport in a manner that suggests I may greet as the magnitude of my error sinks in. The internal 'naughty' line flashes. Steph Lamont, whose sales and promotions clients MacB are, is nearly in tears. She has had to pull into a lay-by on the motorway, shaking.

However, fear not. I'm not really a baddie. We've both been clenching our fists and holding in the laughter talking to folk all calling for our heads for half an hour. Robin is impressed with my convincingly humiliated and remorseful voice whilst dipping the faders every few seconds to let me crack up with laughter. For at 8.15 a.m. we have Becky back on air and reveal to the nation that it has been one big wind-up. Becky is Robin's niece and will be starring in future wind-ups sporadically.

A wee boy comes on for real and wins the money and peace is restored. The response is phenomenal:

'That was the best wind-up ever.' The van boys.

'I vowed never to be caught out by a wind-up, the pair of you played an absolute blinder. I was furious and now I feel like a numpty. You are brilliant.' Joyce, Haddington.

'Cat, I'm sorry I swore at you in my last text you are still a wee sweetheart.' Big Jim and the quarry boys.

Tam is more straightforward: 'You are a pair of tadgers but that was funny.'

Thank goodness I'm off for my holidays now. I need a week in a dark room to lie down and recover . . .

First, though, we have to attend the Enable Scotland Ball in the Radisson Hotel in Glasgow. Robin and I have been asked to host part of the evening with comedienne Karen Dunbar also taking to the microphone. This is a fabulous charity helping people with learning difficulties in a variety of ways.

To be honest, we could be out every night of the week with charity requests and unfortunately have to knock most of them back because of our early bedtimes, but this was one we both really wanted to do. The fact that Jack McConnell's wife Bridget is involved and we both felt a bit guilty about the 'duvet farting incident' is actually coincidental.

Before we take to the floor I get ridiculously star-struck at the bar; Ricky Ross and Lorraine from Deacon Blue are next to me. I've interviewed Sir Alex Ferguson, Ryan Giggs and John Lambie and been fine, but I've had a wee crush on Ricky since I was about thirteen and came over all pink-faced and shy!

Most of the cast of *River City* were present and, I have to say, they are a cracking bunch. It must be a hoot working on that show.

I have a nice chat with Sean Scanlan who is playing Captain Hook in the panto and his hilarious wife Barbara Rafferty who is most famous for being Jamesie Cotter's wife Ella in *Rab C Nesbitt*. They are the nicest wee showbiz couple and bags of fun.

The film shown at the ball, describing how people with learning difficulties can be integrated into the workforce and what it means to the individuals involved, is truly moving and I rue my choice of non-waterproof mascara as I step up for our next slot.

In the auction I bid £500 for a trip round Edinburgh with Ian Rankin, author of the Rebus books, but the prize eventually goes for £1,400. I would expect Ian Rankin to move in and be my houseboy for that.

By half-eleven Robin and I are both very tired. However, the evening managed to raise over £50,000 which is superb. We meet and chat to loads of bubbly listeners as we try to leave, and I finally get home at half past two, twenty-three hours after getting up. I'm not complaining, though. There are so many good people working tirelessly and behind the scenes to help others in Scotland, it just feels good that our tiny wee bit helps.

September

Monday the 4th

I'm back from a two-week break and it feels great. After a ten-day trip to Majorca and Ibiza (coming to a *Sunday Mail* magazine in the shape of a travel feature sometime soon), it is back to the early alarm call and *Breakfast Show* mayhem.

I never slept a wink last night and I now look as if I've been, well, in Ibiza for ten days. My e-mail inbox has closed again with the volume of mail I've to respond to and I've just found out *Offside* is to start again for a short run before Christmas.

The show is filmed on a Monday, my only night off the panto. This now means that from the start of November, I will only have one day off, Christmas Day, until the last week in February when hopefully I will return in one piece from the charity jungle trek. Four months with one day off, working from 5.00 a.m. until 11.00 p.m. Whimper. On the plus side, this schedule will surely do wonders for my liver and waist-line.

I had an interesting chat with Mr Cat about this book on holiday. He's always insisted he has NOT to be mentioned. However, after a few beers, when he found out nearly everybody I know features at some stage, the petted lip came out. The conversation went as follows:

Me: 'But YOU said you didn't want to be in it.'

Him: 'I don't but I never realised everyone else would be in it.'

Me: 'Well do you want to be in it or not?'

Him (huffily): 'Not bothered.'

Me: 'Do you want to be in it?'

Him (staring at feet like a five-year-old): 'Uh-huh.'

Me: 'Well, what would you like me to say, given that you've told me not to include you?'

Him: 'Just say I'm really handsome, dead funny and hung like a donkey.'

At this moment I realise why it HAS been a good idea to keep his appearances to a minimum.

Today's show is all about the two weekend Robbie Williams' concerts and the Scotland game where we thrashed the Faroe Islands 6–0 in the European Championship qualifiers.

I had got off the plane at 3.00 a.m. on Saturday morning and Bobby Harvey, despite being told not to even think about turning up, was the first cheery wee face I saw at the airport. 'Ach Toots; I got up for a pee and couldn't sleep. Your mum doesn't know I'm out.' He really is the best. I got to bed at 4.00 a.m. and was up at 11.00 a.m. to head straight to the Barrowlands where Tartan Army stalwart and delightfully debauched DJ Tam Coyle had organised another magnificent party with 1,500 crazy kilties.

Scotland were 5–0 up at half time; I left ten minutes into the second half and jumped on a bus and the tube to meet the Real Radio girls in Ashton Lane. I walked into the loft as Gary O'Connor scored our sixth. As Walter Smith might say, it is all about timing.

After a nice meal and a karaoke limousine trip to Hampden, it was a night with Robbie, who, I have to say, looked a bit rough. I believe he may have said the same about me. The gig was fun, although dare I say it, not as good as two years ago for the simple reason his new stuff is rubbish.

However, the highlight of the night was our arrival at the Pond Hotel, or 'Bates Motel' as it has been renamed by the girls. The sales team had several clients on a corporate trip which included rooms. They never realised the hotel was due to close the next day and was in running-down mode.

Kenneth the barman became Kenneth the room service man, the receptionist, the cleaner and the porter. Kenneth was not happy at ten girls wanting more than one sherry. When asked if the bar sold crisps or nuts, a not terribly unusual request, he said curtly: 'No, go to the garage.' We did, and returned with enough Doritos and dips to feed the whole of Hampden.

It is worth pointing out that the straining belt on my jeans is now out a full two notches from two weeks ago. Still it was a cracking weekend. Forget the health food; as Robbie might sing, 'I'm loving Nachos instead' . . .

Tuesday the 5th

Today is the day I should have been at Glasgow Airport with Alyson and Janis heading to Lithuania for the football. However, despite booking the trip months ago, I stupidly hadn't realised my summer holiday finished two days ago.

On the show this morning we phone Alyson live at the airport and it sounds mental. It is 6.15 a.m. and she is in the bar with 300 members of the Tartan Army. The girl is a natural loon and is a brilliant on-the-scene reporter despite never having been on air before. She gets the guys to sing some Scotland songs and my sense of longing is acute. I make a mental note to turn my phone off tonight, I'm sure there will be calls.

Last night I popped into the Pavilion for the pantomime auditions for children to be Peter Pan's lost boys. I have to admit I was astonished by the standard; it was like a mini X Factor.

Each kid (between eight and ten years old) was given the chance to read a part for a quick sketch. The elimination process was swift and decisive. Sheridan Nicol, the director, was friendly but firm. I'm now quite nervous about the whole thing, I will be the least experienced actor on the stage and it's all becoming quite real.

I'm finally beginning to catch up on the radio station gossip from my break. The big news is that Baz nearly lost his job after streaking on the *Football Phone In* which is now showing on satellite channel Setanta. I feel partially responsible given that it had been my idea before I left. Robin dared him to go through with it; he did and TWO sets of big bosses were furious. However, once again the cohesive force of people power proved vital and Pollok's finest mentalist lived to fight another day.

Last Friday, while I was in a dodgy Palma Nova bar watching an Abba tribute band, Robin and Bossman Jay were in row A of the Rolling Stones' concert in Glasgow. They made it backstage and were snapped with the band. Standing with Mick and Keith, Bossman 'Brown Sugar' Jay was in his element and must have looked positively youthful! Robin shows me his pictures on his laptop and all I can think of is, 'That would've been a cracker for the book!'

Jake Shears from the Scissor Sisters was also in the station for interviews and photos, but apparently he was a bit fragile from a London party. I've seen the pictures and it looks as if he took his mamma out for about a month . . .

Wednesday the 6th

We have a local farmer to thank for oor Baz being on the show this morning. He was cycling up a hill near East Kilbride last night when his hamstring pinged. The farmer heard his yelp, stuck his bike on the back of his truck and drove our fallen hero all the way back to Pollok. Like my dad picking me up at the airport in the middle of the night, these random acts of kindness deserve recognition and, reassuringly, there are plenty of knights in shining armour out there:

'I was lost a few months ago and asked an old lad for directions. He went and got his car out of his garage and drove in front of me all the way to my destination.' Jason, Kirkcaldy.

'I was on the train on Saturday to see Robbie Williams at Hampden and I was really bursting for the loo. An elderly lady who lived nearby heard me and took me into her house to use hers. How nice was that?' Gina, Glasgow.

'I dropped some postcards in New York I had written for my friends. A family from Florida added a wee message and posted them.' Ann, Glasgow.

[And even strange men on the fifth can be angels in Pringle jumper disguise:]

'I was caught short on the golf course with a partner I had only known for ten minutes, and he gave me his packet of Handy Andies. I've never been so grateful for anything.' Glen Roberts, Wishaw.

This morning I spot another advert in the papers for wacky German supermarket Lidl whose specials this week are telescopic trekking poles and cheap hiking gear. Waterproof walking boots are only £5.99. Not quite as exciting as the previous offer of horse blankets and sub-aqua gear, but impressive nonetheless. They also sell food, I believe!

We get loads of calls from people who have purchased odd things in the store. These include kids' wellies at the freezer counter (thick socks required), a £10 hedge trimmer next to the fruit section (handy for unruly broccoli) and a £4.99 collapsible spade which sounds as useful as a wicker pint glass.

Scotland face Lithuania tonight and kick-off is at 5.00 p.m. Everyone who works is moaning their wee heads off but Robin, Baz and I are delighted. We can watch the game and get to bed at a reasonable hour.

On a positive note, I only put on a pound and a half on holiday, which I consider a bit of a result. Looking at my card, since the Real Radio Scottish Slimmers started eight weeks ago, I have gone up and down and up and down. I am now only two pounds less than when I started while four people in the station have lost over a stone each. I grudgingly admit I am the archetypical yo-yo dieter. Mint ones are my favourites, followed by the orange ones. Yum.

Thursday the 7th

Scotland top group B, five points above World Cup holders Italy. A 2–1 win over Lithuania has given us six points out of six and big smiles all round this morning. We should enjoy the success while it lasts because it certainly vanishes rapidly; just ask wee Craigie 'come on Bravehearts' Broon. The former Scotland manager was refused entry to France v. Italy last night as the security guards had no idea who he was. They said his BBC accreditation looked dodgy and they'd never heard of him.

I have to admit I've always liked wee Craigie Broon, who is like a nice cuddly wee grandpa. He's polite, friendly and a big fan of my dad, Bobby Harvey!

As a young player, he used to sing in a band called Hammy and the Hamsters so he knows his music, and who would have guessed that by the age of sixty-two he would be an international playboy with tabloid stories revealing his complex love life with several women on the go at once, one in her early twenties!

When I did my postgraduate course in journalism at university, our first assignment was to write up a celebrity interview. Craig was in his first season as Scotland manager and I wrote to him asking him for a chat. He replied instantly and booked in three hours of his time up at his SFA office. He was open and helpful and never forgot where we first met in the dozens of times I subsequently interviewed him working for television.

He is passionate about the Tartan Army and loved this tale about when he met a drunken fan before a game in a bar in Estonia: 'I was just heading out to the team bus when I spotted a guy I'd seen at the most dismal and remote places we've ever played and at every reserve game. I asked him why he continued to follow Scotland and he replied: "Following Scotland is like going out with a woman with a permanent period – you know what it could be like but just never get there. I live in hope." I always thought that was a great way of looking at it, and every time we lost a game or didn't do as well as we should, I thought of that guy and how we could improve things for him.'

He did, I should add, have the decency to blush while recounting this tale.

For the record, I got seventy-four per cent for the essay, which was pretty impressive given that the lecturer's red marker in the margin at my title 'Celebrity interview – Craig Brown' said simply, 'Who is he?'

Some things, it seems, never change . . .

Friday the 8th

One of the puzzling phenomena of Woodlands Road in Glasgow is the mystical appearance through the night of random white goods at the bus stop. This morning a large fridge-freezer was poised upright in the centre of the stop with the upper compartment flapping open. This is not a unique occurrence, I reckon there's about five a month and I've no idea where they come from or why.

Baz has a photo in his mobile entitled 'random wardrobe'. It is exactly that – a full-size cupboard in the middle of Pollok.

We've had 'shoe watch' before, where random boots and trainers were reported; this morning for three hours our phone rings off the hook with sightings of unusual objects in unexpected places:

'I was out for a walk in the woods last week and came across a couch with a telly about four feet in front of it. It looked hilarious and quite comfy but there was nowhere to plug the TV in.' Lorraine, Airdrie.

'There is a stuffed pair of overalls with wellies sticking out of a hedge near Tesco in South Queensferry, the poor git has been there for years.' Sharon, Glasgow.

'This topic is so funny because I've just driven past a discarded loo in Paisley Road West near Bellahouston Park.' Jools, Glasgow.

'I've just passed an exercise bike outside the fruit market at Blochairn.' Dee.

[And there are always the comedians:]

'I was at the Muse gig two weeks ago and a girl had lost her shoes. I told her I'd seen many right at the front so she waited until the end and helped herself to someone else's.' From John on a couch floating down the Clyde.

'I saw a girl in Dundee with one shoe on, I said to her, 'You've lost a shoe, hen.' She said 'Naw, I've just found one.' Dunc Clark, Dunfermline.

I'm slightly scared today as we are all off to Leeds for the weekend to learn how to be a better *Breakfast Show*. All of the GMG radio bigwigs are going for an intense training course with lectures from leading international industry figures.

The invite letter informs us: 'Whilst alcohol can help you relax please don't spoil the company's reputation by overindulging!' Whilst this letter was sent to all twenty-six people attending, Robin and I are in no doubt it has been included for our benefit after THAT FRIDAY.

True to form, John Simons, our strict but likeable group programme director, is due in the station today. He walks in the door and comes straight over to me with a massive smile, he gives me a peck on the cheek and says warmly: 'Are you looking forward to the weekend? You're not going to let me down, are you, Cat?'

I'm now confused. Is it a warning, does he want me to behave impeccably, or does he want me to live up to the legend one particularly messy night out has created? I think I shall be cautious and moderately angelic; who knows, the next random object spotted in a weird place could be my rather chunky bottom booted out the Real Radio door . . .

Monday the 11th

We are still on air, folks, which is something of a miracle after our weekend *Breakfast Radio* boot camp. At the very beginning of the conference Simo told the distinguished gathering: 'We know Scotland can party everybody under the table, they do NOT have to prove it.' So from the word go we were under close inspection.

The seminar started with a speech from respected controller of Radio Two, Lesley Douglas. She opened with this cracking line: 'Management should remember you can never, ever, ever, ever manage talent.' The timing of this was sensational as Simo shot us both a look that implied, 'Don't even think about it.'

The hotel – in a remote industrial estate to keep us away from the Leeds nightlife – was packed with people going to the Robbie Williams concert. However, just as the banter was beginning to flow in the bar we were told to finish up. We were then actually physically escorted to bed.

I knew when my mobile rang fifteen minutes later it would be Robin. He only had to utter two words. 'Shall we?' And with that, your gruesome twosome sneaked out of their respective rooms, tip-toed down the corridor and headed back to the action until four in the morning.

Not since I escaped, when Mr Galbraith caught my friends Denise and Rhona with half a bottle of cider in the hotel fire escape on our school trip to Paris in 1989, have I felt such impish exhilaration. I think we felt we had to rebel to retain some individuality. I also believe Simo, in HIS on-air days, would've done exactly the same.

To be honest, the weekend was a lot more instructive and enjoyable than I had ever imagined. Simons and Myers, the Lennon and McCartney of commercial radio, were thorough and informative, talking about expectations and improvements. Phil Dowse, the tough-talking Aussie, delivered a fascinating insight into 'hot buttons' – basically what people like to listen to and why.

On this morning's show we try to implement all the top tips we've learned to keep those in charge happy. However, we run a wee sketch at 8.30 a.m. entitled 'What happened after lights out.' If the bosses hadn't known about our nocturnal adventures, they certainly do now. That Radio Two wifie was right . . .

Tuesday the 12th

In case you were wondering, this is National Advice Week. I'm not sure who you're meant to ask for it or why, but it gets us gabbing enthusiastically. Ever since my dad's infamous 'Keep yir hand on yir ha'penny' incident, I've been open to further suggestions. Jim the crane driver calls in first with this advice for trainee crane operatives: 'Never pee into the wind, I learned the hard way.' Other top advice includes:

'My mum told me if I had any trouble from boys to lift my knee to them.' Kate.

'Keep your eye on the ground there's things to be found, keep your eye on the sky you'll get sh** in your eye!' Rob, Edinburgh.

'Be true to your teeth or they'll soon be false to you.'

'Don't pick your nose in turbulence.'

'If he wants breakfast in bed tell him to sleep in the kitchen.' Fiona, Motherwell.

'If you go to bed with an itchy bum you'll wake up with stinky fingers!' Mark, Dunfermline.

'Never trust a dog with orange eyebrows.' Alec.

'If you're not in bed by ten o'clock then go home.' Big Col the trucker.

'You only have one mammy so look after her.' Davie, Hamilton.

[However, I think my favourite is this one from Lorna in Paisley:]

'My dad always told me never to trust a doctor whose house plants were dead.'

There is logic there somewhere, you know.

I have a very odd phone call when we come off air. Russell Kyle, Scottish PR guru, my first employer and all-round good guy, has an odd request.

Russell: 'Hi, Cat, I know this is a bit unusual but do you think you would let Celtic captain Neil Lennon on your show?'

Me: 'Eh, what for?'

Russell: 'Well, he has a book to promote, but he's said the only show he wants to go on is the *Breakfast Show* with you and Robin. He listens every day and is a massive fan.'

Me: 'Aye, right! Are you trying to sweet-talk us?'

Russell: 'No, I'm not kidding – he's just phoned me and asked if I knew either of you. He's knocked back Clyde and a few others but he really wants to go on your show.'

Me: 'Well, he must know what we are like. We'll ask him about everything apart from football.'

Russell: 'Yes, I know – I heard the Jack McConnell interview. He is aware of what lies in store. You will be doing me a massive favour – he never asks for anything but he really wants on your show.'

I know Neil from my *Scotsport* years and I happen to think he would actually be very funny on the show; Robin agrees. I find it extremely comical that Celtic are currently in Manchester ahead of tomorrow night's Champions League game with United and their skipper is trying to work out how to get on our show! We agree in principle, and await further details as to when suits us and him. I'm sure he would've loved to have been on today's show, particularly when overnight legend Willie D parted with his top piece of advice – 'Never trust a ginger.'

Wednesday the 13th

The hills are alive with the sound of squabbling. We have another classic Robin v. Cat debate this morning which provokes an incredible response. Robin's argument is quite basic: 'Musicals are for girls.' He reckons they're all boring, overrated and staged purely for females. He claims *Les Misérables* succeeded in making him totally miserable and was the worst three hours of his life. Andrew Lloyd Webber, according to the man who once starred with Dana, is the devil reincarnate.

I love most musicals (ironically I think *Cats* is drivel) and open the melodious can-can of worms by insisting most men would probably like them too if they gave them a chance:

'I dragged my boyfriend to see Jason Donovan in *Joseph and his Amazing Technicolor Dreamcoat*. He'd a face like a mince pie, but he reluctantly enjoyed it and we've now been married fourteen years.' Dee.

'Well, I'm a big hairy trucker and I like them a lot.' Phantom Jim from Bo'ness.

'I saw *Chicago* in London and thought it was excellent, even Darius didn't spoil it and I'm a man's man!' Brian, Maryhill.

Robin reluctantly admits he's seen *Chicago* in New York and loved it.

Me: 'But that is a musical and you raved about it.'

Robin: 'Yes, eh, but . . .'

He smiles sheepishly; I sense an Achilles heel and go in for the kill thanks to the following text: 'I love musicals. *Les Misérables* was great but the Abba one was my favourite.' Wullie McGovern, Bannockburn.

Me: 'Ah yes, the Abba one – *Mamma Mia* – the one we both went to and you ended up dancing in the aisles and then taking your daughter to the following week because it was so good.'

He smiles at me defiantly but knowing the battle is over. Comedy moment of the day comes courtesy of Scotland legend Roughie who calls in at 8.30 a.m. He is absolutely furious: 'I love musicals and I've been to them all. I've been hooked since I was taken to the *Sound of Music* when I was a kid. I'm a masculine man but I'm not scared to admit that they're great. *Phantom of the Opera* is one of my favourites.'

Robin's stunned look is priceless; Baz and I are in stitches. Roughie continues enthusiastically: 'I even like the ballet, my favourite is *The Nutcracker*. Robin you are wrong on this one!' His pro-musical outburst amuses the listeners who, it appears, still haven't forgiven him for Argentina: 'I can't believe Roughie goes to the ballet. If only he'd taken lessons in 1978 he might have known how to use his legs and his arms.' The Dodge.

Robin may claim not to enjoy musicals but at least he's not made to watch them like the anonymous sender of this final text: 'My wife makes me sit through her *Phantom of the Opera* DVD if I want a bit of you know what.' Ah well, if he doesn't watch it ever again at least he'll have his 'Memories . . . all alone in the moonlight . . .'

Thursday the 14th

Our fascination for wacky German supermarket Lidl reaches new heights today as we launch Lidl Idol – the search for a supermarket correspondent. It's tongue-in-cheek fun for three hours and we're bombarded with eager would-be reporters.

Specials this week are office shredders at £14.99, ladies' lemon crop top and pants sets at 99p and £4.99 blow torches. Like supermarket wars all over Scotland, competition is fierce.

'My husband bought a chainsaw for £50 in Lidl because he thought it was a bargain. It is still in its box and I'm terrified to think what it's for!' Pauline, Renfrew.

'I bought a great pair of padded cycling pants, not shorts but pants. I suppose I should buy a bike now. I only went in for some cheap fruit.' Nicky.

'I bought my grandson who is six a wetsuit. He now wants me to take him surfing which there really is no call for in Dunfermline!' Derek.

'My dad Ian Watts from Edinburgh is seventy-two and the Lidl king. He swears by it and drives us mad with his cheap sandals and hiking socks.'

[Mark Johnstone from Wishaw e-mails the show:] 'We all start the day with a Lidl breakfast listening to Real Radio; they do great toasting croissants and cappuccino coffee. However, I bought a cheap portable satellite system and ended up buying a caravan to use it.'

[The most ingenious text of the day came from Davie in Glasgow:] 'I've just heard Lidl and Aldi are going to merge. Their Scotland branches are going to be called Laldi!'

Our title of Lidl Idol goes to Lisa from Glasgow who sounds like a complete and utter nutcase. She is hyper when describing her love of the store:

> 'I buy all my presents there and go three times a day. I can tell you every price on every aisle and I've bought pretty much every bargain going. I bought the £4.99 foldable spade, I don't have a garden yet but you never know. I have the wetsuit and my mum has the horse blanket. She doesn't have a horse but she put it on her couch and it looks nice as a throw.'

Robin and I are doubled over. She hasn't even paused for a breath. When we call her back and tell her she has won – the grand prize of hee-haw – she goes mental. 'You are kidding; this is the best day of my life, ever. I never win anything, this is brilliant.' We point out she has still won nothing apart from the title of Lidl Idol that we made up earlier. She gets to come on weekly to let us know about forthcoming specials, but her reaction is like an Oscar triumph.

It's being allowed to gamble on these wacky ideas that may or may not work (this was a cracker) and the characters that rise to the occasion that makes this show such fun to work on. Lisa will be a star. We may even buy her the shredder as a token of our appreciation . . .

My big weigh-in yesterday was another anticlimax for Robin who, bless him, has more faith in me than I do. I stayed exactly the same again which I am fairly pleased with, given my Crunchie consumption at the weekend. This really is a long and exceptionally tedious process and my motivation is at an all-time low, not helped by the arrival of the most magical pleasure-filled vending machine.

No word from Neil Lennon so far. Celtic lost 3–2 at Old Trafford last night and I'm sensing he may have bottled it. Shame really, we could've given him a foldable spade to dig Celtic out of European trouble . . .

Friday the 15th

I'm in a cracking mood this morning. I think the fact that we worked straight through last weekend has made me ridiculously excited about this one. Or maybe it is the fact that I've organised a girlie-only soirée in the West End tomorrow and the current uptake is eleven. We haven't been out *en masse* for a while and there is plenty of gossip to catch up on.

We chat about our plans for the weekend on air when I happen to mention my mates Dolina and Mini-Me are coming out to play and they dance to anything from 'YMCA' to 'The Birdie Song'. Baz looks at me curiously: 'What dance to "The Birdie song"?' He must be the only person on the planet who has never wiggled through this, erm, classic by the Tweets.

Robin and I show him how to do the dance with the basic hand snap, arm flap, bum wiggle and clap formula and then go into hysterics when we do the maypole rotation bit in the studio with the 'la la la la la la la la la' then the turn and then the same again. We threaten to play the song in full, but know after the 'Hucklebuck incident' we are treading on thin musical ice. Thankfully our loyal bams are straight on the blower and we've enough textual evidence to endorse the selection. So at 8.45 a.m. Real Radio are probably the only station in the world to play – and dance to – 'The Birdie Song' in full, and let me tell you, it goes on a lot longer than I remembered. It certainly gets the country flapping:

'Falkirk has gone mad. There is a taxi driver doing "The Birdie Song" in the car in front of me. I may wet myself.' Mary.

'Chaos on M8, white vans wiggling all over the place.' Boab.

'This is brilliant, everybody on my coach is doing the dance. You lot are mental.' Jimmy the coach driver.

'Great to hear a classic, our whole factory have been clapping, flapping and singing along. Thank you.' Glen, Wishawhill.

I come off air with a massive smile and a sweaty face. I wonder if they ever feel like this on BBC radio . . .

I have to dash off early today for a big glamour photo-shoot of sorts. Alyson and I have a date with the young strapping Partick Thistle team in the dressing room at Firhill. I know, it is a dirty, tough shift but somebody has to do it. The Jags' manager Dick Campbell and the players are supporting our efforts as we try to raise funds for the Thai jungle trek. Next Saturday, at the home game against Gretna, we will be collecting with buckets, in the rain no doubt, for five hours. This could prove hilarious, given that I know most of the supporters. I hope they give generously.

I'm beginning to get a bit apprehensive about the whole trek thing now. I received an e-mail yesterday from Shaz, a prison officer from Polmont who is coming on the trek too. She informs me her training is going well. At the weekend she completed three Munros (mountains over 3,000ft) in Aviemore. I'm thinking the 5km I managed to run a few months ago is perhaps not enough. Still, I hope to dance off some calories at Body Jam, some sticky-sounding dance class Alyson has persuaded me to go to tonight, and by sprinting to the bar afterwards for last orders. Come on, it is anoher start . . .

Monday the 18th

My bum hurts. It's not a sentence I wish to start my week of extreme happiness with (more of which later) but quite frankly I have no choice. It hurts to sit still, it hurts to move and bending down is an absolute no-no. Body jam, as funky dance types would say, is hi-N.R.G and my R.S.E. is still in tatters.

The hour-long class was a fusion of dance styles incorporating jazz, funk and salsa. What my lovely ex-mate Alyson forgot to tell me was that my début class was the final week of the run and that everyone else has been learning the routines for eight weeks.

So heid-the-ba here turns up with the baggy trackies and 99p-in-the-sale maternity T-shirt from Dorothy Perkins (great if you like hiding a roly-poly paunch) to join in with Greens gym's version of the Pussycat Dolls.

I stood at the back of the class and tried to follow as the cries of 'pony weave for eight, into bow and arrow and step ball change' resonated through my vacant head. I never knew you needed another language to participate, but if truth be told I actually quite enjoyed it, particularly the high kicking routine to Guns N' Roses' 'Welcome to the Jungle'.

I should come clean here and admit the sore bahooky is not a direct result of the body jam class. Oh no, the fact that Alyson and I decided, somewhat predictably, to recreate the full routine with no warm-up in front of the troops on Saturday night on the Òran Mór dance floor is without doubt the cause of my discomfort. But hey, we rocked! Still, as I mentioned earlier, it's my week of extreme happiness so I shall grin through the discomfort.

To explain, on Sunday after moaning at Mr Cat that I was too tired, there's no chocolate, my kitchen's a disaster, my new neighbour appears to be a late night Lothario intent on sharing his joy with everyone within ten miles, my flat is too dark, the telly is rubbish, my bin smells, the bulging ice compartment in my fridge is preventing the door from shutting and there's no Diet Bru, I suddenly listened to myself and completely ran out of steam.

'That's it.' I declared with finality. 'I'm going to have a week of extreme happiness.' This was the actual line that came out of my mouth and I'm now going to see if the power of positive thinking really does work. Mr Cat just laughed that knowing 'aye right' laugh but I shall prove him wrong.

For the next seven days I shall be super nice to everybody, I shall go to the gym at least three times, I shall buy my mum flowers and pay my bills on time for once. I shall smile at traffic wardens and possibly even unload the dishwasher at work. I shall make no-check skinny soup and enjoy it. I shall embrace healthy eating and help old ladies cross the road. I shall take things to the charity shop and be patient and understanding towards the wee shits that skateboard past my flat at two in the morning.

Robin's taken my new manic cheerfulness with a pinch of lo-salt and reckons I will crack by Wednesday. I sense he will try to break me with the one thing he knows I can't handle – a Dido record. But this lady is not for turning; I shall simply appreciate her dusky vocals and haunting melodies and rue her melancholic state of mind.

My euphoria wavers temporarily when I realise I was in the loo with the *Daily Record* (come on, we all do it) and missed a fleeting visit to the station by my teen heart-throb Marti Pellow. However, the general consensus from the girls in the news team is that he looked scrawny and in need of a good feed, so it is probably for the best.

It is fate, you see – I'm destined to be extremely happy all week and I'll be very annoyed if I'm not . . .

Tuesday the 19th

This morning the papers are full of magnificent pictures of the Clyde Arc – the first new vehicle bridge over the river in thirty years. Known locally as the squinty bridge because of its angled appearance, the bridge links Pacific Quay to the Finneston area. Until today nobody knew what the bridge was to be called. The Clyde Arc is a rather grand title so naturally we ask for alternative suggestions:

'The empty bridge – nobody knows how to get on it yet.'
Ricky Morgan.

'The Weegie hump.' Ally.

'The Govan gateway.' Marc.

'What about the Lara Croft bridge – it is curvy, well built but not worth crossing.' Gus.

'The curvy Clyde crossing', 'the banana bridge' and 'the boomerang bridge' are also popular choices. And spare a thought for poor Charlie in Motherwell; he clearly needs a bit of my extreme happiness to rub off: 'Surely if it is that twisted it should simply be called – the wife.' My favourite call is from Gary, one of the construction workers: 'We've been working on it since last April and believe me it has plenty of names you couldn't mention on the radio! However, at home my wee two-year-old Leah calls it "Daddy's bridge over the water". I quite like that.'

I can hear the collective 'aaaaaaaawwwww' across the nation. Anyway, we were just having a bit of fun and the Clyde Arc it is – the winning name apparently coming from a school kid in a competition for Glaswegian children. How cool is that? In my day we drew pictures for book tokens . . .

I come off air to find seven texts waiting for me. All week I've been bombarded by people hoping to scrounge Scotland v. France tickets. I know loads of people who work in football but I'm afraid I only have access to six and they're taken.

The game is in October but last Thursday people queued overnight for tickets at Hampden and they're changing hands on eBay for hundreds of pounds. To be honest, I'm delighted that interest in the national side is on the up. Not since the World Cup finals in France 1998 have we been in such fine voice. I had a ball in Paris, Bordeaux and St Etienne and even bumped into Shareen Nanjiani and Kaye Adams at the Morocco game. Actually, I've only mentioned this because I found a nice photo of the three of us when I was searching for pictures for this book at the weekend and thought, ah, that's a good celebrity photo, I think I'll include that and pretend they're my friends! It's quite shameless really. I love Shareen, who I worked with at STV, but that's the only time I've met Kaye who seemed lovely too. Still, the bored folk who only flick through the photo section in the bookshops won't know this, will they?

My celebrity miss list is higher than the hit-rate at the moment; following on from missing Marti, Robin and I chose NOT to interview former Westlife star Brian McFadden. His 'people' said he could possibly slot us in if we didn't talk about Kerry, Delta, his love-life or Westlife. In fact his new single was all we were allowed to discuss. We said thanks but no thanks. I preferred Take That anyway.

Just to let you know, my W.O.E.H is going very well. I did indeed go to the gym yesterday, I made no-check soup and I sent flowers to my mum. The fact that I got a text from my dad on their arrival saying, 'Right, what have you done now?' says it all . . .

Wednesday the 20th

This diary entry will take me longer to write than any other so far. I've not run out of frivolous chat, I just have the most ridiculous finger injury caused by my latest kitchen disaster. That feng shui man was so right. I am a danger to myself and as such should have staff, I've decided!

Last night, I cooked a healthy tea of organic salmon and spinach at just eight Scottish Slimmers' checks. Taking the pot of boiling spinach to the sink, I spotted what looked like a perfect handy implement to strain my greens. In retrospect, I can see that a flat cheese grater should be used for that and that alone.

My middle finger on my left hand is currently smothered in antiseptic cream and bandaged like a puffy pink beef olive. I'm sure Mr Cat enjoyed the romantic vision of me, tear-stained and girny, shovelling salmon into my gub with a fork in one hand, the other throbbing and submerged in a large pot of cold water.

Fear not, though: once the pain dispersed I was still extremely happy. I think I am beginning to do Robin's head in with my super-friendliness. I've made him more tea this week than his bladder can handle, while Baz has been gifted so much Irn-Bru that the machine has actually run out.

Today we get a lovely wee text from Mark in Stewarton: 'My wee seven-year-old daughter was really upset after tidying her room yesterday. She said to me, "Daddy remember that hotel where we stayed in Spain, well I've taken the pen home by mistake. I'm really sorry." Such innocence eh?'

We start discussing what you're actually allowed to take home and our listeners have very interesting ideas on hotel etiquette:

'I owned a hotel and we had guests that swapped our nice new duvets for old skanky smelly ones!' Fran in Edinburgh.

'I always take the lot. In the Dhow Palace in Dubai, I even took the writing blotter as it was so lovely.' John in Edinburgh.

'My wife is a towel thief.' Dougie in Carluke.

'My partner was working abroad and brought me back a dressing table stool.' Annette, Dunoon.

'I'm not sure if you count Butlins in Ayr as a hotel, but every year my family came home with a lovely new set of cutlery.' Robert, Wishawhill.

'After a night out, I got home to discover I had packed the TV remote from the hotel instead of my electric shaver.' Jim.

'The hot chocolate and coffee sachets are handbag sized and exceptionally useful, I feel it would be rude not to. I'm not sure what I need with eleven sewing kits right enough.' Pauline, Morningside.

I have to admit my only bad hotel habit is pinching the Molton Brown hair and body products from posh establishments. That is a real kleptomaniac's treat. Today I could do with 'borrowing' one of those swanky Moët & Chandon champagne ice buckets to stick my gimp digit in.

One place I won't be stealing from is Firhill, home to my beloved Partick Thistle and as of today, drum roll please, the official home to *The Cat's Whispers* book launch. I'm sure the lovely Edinburgh publishers are appalled at inviting literary types to a football stadium in Maryhill, but I think it's perfect. I wouldn't be comfortable in a luxurious venue, particularly because we all have to wear pyjamas. *No. 1* magazine has confirmed they'll cover the event, and travel Gav, our occasional traffic legend, is providing his DIVA spectacular show for entertainment. That and Bobby Harvey on his fiddle of course and my wonderful Mydas mates with their guitars.

This book may not be that memorable, but the party has the makings of a classic . . .

Thursday the 21st

What is in a name? More than you might think, it appears. Whilst sipping his seventh free can of Irn Bru this week (stocks have been replenished and I just keep giving and giving) Baz reveals he is actually named after his favourite tipple: 'My mum drank so much Barrs' Irn-Bru when she was pregnant she called me Barrie. It could be worse, though: she was reading a nineteenth-century novel when she was carrying my brother and called him Tremayne. There are not many of them in Pollok I can tell you.'

I subsequently learn that the bold Tremayne is super-fit and not to be messed with, which is not entirely surprising.

I'm named Catriona which is Gaelic for Catherine, my mum's name. I've always thought it was quite a nice name despite the fact nobody can ever pronounce it correctly and that as a youngster I could NEVER get any cool stuff like stickers, pens or door plaques with my name on it.

Robin says his mum was the president and spokesperson of the Aberdeen Ornithological Society and he was born in December – hence his feathery festive moniker. Personally, I see that wind-up glint in his eye again, but he smiles not very innocently and says it is true.

There are a few classics:

'My name is Alison Berry. My mum named me so she could sing the song 'Ali Bali Ali Bali Be'. The worst thing is all my pals call me Ali, so I am Ali Berry like the Bond girl.'

'Hi, Kay from Fife, I was named after Kay Kendal, my sister Joni is named after Joni Mitchell while my other sister Vicki was named after the page three girl on the day she was born.'

'I am the youngest of eight. My mum called me John-nie to remind my dad of how it would be from now on!'

We have another 'wee Becky' wind-up this morning which is hilarious; she really is a star being guided by the master. In this call she phones the Ballieston Parish Church wanting a wedding date for her and her nine-year-old boyfriend Mikey. The minister is a natural comedian and an unexpected match for our intrepid youngster:

'I'm nine and I want to get married next week.'

'Oh do you now, well you'll need to give me more time.'

'How much more time?'

'I think maybe about fourteen years?'

Robin has now recorded over 10,000 wind-ups and they're more popular than ever. Wherever we go people shout catch-phrases from his characters Old Mrs Galloway, Hector Brocklebank and Cecil with his Boaby. He's often asked his favourites, so here are his thoughts:

'My favourite call ever was to a guy called William Greenan who was set up by his brother. He kept pigeons and I phoned pretending to be a neighbour complaining about the noise. He just went completely off his head from the start, so I sat back, threw in a few random lines and listened to him explode. He called me everything under the sun and the bleep machine nearly broke in the edit. He took it well, though, and seemed like a nice bloke who is clearly very fond of his doos.'

His favourite Hector call was phoning the *Aberdeen Press and Journal* to place an obituary for his friend with the touching message, 'Peter Reid fae Peterheid is deid.' Cecil getting his Boaby stuck up his exhaust and Old Mrs Galloway's runaway lawnmower through the greenhouse calls are also in his top five.

Just as I'm about to leave (to take my bags to the charity shop, honestly this happiness week is working) Robin laughs at a text message he's just received. My nose is bothering me and I ask what is so funny. He grins: 'My wee brother has just sent me a text asking why he never knew Mum was involved in the local bird club!'

I bloody knew it . . .

Friday the 22nd

Buckets at the ready – the girls are coming your way. Tomorrow Alyson, Rhona, Jane, Michelle and I will be outside Firhill collecting for NCH Scotland, the children's charity.

On the show I ask for top fundraising tips and I have to confess I never knew it was such a complicated process. We've had to get written permission from the police, NCH and the football club. Loads of listeners get in touch with charitable tips:

'Take Ewen Cameron along and charge a pound a punch.' Kenny, Fife.

'Take wee Becky with you, she sounds like she could get money out of anybody.' Terry, Glasgow.

'Make sure you stand next to the munchies van or the programme sellers, anywhere people have their cash out. Good luck.' Steve.

'Stick on a Burberry cap, a Berghaus jacket and carry a baseball bat. You'll have no trouble getting cash from people.'

'Just shake your cans!'

Hmm, an interesting proposition. However, it is apparently illegal to shake our buckets because that is classed as begging. The buckets are also sealed and the cash can only be counted by charity officials. I can fully understand this; I might need pie money at half-time!

At 8.30 a.m. I'm all set to do a funny little segment about *No. 1* magazine; they've cut Robin out of our picture for the second time which I find hilarious given that he is the good-looking one. Gaynor, the assistant editor, wants me to do a full glamorous shoot and interview with them for the next issue. I'm a bit scared as I hate the thought of clothes I'm not familiar with, i.e. if it's not baggy, covers everything and comes with a hood I won't be comfy. Robin is going to dare me to blag my way on to the front cover wearing a hoodie.

I WAS about to chat about this but he threw me with the line I dread the most: 'Cat, you don't know anything about this but . . .' It turns out Alyson has written an article in the Thistle programme offering my services for cash! For a fiver, I have to kiss people outside the game. I'm not sure who has to pay. Robin hands me the match programme and I am actually lost for words. I shall, as they often say in Robin's wind-ups, kill her!

Gifted songstress Lucie Silvas pops into the studio today. She seems nice and friendly. The fact that she is stunning as well as a talented musician is not lost on Bossman Jay and Robin who are VERY accommodating. They are meant to be professionals; as if I would behave in that manner if someone like Shane Ward came in!

I end my week of extreme happiness on a very tasty note – I treat everyone in the office to something delightful from the fast food van. My roll and square sausage with a thick dollop of tomato sauce is unadulterated pleasure on a plate. I have no slimming anxieties, as I eat safe in the knowledge I shall bop it off at body jam later.

This positive thinking lark is amazing I've had a brilliant week and I'm optimistic about tomorrow. We shall raise thousands for underprivileged kids and all the men shall be taut, half-naked visions that look like Johnny Depp . . .

my real conclusion

The printing deadline has arrived and I'm afraid I must leave you here, my friends. Writing this diary has been a journey in itself; there have been amazing times, emotional times and some pretty tough times. I've battled insomnia, unsocial hours and the depressive rain cloud of the perpetual dieter but the show has kept me cheery all the way.

I am deeply indebted to many people for helping me complete this crazy wee project, but most of all I'd like to thank the person who invented spell-check. (I shall let them know later what 'the boaby' and 'Jakeys' are!) Like the show itself, I could not and would not have chosen to embark on this mission without the help of Robin and our listeners.

I'm often asked the best thing about my job and it is the stories, the banter and the affection we receive on a daily basis from the Scottish public. You really are the best. So, before I get shamefully weepy and girlie like Gwyneth Paltrow at the Oscars, here are my *Real Radio Breakfast Show* highlights of the year:

- MOST MEMORABLE MOMENT: The reindeer horned eureka moment at Jack's house.
- PARTY OF THE YEAR: Torremolinos, Real Radio's trip away.
- JAMMY GITS' AWARD: Celebrating Chinese New Year in Hong Kong.
- BEST WIND-UP: Beating the kid in the competition and claiming the £500 prize.

- MOST FANCIABLE FEMALE: Robina in her frock. Those pins!
- MOST FANCIABLE MALE: Shane Ward, he wanted me.
- NAKED AMBITION AWARD: Young Baz, for getting his bits out. Lots.
- PROUDEST ACHIEVEMENT: Speaking to 12,000 people at the Cancer Research Race for Life 5km and completing it in a decent time.
- BIGGEST DISASTER: THAT Friday.
- MOST REGRETTABLE PERFORMANCE: (apart from the above) Engaging in flirty banter with a senior royal.
- BIGGEST SHOCK: The pink car.
- MUSICAL HIGHLIGHT: T in the Park.
- MUSICAL LOWLIGHT: Robin and Cat play Big in Falkirk.
- BIGGEST CHALLENGE AHEAD: Getting fit enough for NCH Thailand trek.

I finish this book a whopping three pounds lighter than this time last year and remain naively optimistic that by my eighty-fifth birthday I shall be able to tuck in a top. I've made a lot of friends along the way and continue to count my blessings that I've been teamed up with Robin, a truly gifted broadcaster and one hell of a nice guy.

I've no idea what the future holds for me in this funny industry, but if I chuck it all in tomorrow to become a sandal-wearing hermit in Bolivia or find myself being pointed to the door after another spontaneous misadventure, I've loved my time at Real Radio. It is quite a unique media organisation in that everybody gets on. The emphasis is on fun rather than on the cost-cutting emphasised in most others at the moment. The management are friends. They are professional and dedicated but best of all they are head-cases. I admire these qualities greatly.

As I've mentioned, I only have one day off in the next four months. My career as a sensible respected journalist is clearly over but I shall continue to try and have fun for a living with the *Real Breakfast Show*, *Offside*, travel writing and panto before trekking through the jungle and hopefully emerging with over £60,000 for the National Children's Homes in Scotland.

I hope you've enjoyed my random exploits – the First Minister and his Christmas party have a lot to answer for . . .